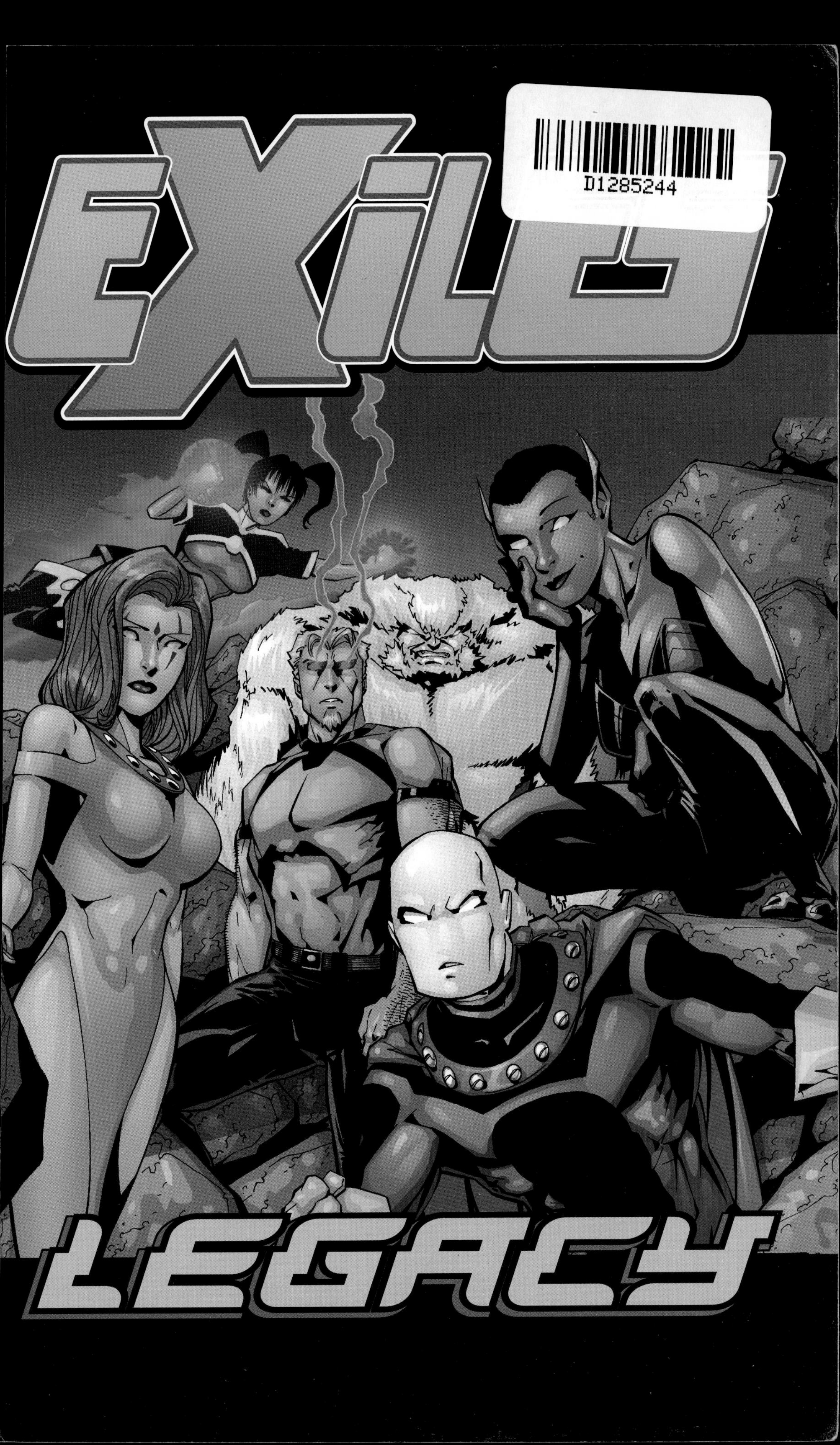
EXILES
LEGACY

EXILES

BLINK
Clarice Ferguson
Teleportation

MORPH
Shape-Shifting

SASQUATCH
Dr. Heather Hudson
Super-Strength
& Senses

SUNFIRE
Mariko Yashida
Flame Control/Flight

NOCTURNE
TJ Wagner
Hex Bolts, Possession

MIMIC
Calvin Rankin
Mimics the Powers
of Five Mutants

LEGACY

ISSUES #20-22

Writer: **JUDD WINICK**

Penciler: **JIM CALAFIORE**

Inker: **JON HOLDREDGE w/ERIC CANNON**

WITH AN IRON FIST

ISSUES #21-23

Writer: **JUDD WINICK**

Pencils: **KEV WALKER**

Inks: **KEV WALKER & SIMON COLBEY**

Colors: **TRANSPARENCY DIGITAL**

Letters: **PAUL TUTRONE**

Assistant Editor: **NOVA REN SUMA**

Editor: **MIKE RAICHT**

Supervising Editor: **MIKE MARTS**

Collections Editor: **JEFF YOUNGQUIST**

Assistant Editor: **JENNIFER GRÜNWALD**

Book Designer: **PATRICK MCGRATH**

Editor in Chief: **JOE QUESADA**

President: **BILL JEMAS**

They are the EXILES, reality-hopping nomads forced to repair the broken chain of time. In each new universe, they must complete a mission before moving on. Their only guide is the mysterious Tallus, a bracelet talisman that provides direction, although sometimes oblique, as to what the EXILES are there to rectify.

To fail at a mission means returning to their worlds to live a life in a fractured timeline. If they succeed, the team moves to the next reality and the next mission. Their final goal is to repair their own timeline and return to it.

The dangers they face are real. Some may never return home.

Recently, the EXILES were interrupted from a mission and thrown into a world they weren't meant to visit. This was the Mojoverse, a bizarre reality lorded over by the maniacal and vicious Mojo who keeps his people sedated by television.

Mojo had captured the EXILES in order to put his favorite performer, Morph, on the air. By torturing Nocturne, Mojo was able to force Morph to do his TV show. In the meantime, the other EXILES teammates—Blink, Mimic, Sasquatch and Sunfire—located the only man in Mojoverse capable of defeating Mojo, a resistance leader named Longshot who had been imprisoned after the last uprising. With Longshot's help, the EXILES succeeded in rescuing their friends. In the end, their timeline was repaired and the EXILES were returned to their reality-hopping fate.

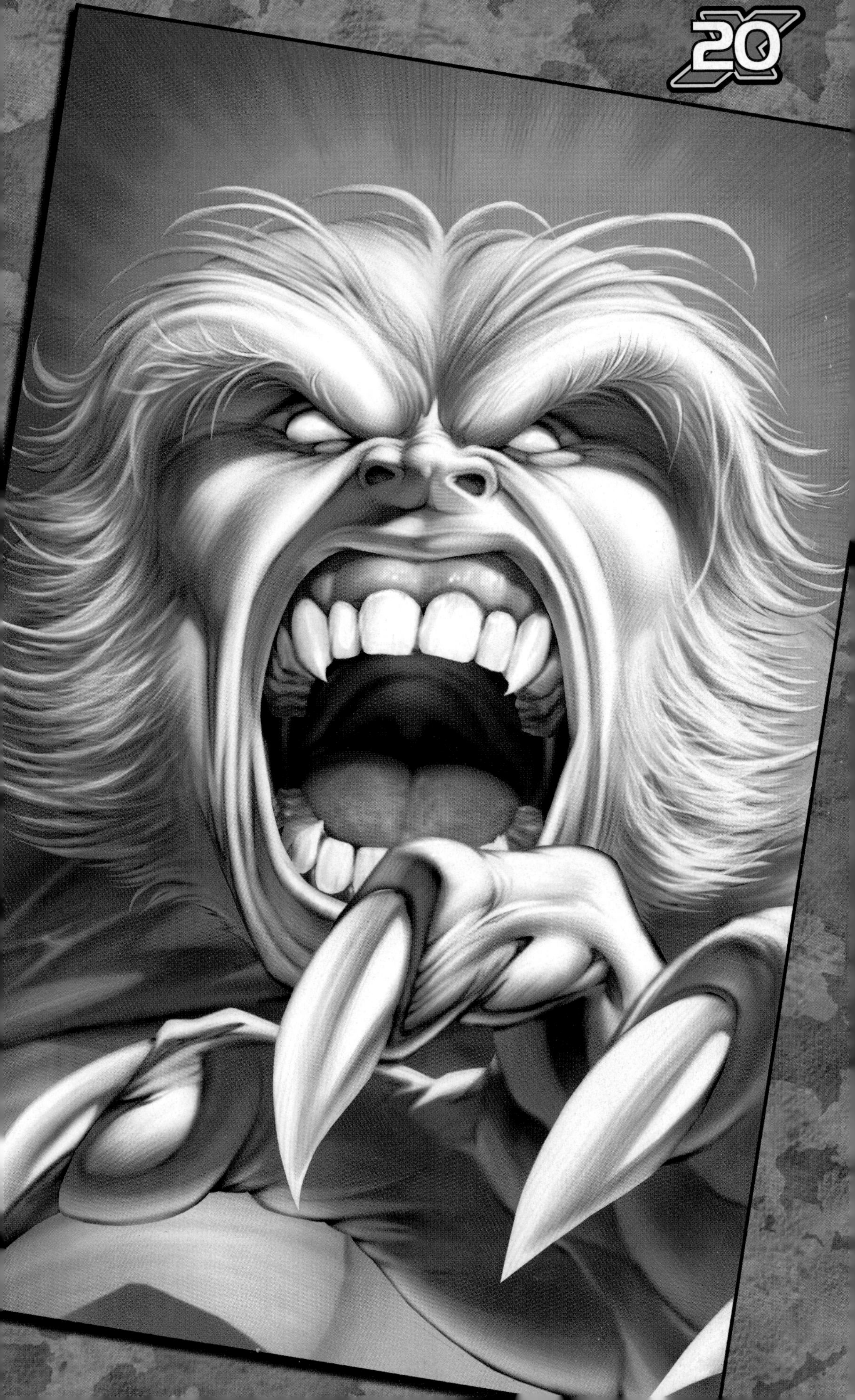

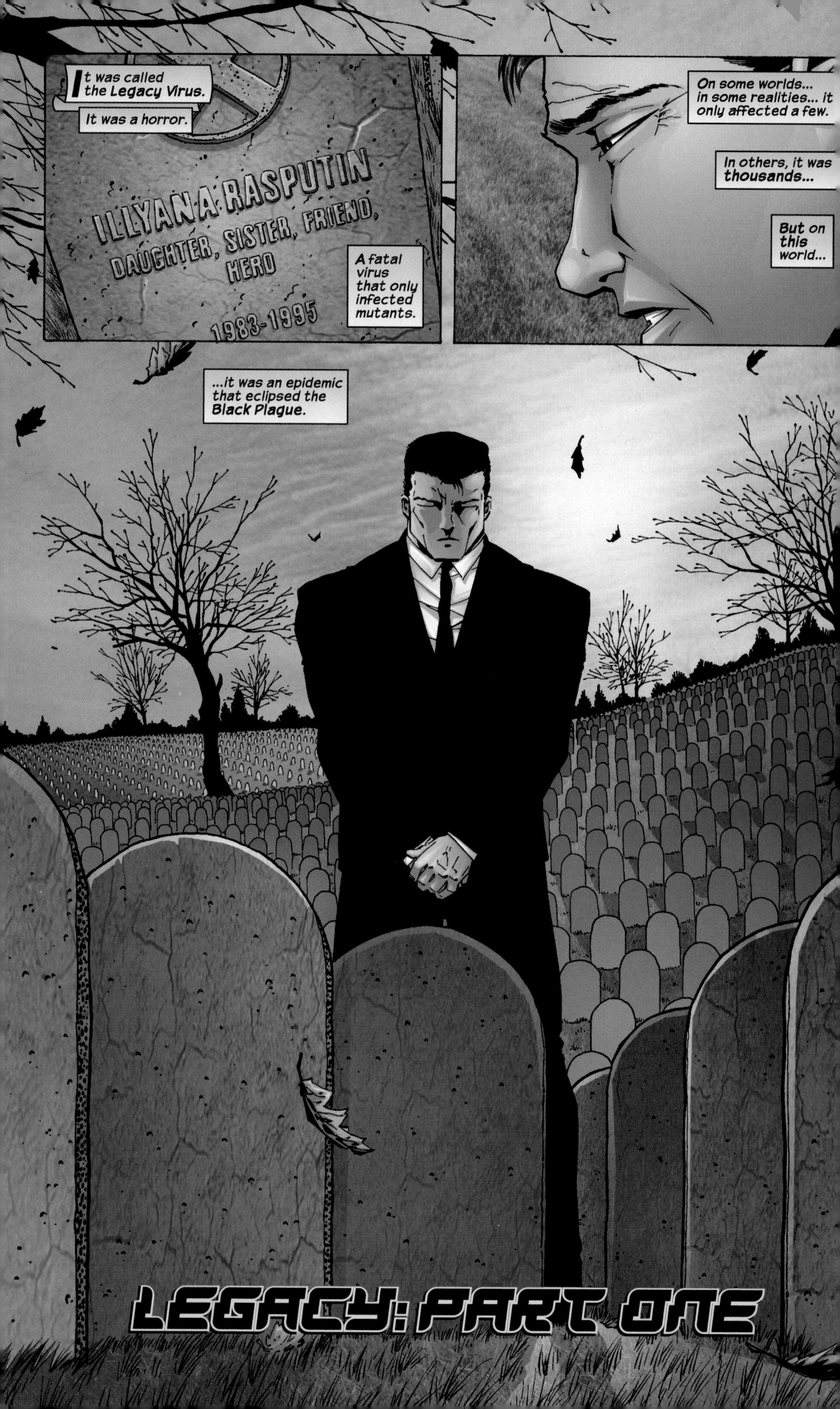

It was called the Legacy Virus.
It was a horror.
ILLYANA RASPUTIN
DAUGHTER, SISTER, FRIEND, HERO
1983-1995
A fatal virus that only infected mutants.
On some worlds... in some realities... it only affected a few.
In others, it was thousands...
But on this world...
...it was an epidemic that eclipsed the Black Plague.
LEGACY: PART ONE

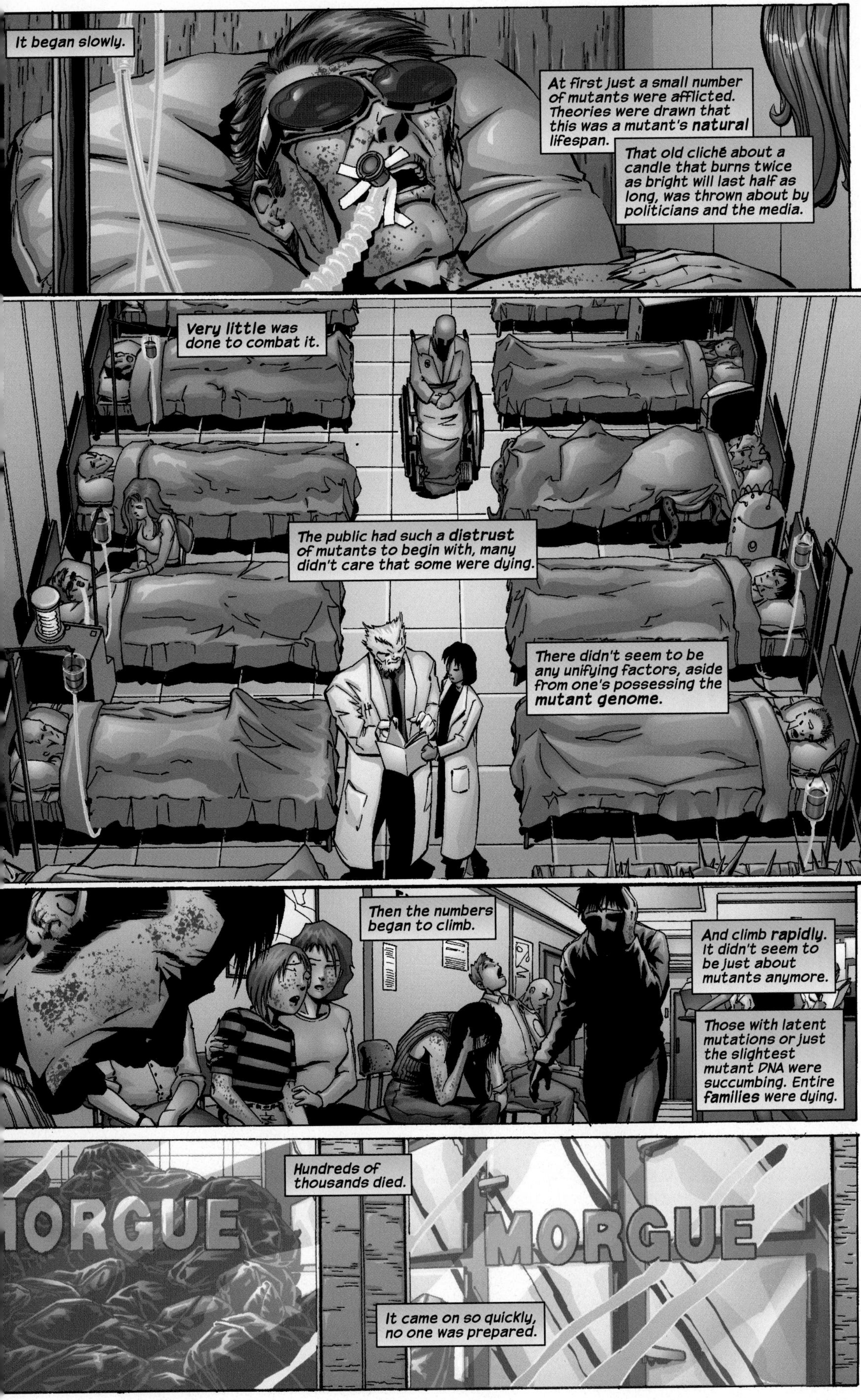

It began slowly.
At first just a small number of mutants were afflicted. Theories were drawn that this was a mutant's natural lifespan.
That old cliché about a candle that burns twice as bright will last half as long, was thrown about by politicians and the media.
Very little was done to combat it.
The public had such a distrust of mutants to begin with, many didn't care that some were dying.
There didn't seem to be any unifying factors, aside from one's possessing the mutant genome.
Then the numbers began to climb.
And climb rapidly. It didn't seem to be just about mutants anymore.
Those with latent mutations or just the slightest mutant DNA were succumbing. Entire families were dying.
Hundreds of thousands died.
MORGUE
MORGUE
It came on so quickly, no one was prepared.

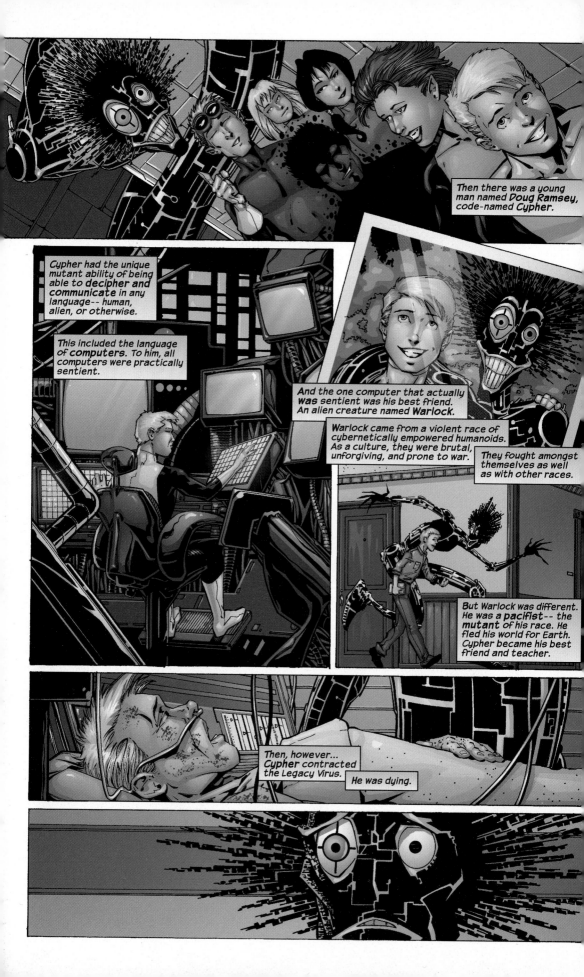

Then there was a young man named **Doug Ramsey**, code-named **Cypher.**

Cypher had the unique mutant ability of being able to **decipher** and **communicate** in any language-- human, alien, or otherwise.

This included the language of **computers.** To him, all computers were practically sentient.

And the one computer that actually **was** sentient was his best friend. An alien creature named **Warlock.**

Warlock came from a violent race of cybernetically empowered humanoids. As a culture, they were brutal, unforgiving, and prone to war.

They fought amongst themselves as well as with other races.

But Warlock was different. He was a **pacifist**-- the **mutant** of his race. He fled his world for Earth. Cypher became his best friend and teacher.

Then, however... Cypher contracted the Legacy Virus.

He was dying.

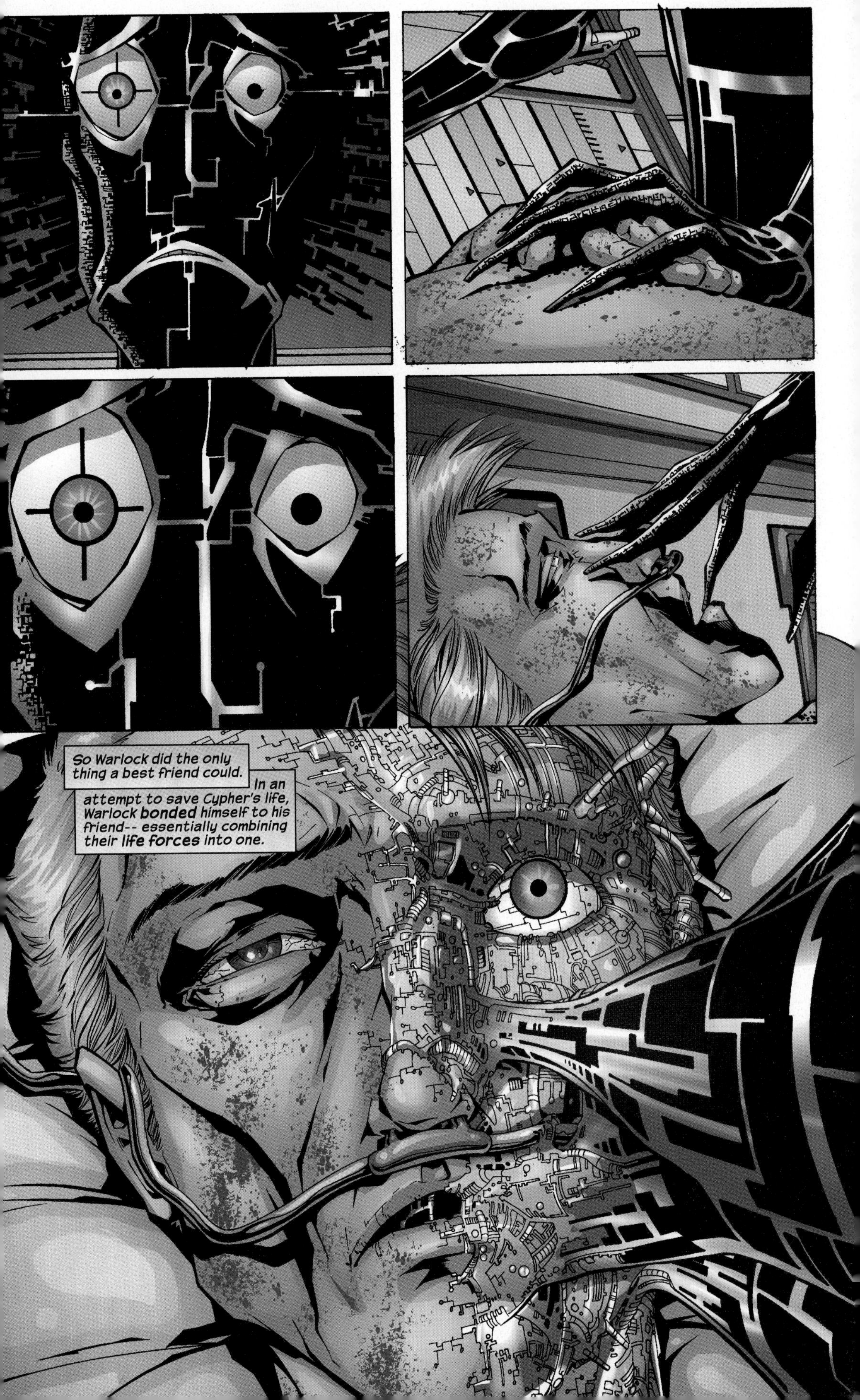

So Warlock did the only thing a best friend could.
In an attempt to save Cypher's life, Warlock **bonded** himself to his friend-- essentially combining their **life forces** into one.

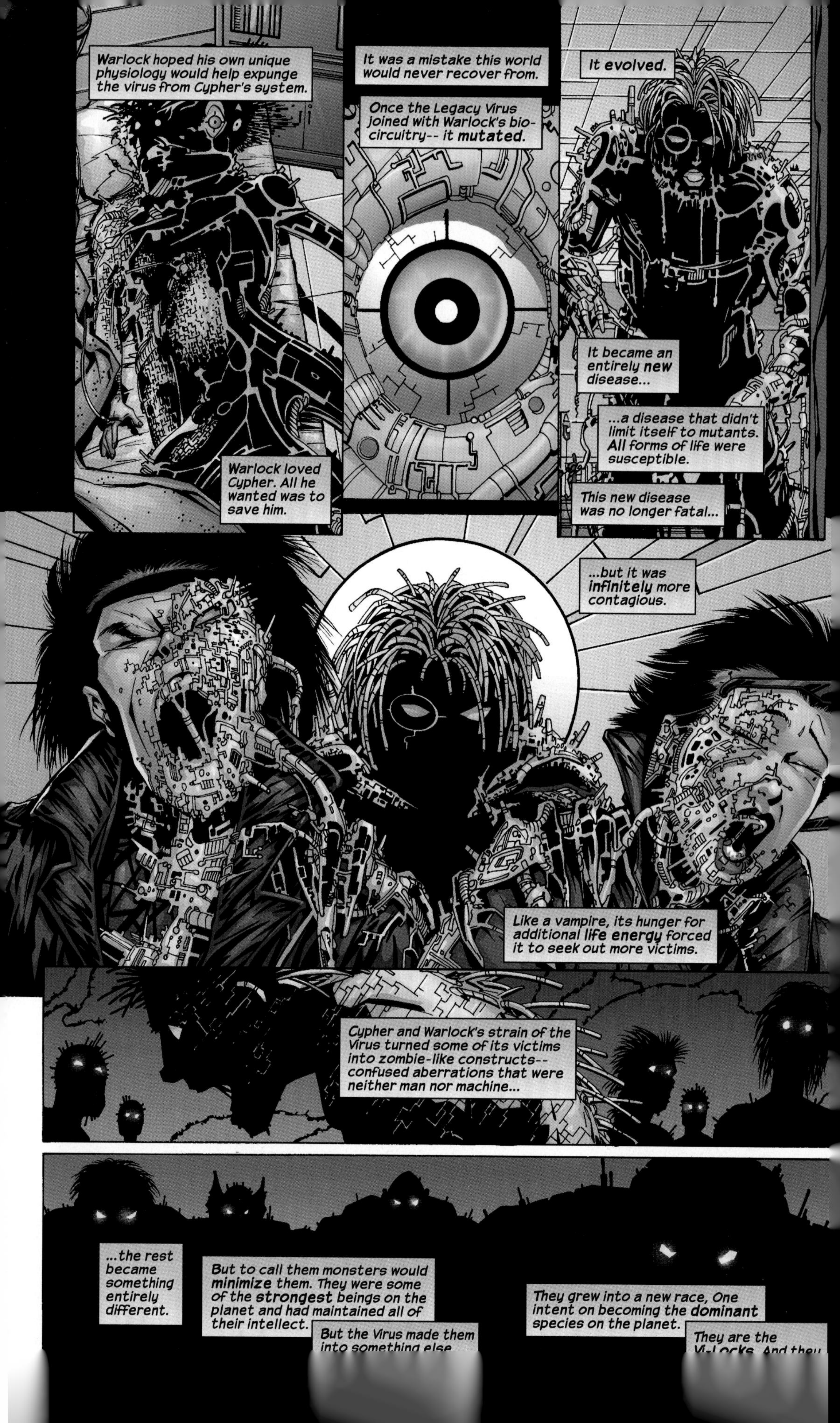
Warlock hoped his own unique physiology would help expunge the virus from Cypher's system.
Warlock loved Cypher. All he wanted was to save him.
It was a mistake this world would never recover from.
Once the Legacy Virus joined with Warlock's bio-circuitry-- it mutated.
It evolved.
It became an entirely new disease...
...a disease that didn't limit itself to mutants. All forms of life were susceptible.
This new disease was no longer fatal...
...but it was infinitely more contagious.
Like a vampire, its hunger for additional life energy forced it to seek out more victims.
Cypher and Warlock's strain of the Virus turned some of its victims into zombie-like constructs-- confused aberrations that were neither man nor machine...
...the rest became something entirely different.
But to call them monsters would minimize them. They were some of the strongest beings on the planet and had maintained all of their intellect.
But the Virus made them
They grew into a new race, One intent on becoming the dominant species on the planet.
They are the

We're gonna get in *so* much trouble.

Stop being such a *wuss*. Do you want to catch lizards or not?

We can catch lizards in the city.

Not *big* ones, buttface, just the little baby ones.

We have to get *outside* the city if we're gonna get anything *decent*.

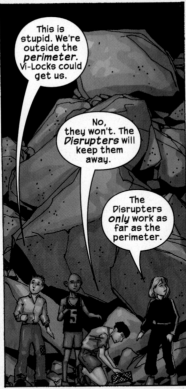

This is stupid. We're outside the *perimeter*. Vi-Locks could get us.

No, they won't. The *Disrupters* will keep them away.

The Disrupters *only* work as far as the perimeter.

My *dad* says that they are just being *overly* careful. He says, the Disrupters work *a lot* further than the outer fence.

They just want to keep people scared. That way they do what they're told.

I don't like this. I'm going back.

David! Man, you're *such* a tool. I'm just gonna set the traps and we can go.

Nothing's out here. We're--

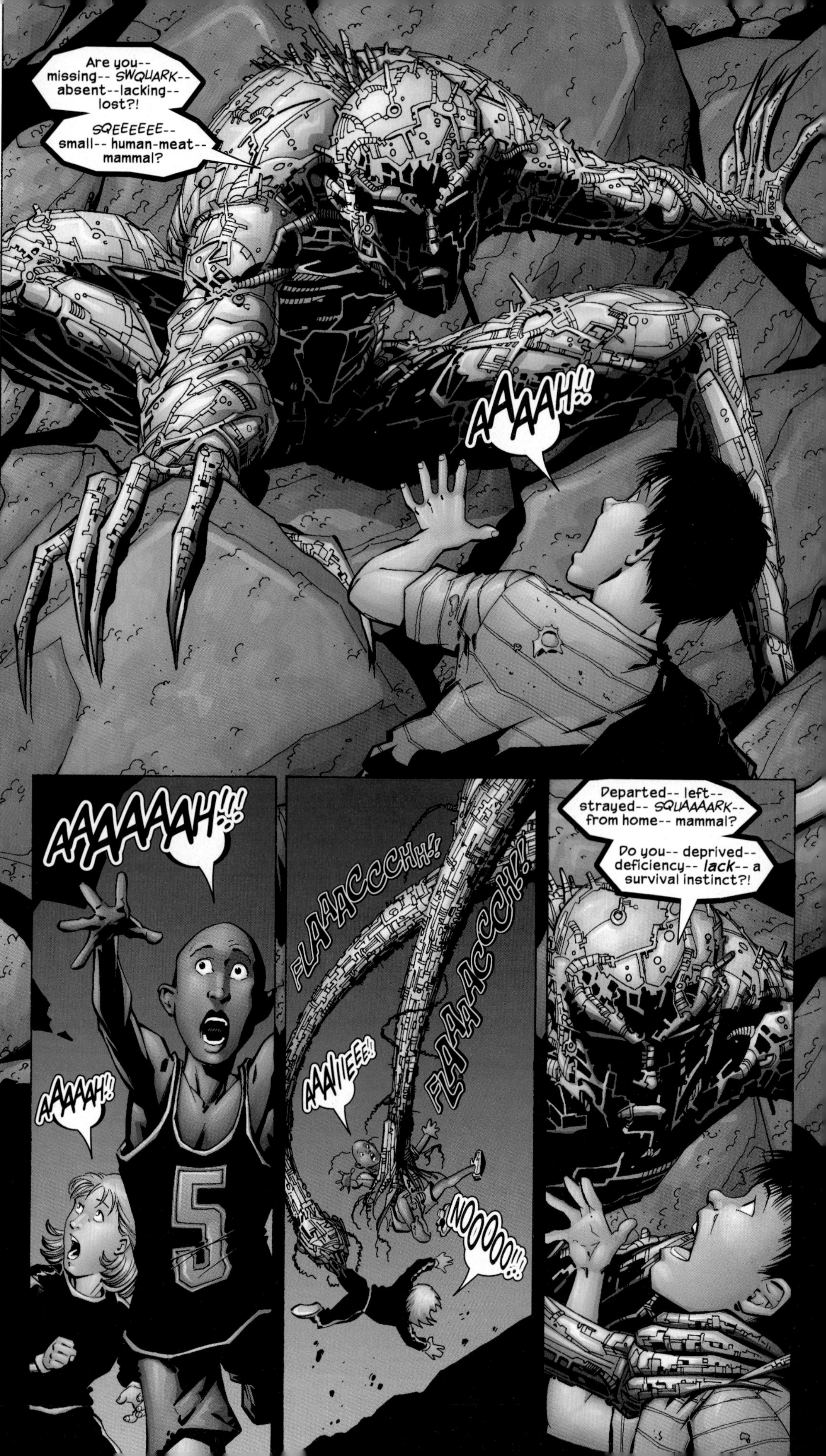

Are you-- missing-- SWQUARK-- absent--lacking-- lost?!
SQEEEEEE-- small-- human-meat-- mammal?
AAAAH!!
AAAAAAAH!!!
AAAAAH!!
FLAAACCCHH!!
AAAIIEEE!!
FLAAAACCCH!!
NOOOOO!!!
Departed-- left-- strayed-- SQUAAAARK-- from home-- mammal?
Do you-- deprived-- deficiency-- lack-- a survival instinct?!

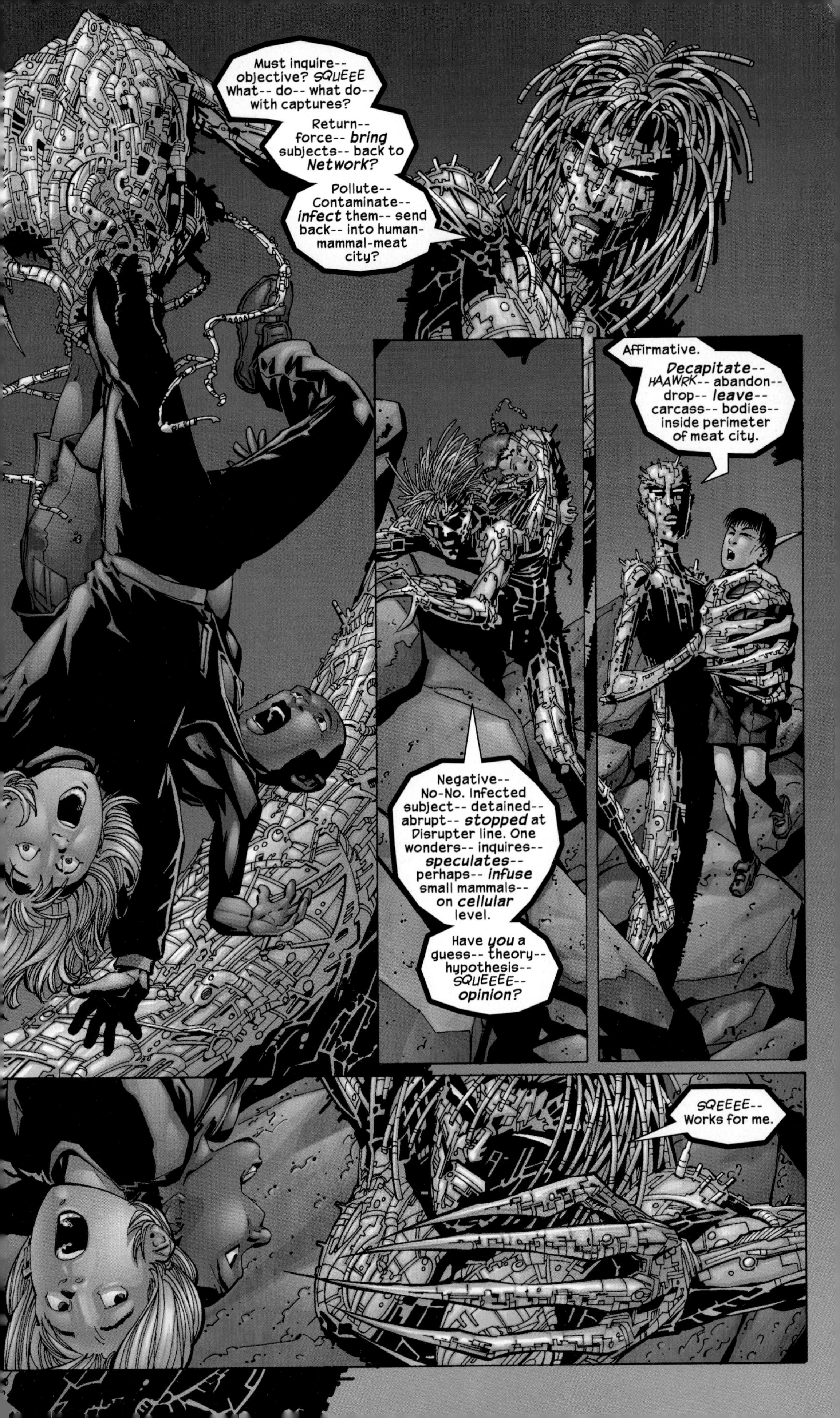
Must inquire-- objective? SQUEEE What-- do-- what do-- with captures?
Return-- force-- bring subjects-- back to Network?
Pollute-- Contaminate-- infect them-- send back-- into human-mammal-meat city?
Negative-- No-No. Infected subject-- detained-- abrupt-- stopped at Disrupter line. One wonders-- inquires-- speculates-- perhaps-- infuse small mammals-- on cellular level.
Have you a guess-- theory-- hypothesis-- SQUEEEE-- opinion?
Affirmative.
Decapitate-- HAAWRK-- abandon-- drop-- leave-- carcass-- bodies-- inside perimeter of meat city.
SQEEEE-- Works for me.

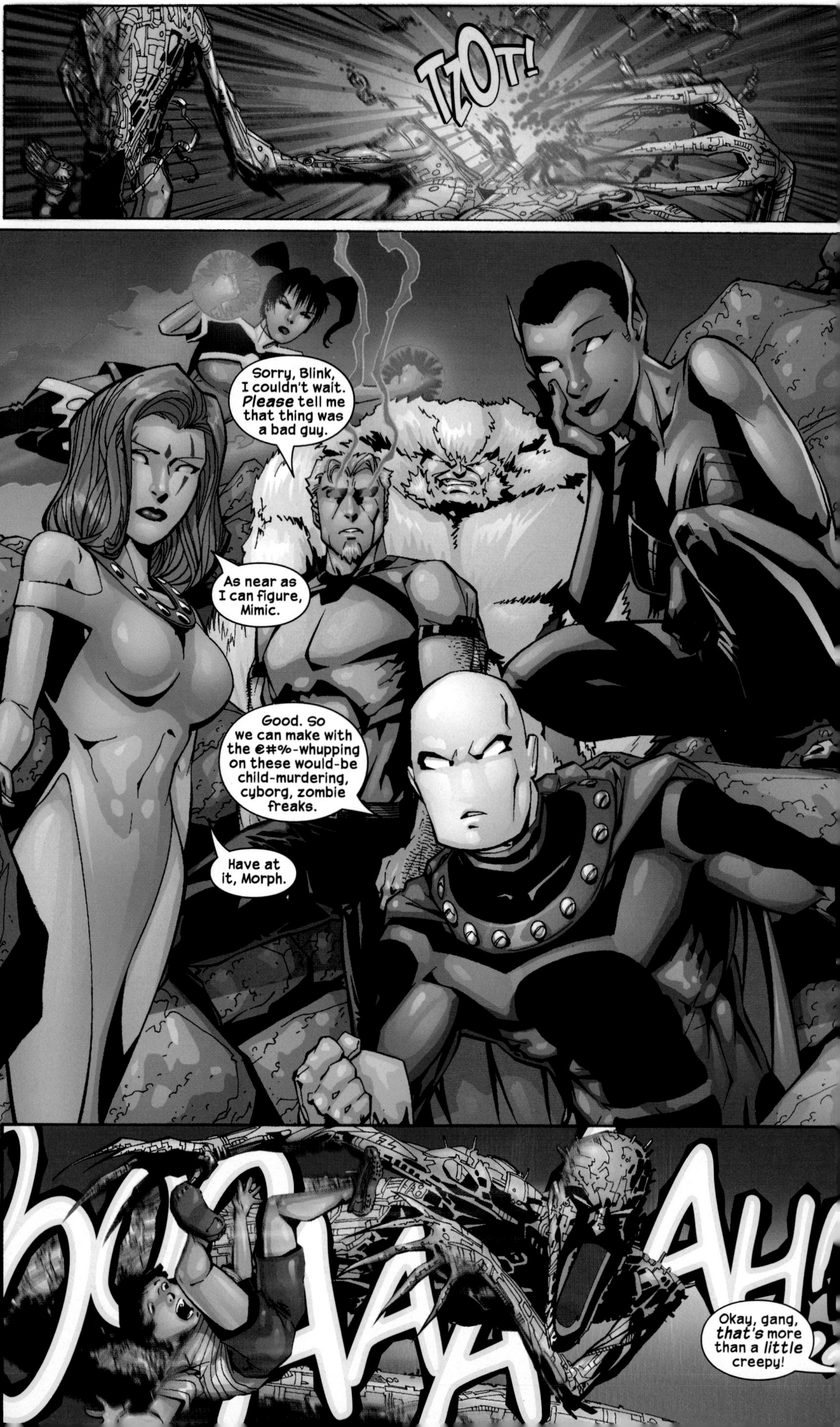
TZOT!
Sorry, Blink, I couldn't wait. *Please* tell me that thing was a bad guy.
As near as I can figure, Mimic.
Good. So we can make with the €#%-whupping on these would-be child-murdering, cyborg, zombie freaks.
Have at it, Morph.
Okay, gang, *that's* more than a *little* creepy!

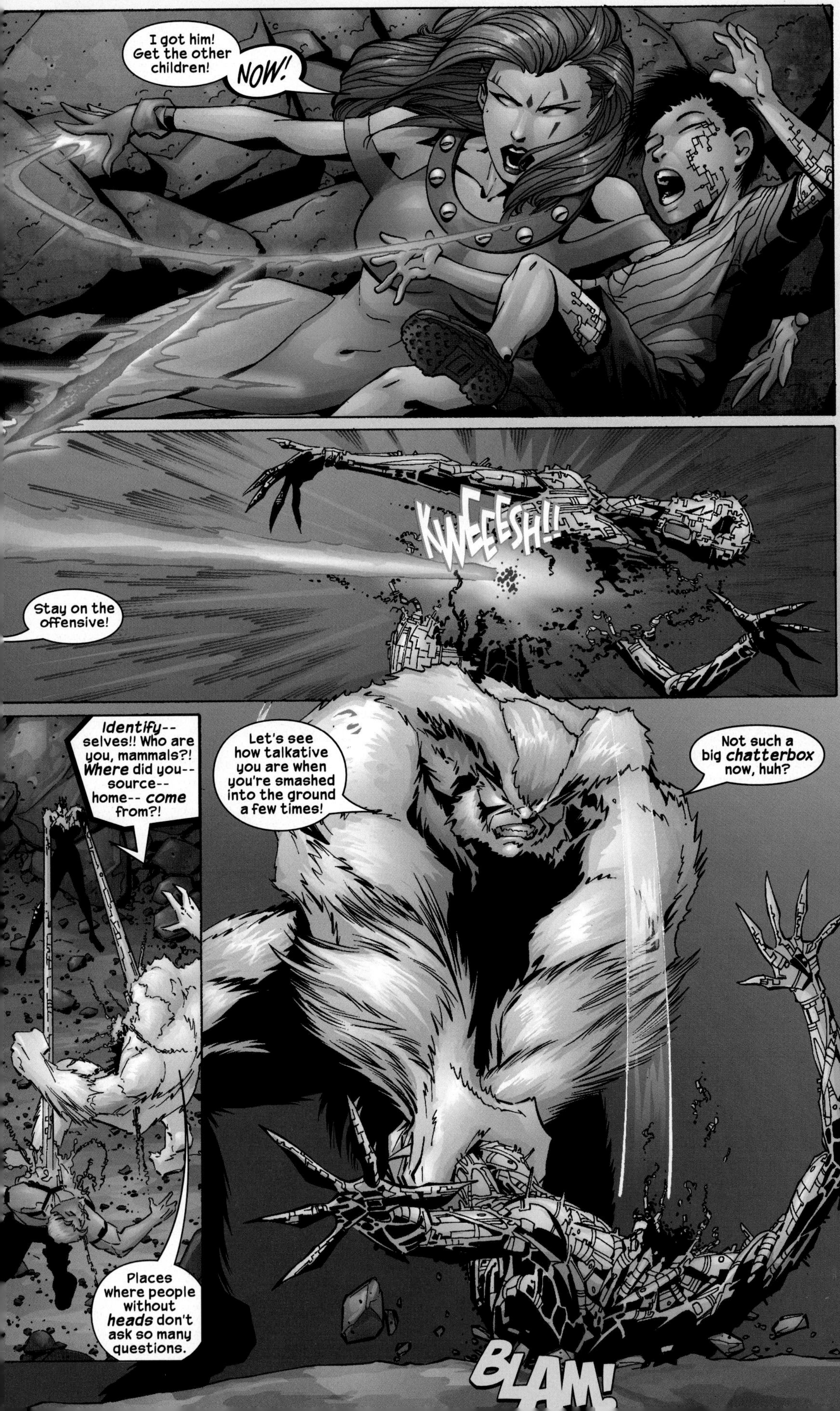
I got him! Get the other children! NOW!
Stay on the offensive!
KWEEEESH!!
Identify-- selves!! Who are you, mammals?! Where did you-- source-- home-- come from?!
Places where people without heads don't ask so many questions.
Let's see how talkative you are when you're smashed into the ground a few times!
Not such a big chatterbox now, huh?
BLAM!

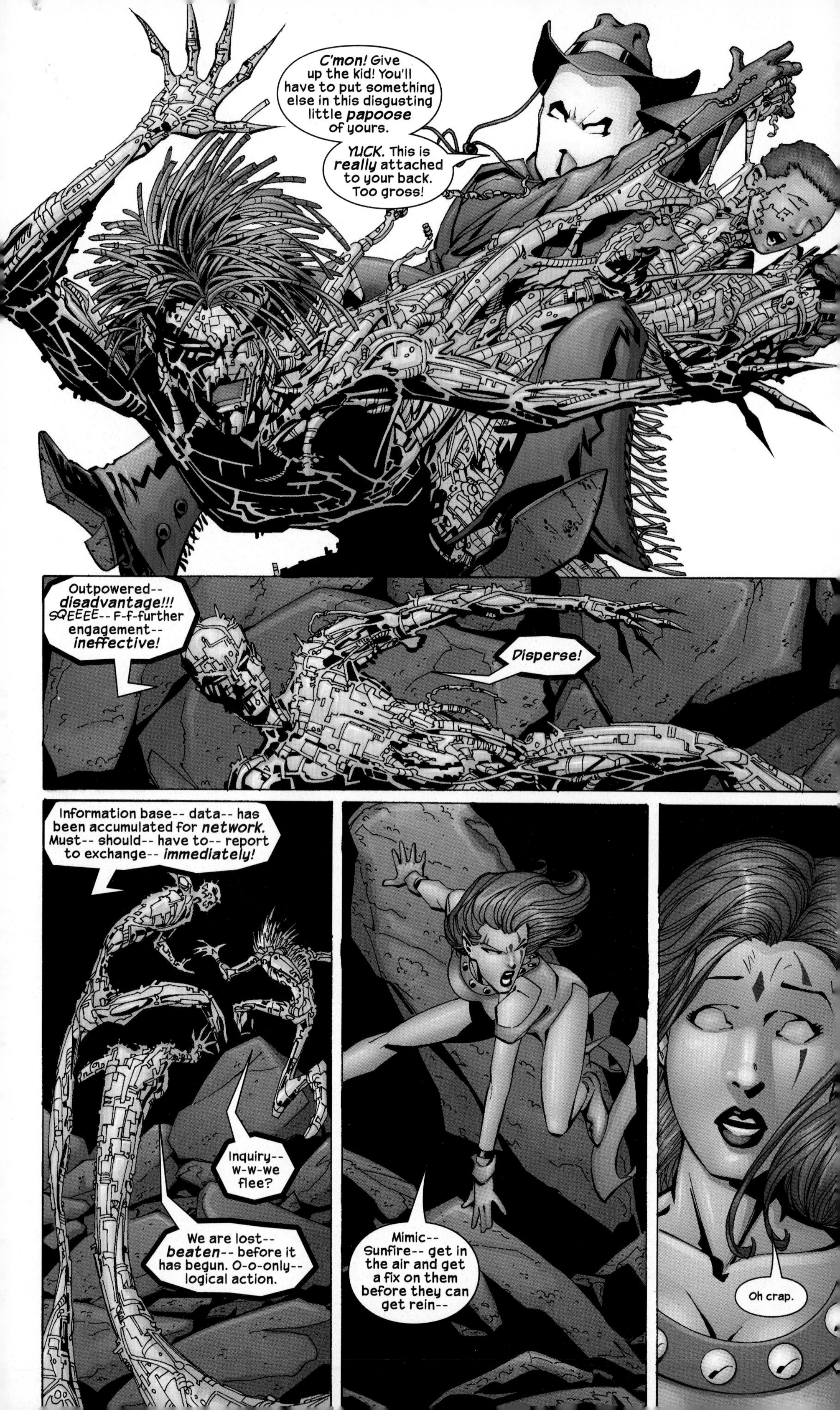

C'mon! Give up the kid! You'll have to put something else in this disgusting little papoose of yours.
YUCK. This is really attached to your back. Too gross!
Outpowered-- disadvantage!!! SQEEEE-- F-f-further engagement-- ineffective!
Disperse!
Information base-- data-- has been accumulated for network. Must-- should-- have to-- report to exchange-- immediately!
Inquiry-- w-w-we flee?
We are lost-- beaten-- before it has begun. O-o-only-- logical action.
Mimic-- Sunfire-- get in the air and get a fix on them before they can get rein--
Oh crap.

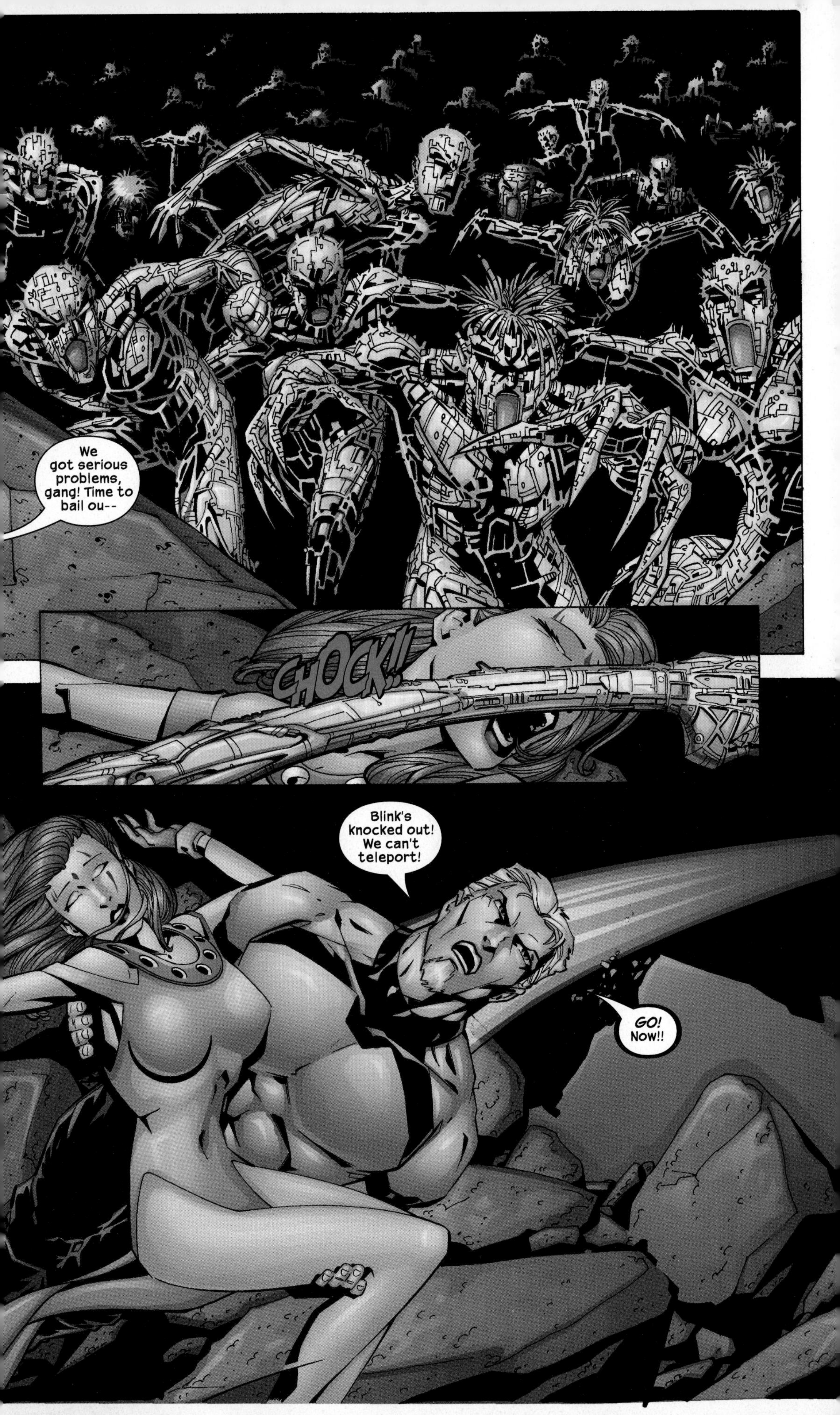
We got serious problems, gang! Time to bail ou--
CHOCK!!
Blink's knocked out! We can't teleport!
GO! Now!!

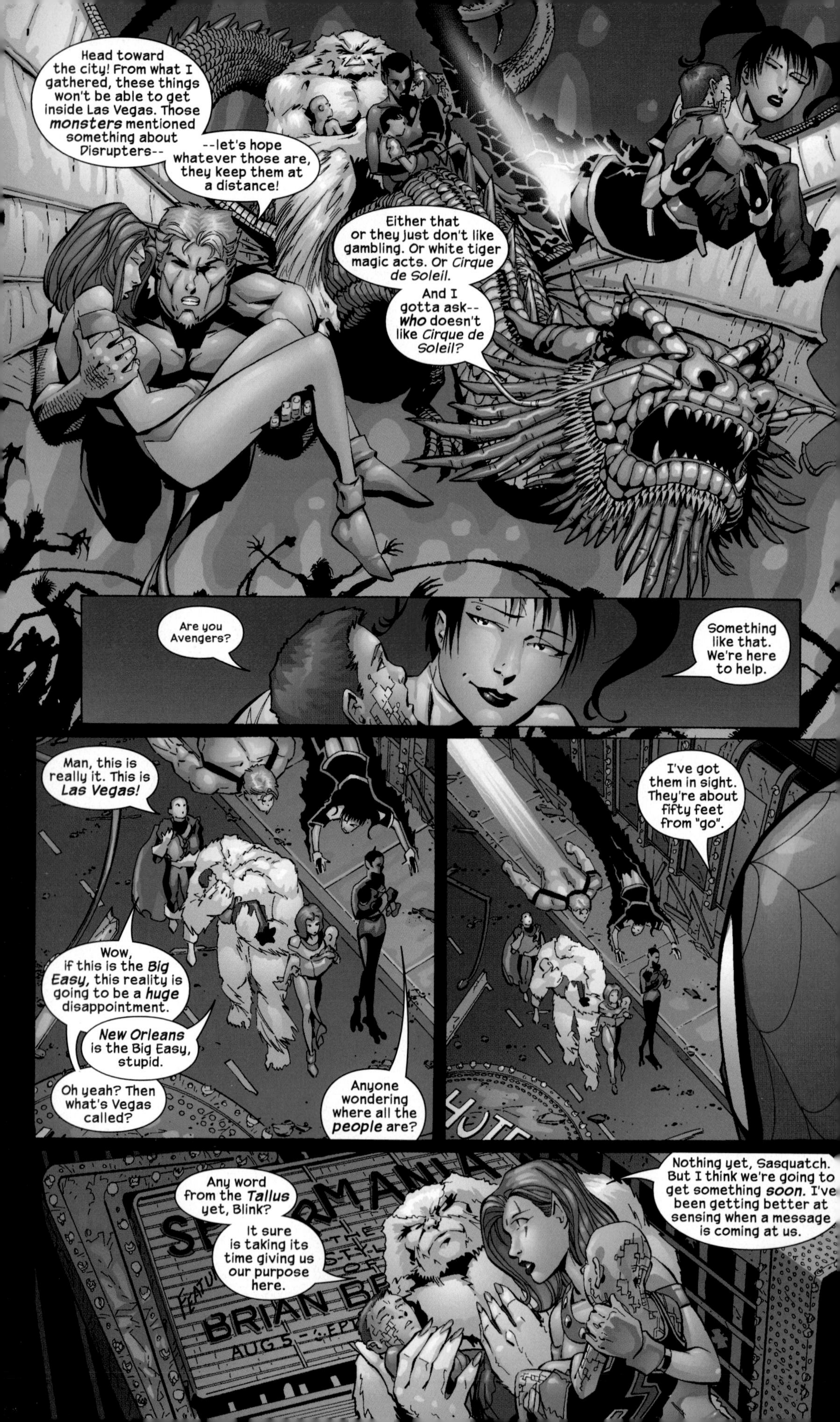
Head toward the city! From what I gathered, these things won't be able to get inside Las Vegas. Those monsters mentioned something about Disrupters--
--let's hope whatever those are, they keep them at a distance!
Either that or they just don't like gambling. Or white tiger magic acts. Or Cirque de Soleil.
And I gotta ask-- who doesn't like Cirque de Soleil?
Are you Avengers?
Something like that. We're here to help.
Man, this is really it. This is Las Vegas!
Wow, if this is the Big Easy, this reality is going to be a huge disappointment.
New Orleans is the Big Easy, stupid.
Oh yeah? Then what's Vegas called?
Anyone wondering where all the people are?
I've got them in sight. They're about fifty feet from "go".
Any word from the Tallus yet, Blink?
It sure is taking its time giving us our purpose here.
Nothing yet, Sasquatch. But I think we're going to get something soon. I've been getting better at sensing when a message is coming at us.

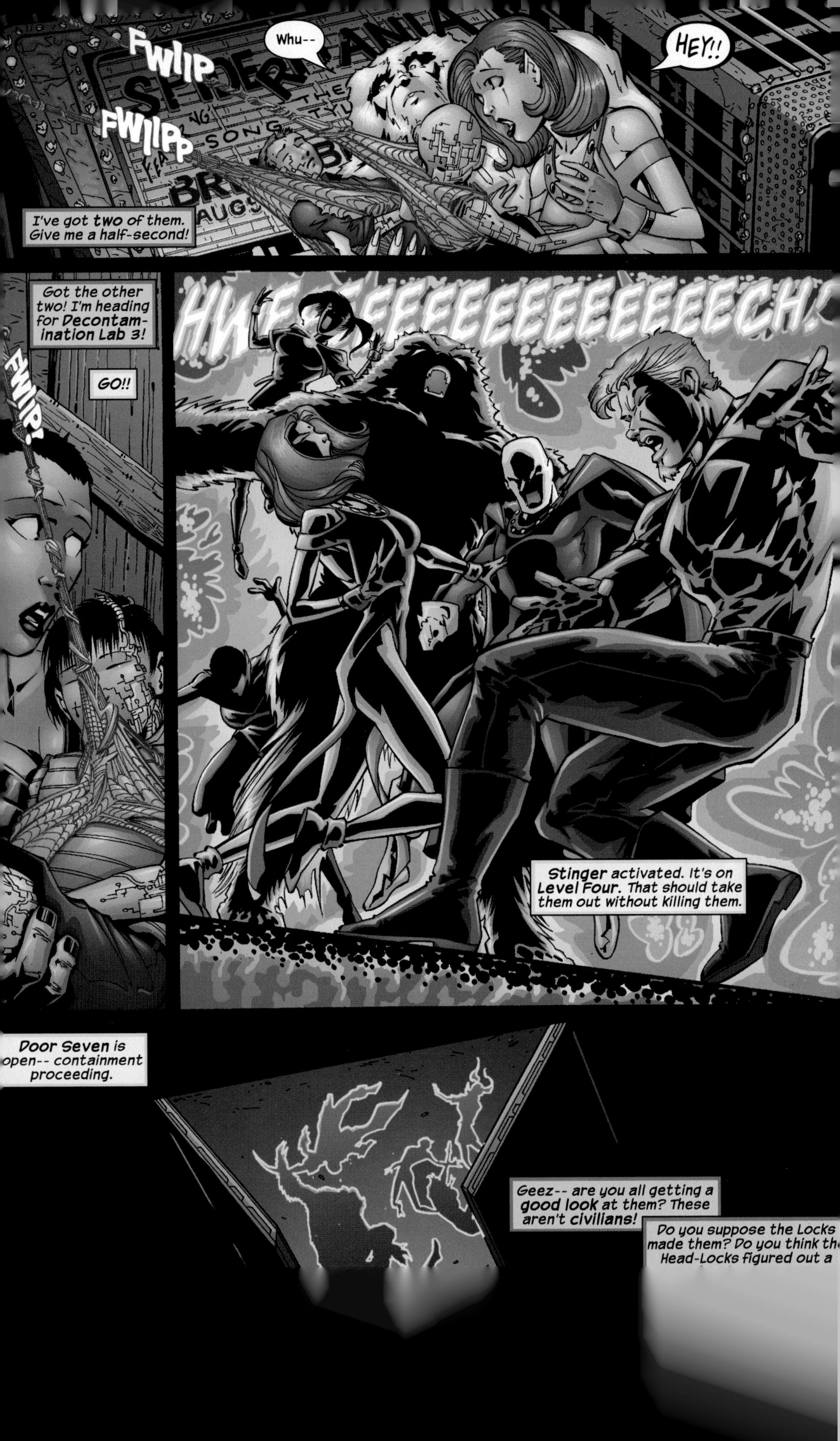
FWIIP
FWIIPP
Whu--
HEY!!
I've got two of them. Give me a half-second!
Got the other two! I'm heading for Decontamination Lab 3!
GO!!
FWIIP!
HWEEEEEEEEEEEEEEEEECH!
Stinger activated. It's on Level Four. That should take them out without killing them.
Door Seven is open-- containment proceeding.
Geez-- are you all getting a good look at them? These aren't civilians!
Do you suppose the Locks made them? Do you think the Head-Locks figured out a

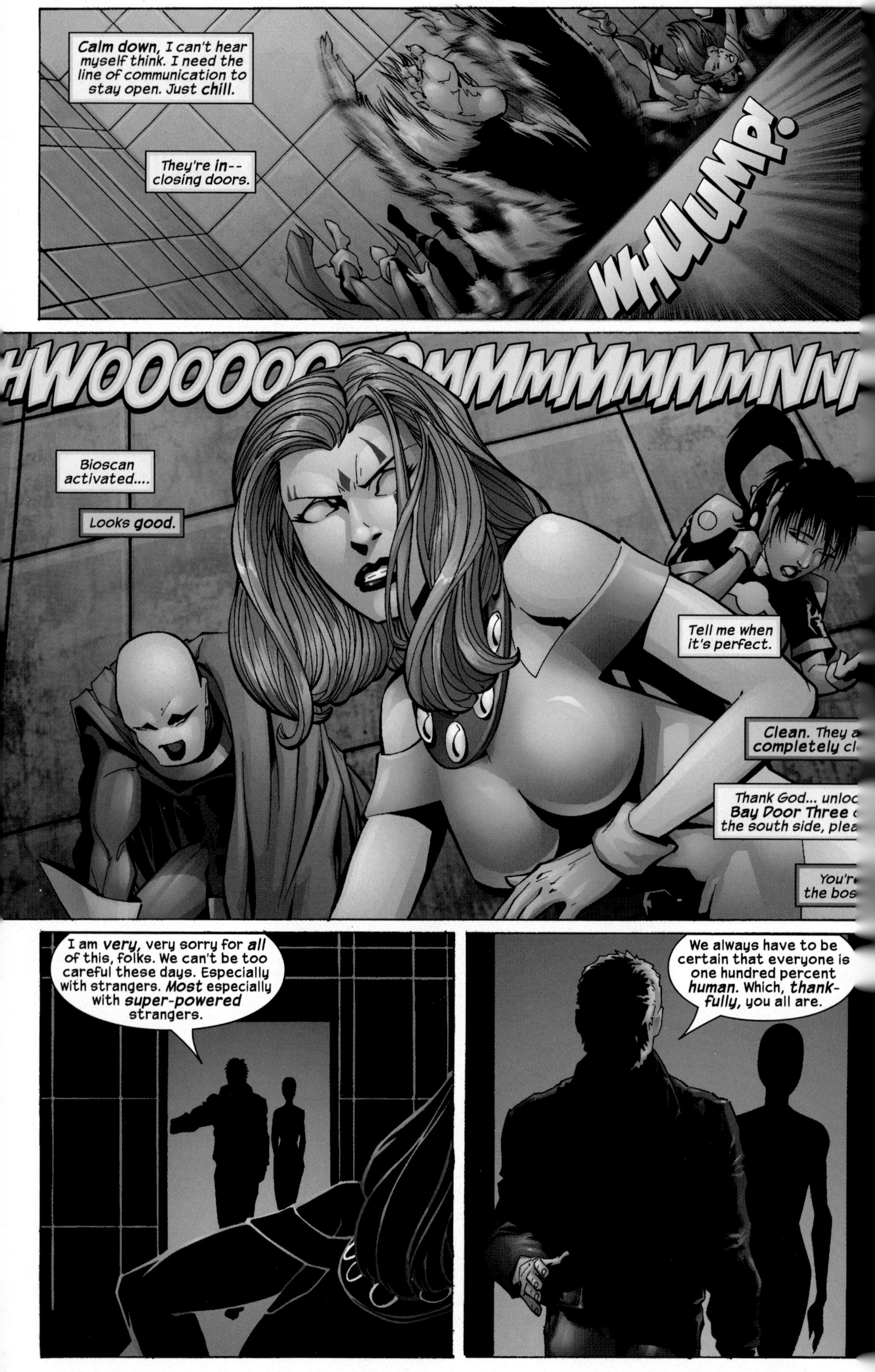

Calm down, I can't hear myself think. I need the line of communication to stay open. Just chill.
They're in--
closing doors.
WHUUMP!
HWOOOOOOOMMMMMMMMMNN
Bioscan activated....
Looks good.
Tell me when it's perfect.
Clean. They a
completely cl
Thank God... unloc
Bay Door Three
the south side, plea
You'r
the bos
I am very, very sorry for all of this, folks. We can't be too careful these days. Especially with strangers. Most especially with super-powered strangers.
We always have to be certain that everyone is one hundred percent human. Which, thankfully, you all are.

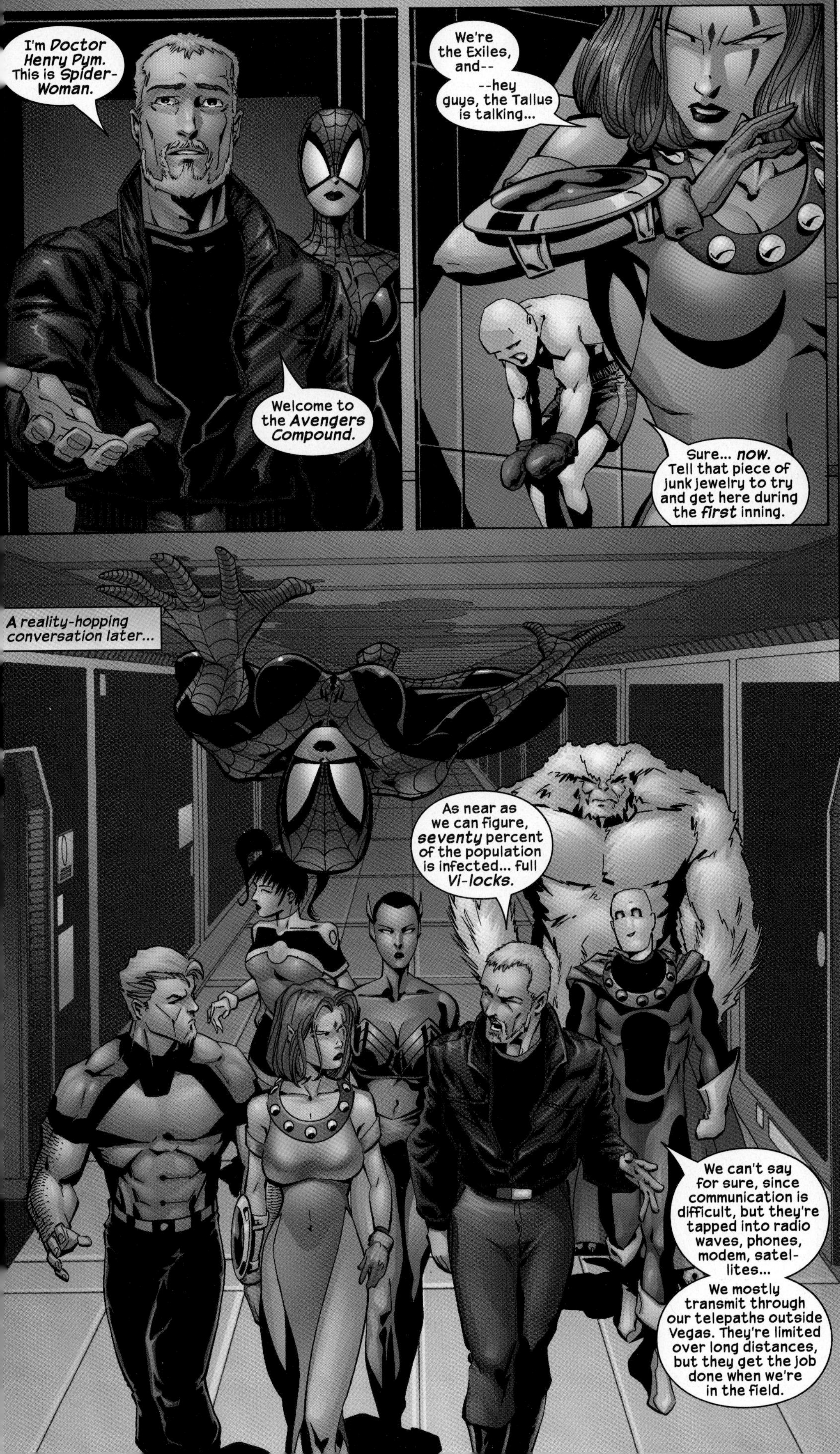
I'm *Doctor Henry Pym.* This is *Spider-Woman.*
Welcome to the *Avengers Compound.*
We're the Exiles, and--
--hey guys, the Tallus is talking...
Sure... *now.* Tell that piece of junk jewelry to try and get here during the *first* inning.
A reality-hopping conversation later...
As near as we can figure, *seventy* percent of the population is infected... full *Vi-locks.*
We can't say for sure, since communication is difficult, but they're tapped into radio waves, phones, modem, satel-lites...
We mostly transmit through our telepaths outside Vegas. They're limited over long distances, but they get the job done when we're in the field.

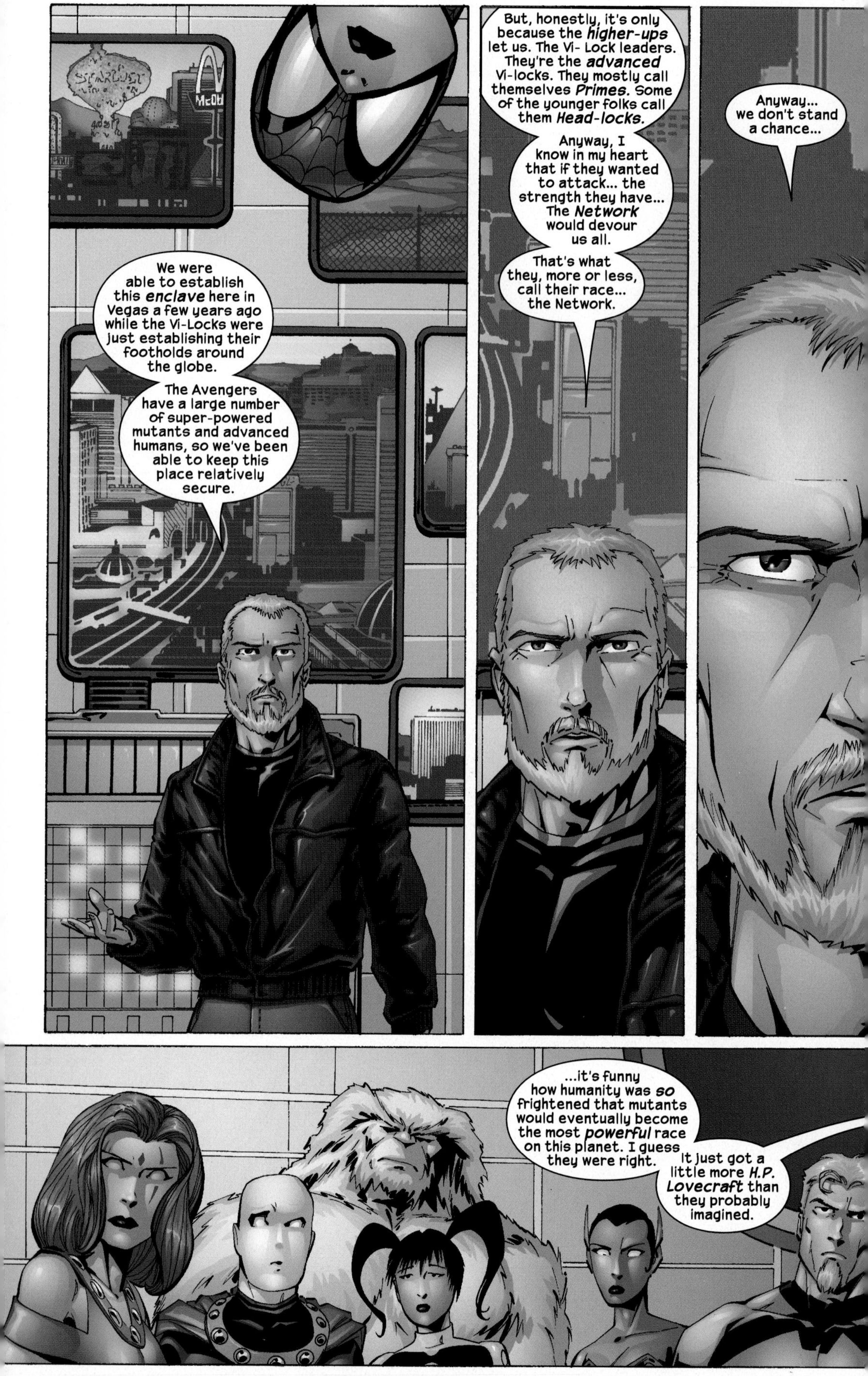

We were able to establish this *enclave* here in Vegas a few years ago while the Vi-Locks were just establishing their footholds around the globe.
The Avengers have a large number of super-powered mutants and advanced humans, so we've been able to keep this place relatively secure.
But, honestly, it's only because the *higher-ups* let us. The Vi- Lock leaders. They're the *advanced* Vi-locks. They mostly call themselves *Primes.* Some of the younger folks call them *Head-locks.*
Anyway, I know in my heart that if they wanted to attack... the strength they have... The *Network* would devour us all.
That's what they, more or less, call their race... the Network.
Anyway... we don't stand a chance...
...it's funny how humanity was *so* frightened that mutants would eventually become the most *powerful* race on this planet. I guess they were right.
It just got a little more *H.P. Lovecraft* than they probably imagined.

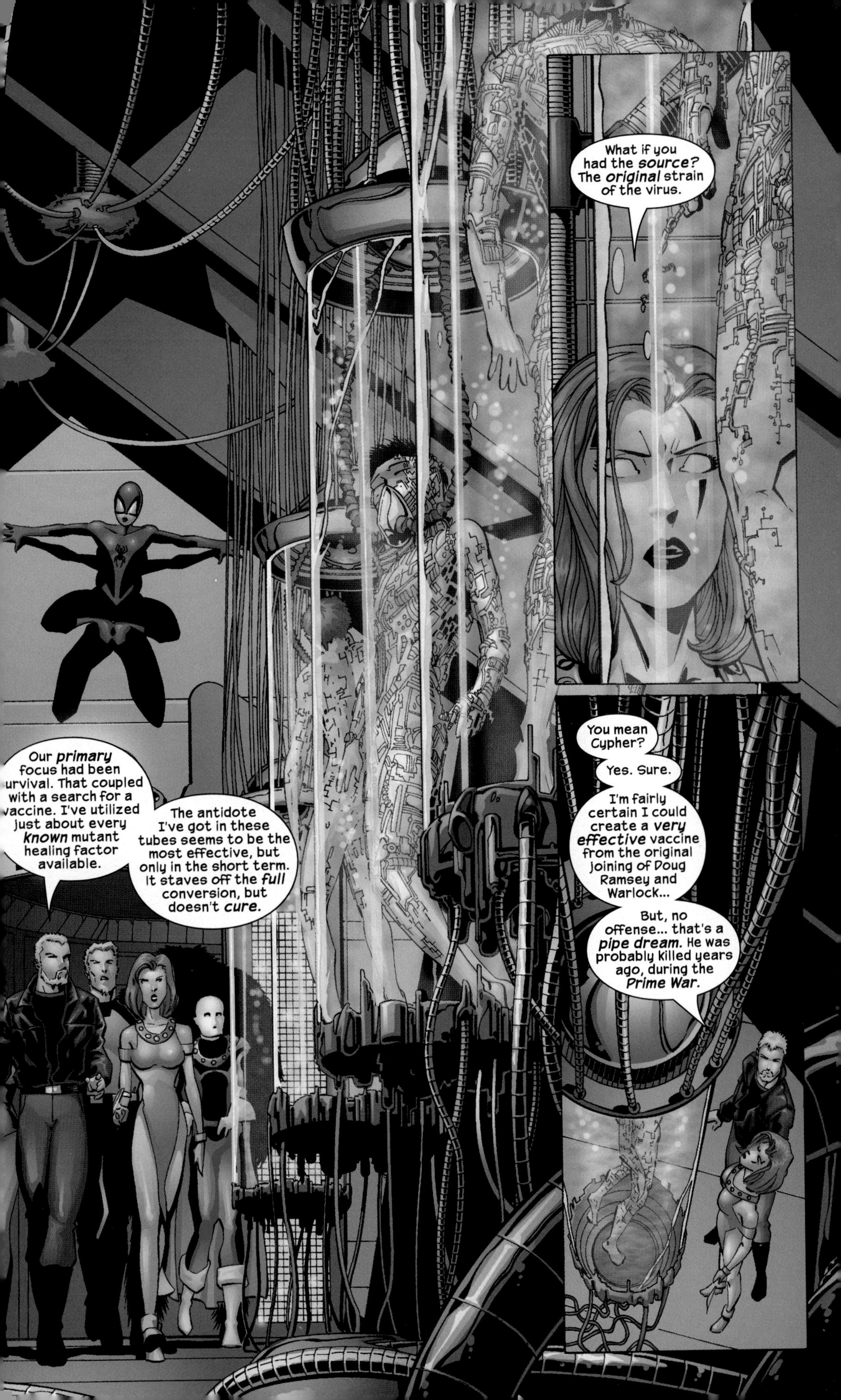

Our *primary* focus had been survival. That coupled with a search for a vaccine. I've utilized just about every *known* mutant healing factor available.
The antidote I've got in these tubes seems to be the most effective, but only in the short term. It staves off the *full* conversion, but doesn't *cure*.
What if you had the *source?* The *original* strain of the virus.
You mean Cypher?
Yes. Sure.
I'm fairly certain I could create a *very effective* vaccine from the original joining of Doug Ramsey and Warlock...
But, no offense... that's a *pipe dream.* He was probably killed years ago, during the *Prime War*.

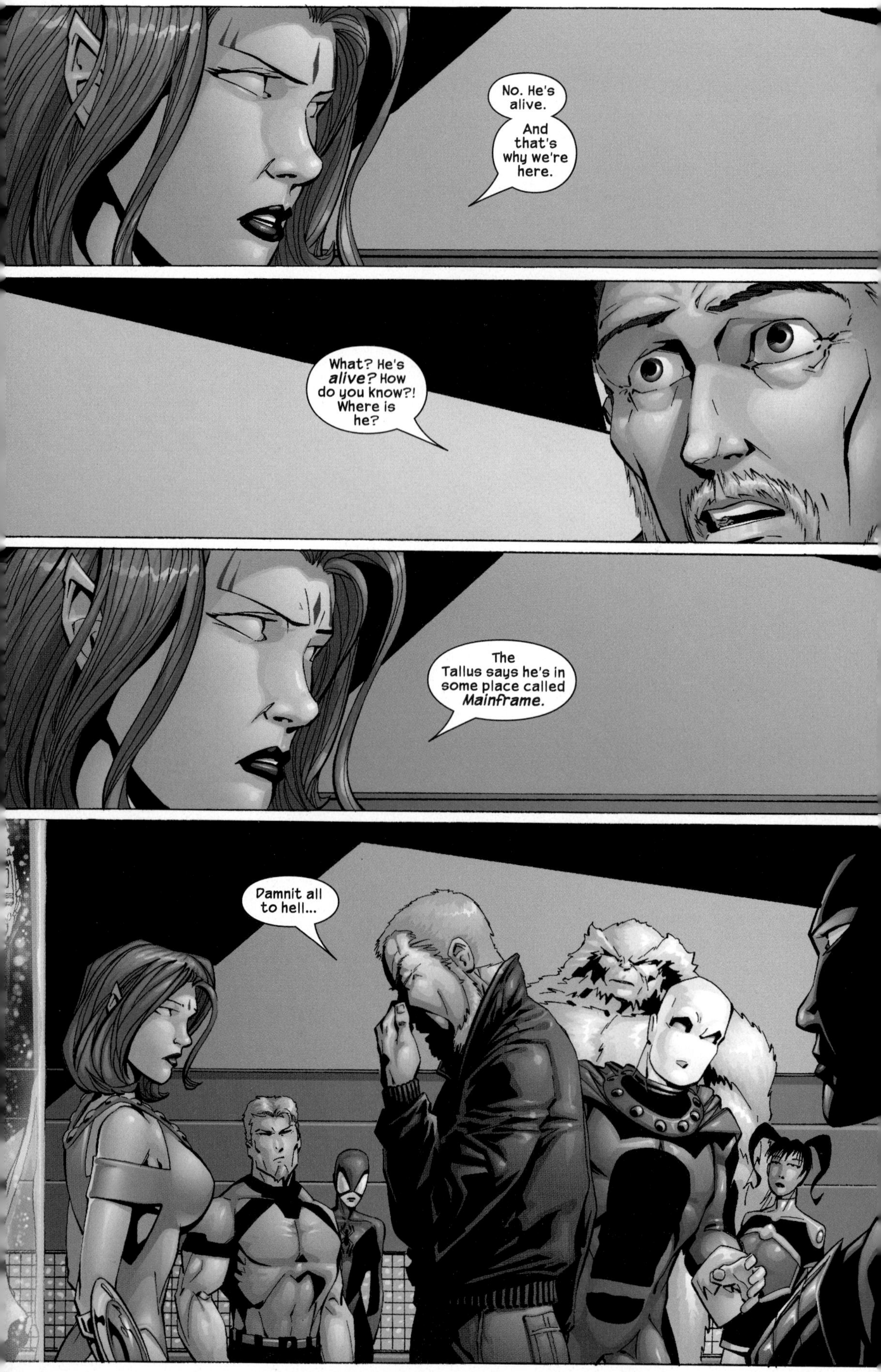
No. He's alive.
And that's why we're here.
What? He's *alive?* How do you know?! Where is he?
The Tallus says he's in some place called *Mainframe.*
Damnit all to hell...

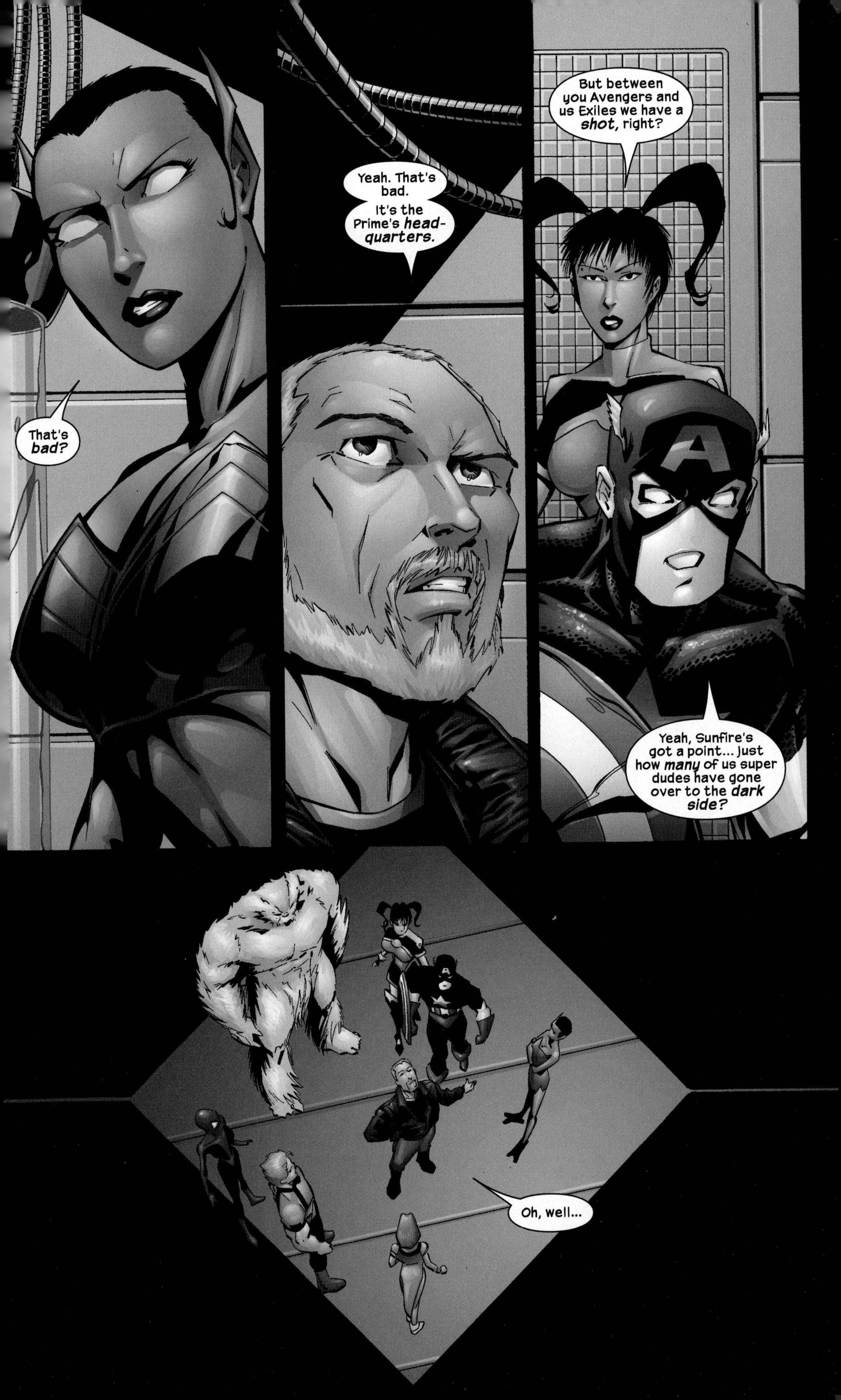
That's bad?
Yeah. That's bad.
It's the Prime's head-quarters.
But between you Avengers and us Exiles we have a shot, right?
Yeah, Sunfire's got a point... just how many of us super dudes have gone over to the dark side?
Oh, well...

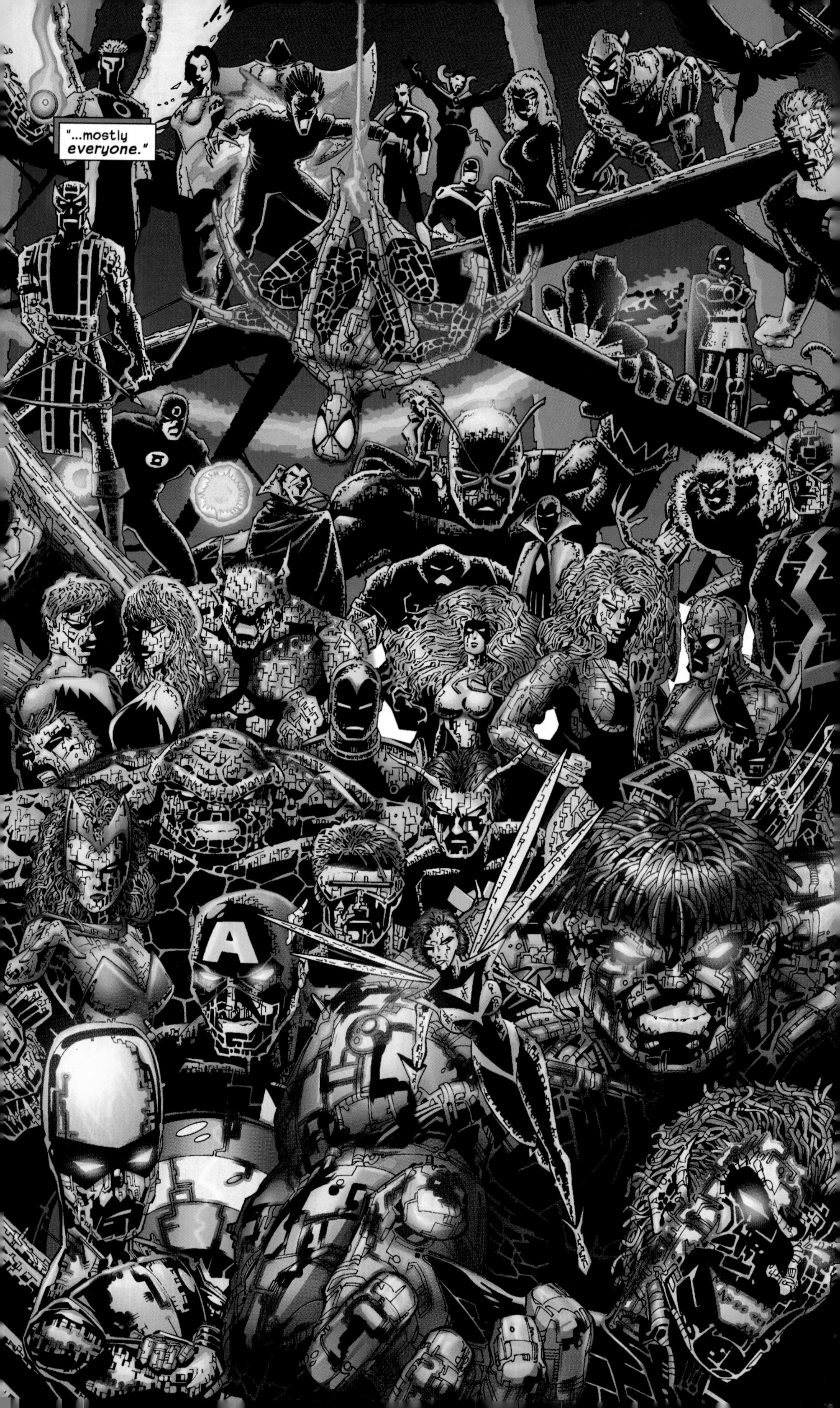
"...mostly
everyone."

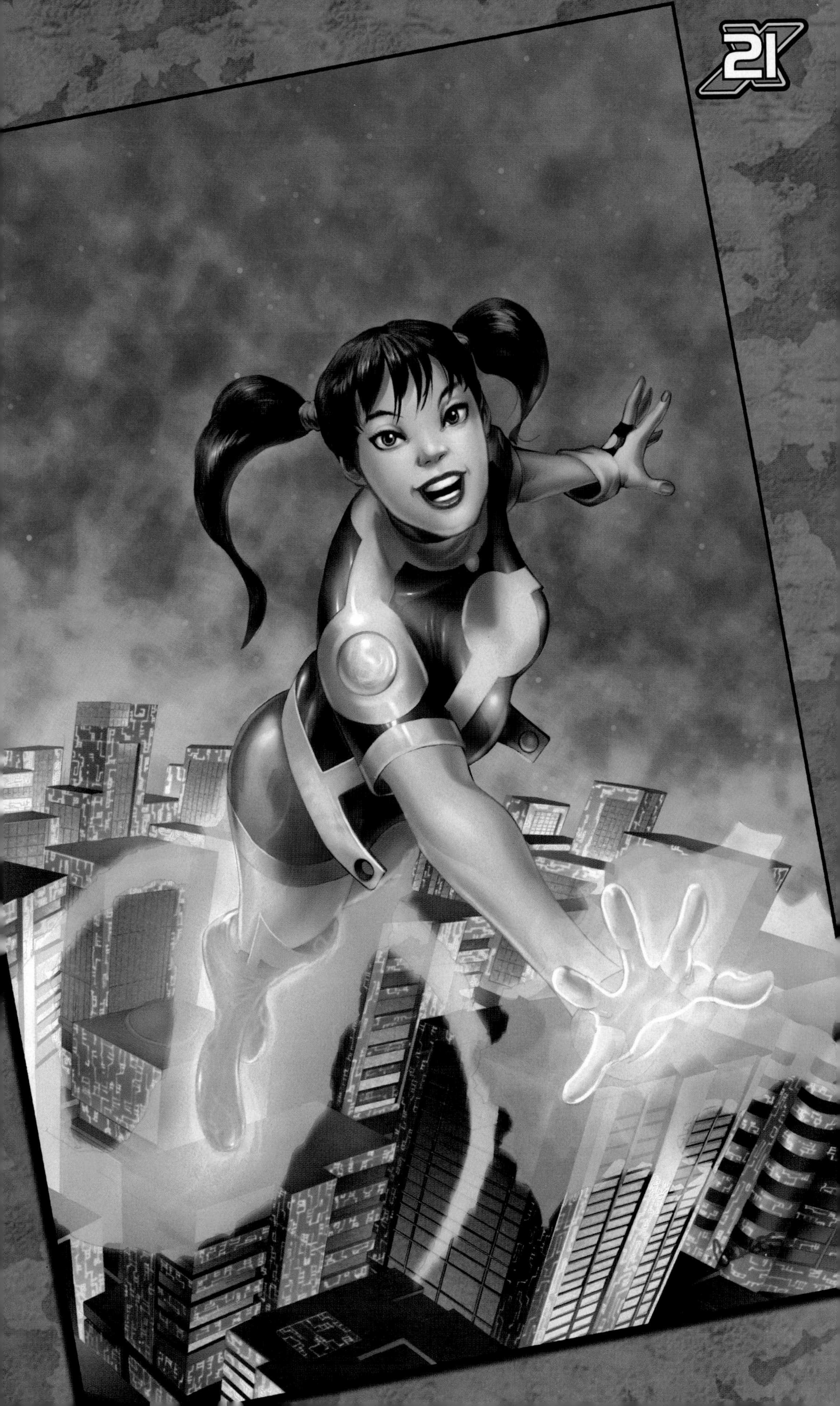

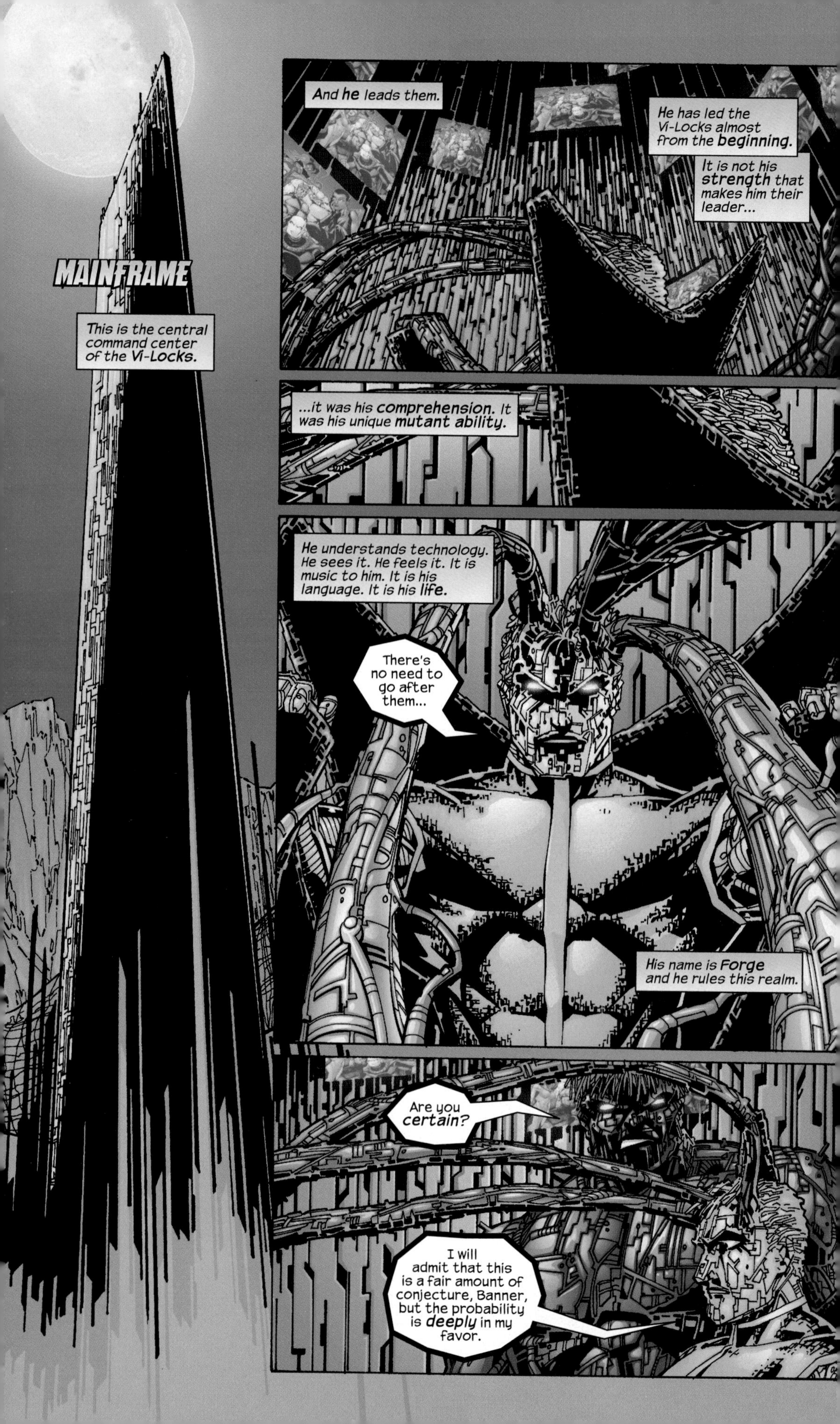
MAINFRAME
This is the central command center of the Vi-Locks.
And he leads them.
He has led the Vi-Locks almost from the beginning.
It is not his strength that makes him their leader...
...it was his comprehension. It was his unique mutant ability.
He understands technology. He sees it. He feels it. It is music to him. It is his language. It is his life.
There's no need to go after them...
His name is Forge and he rules this realm.
Are you certain?
I will admit that this is a fair amount of conjecture, Banner, but the probability is deeply in my favor.

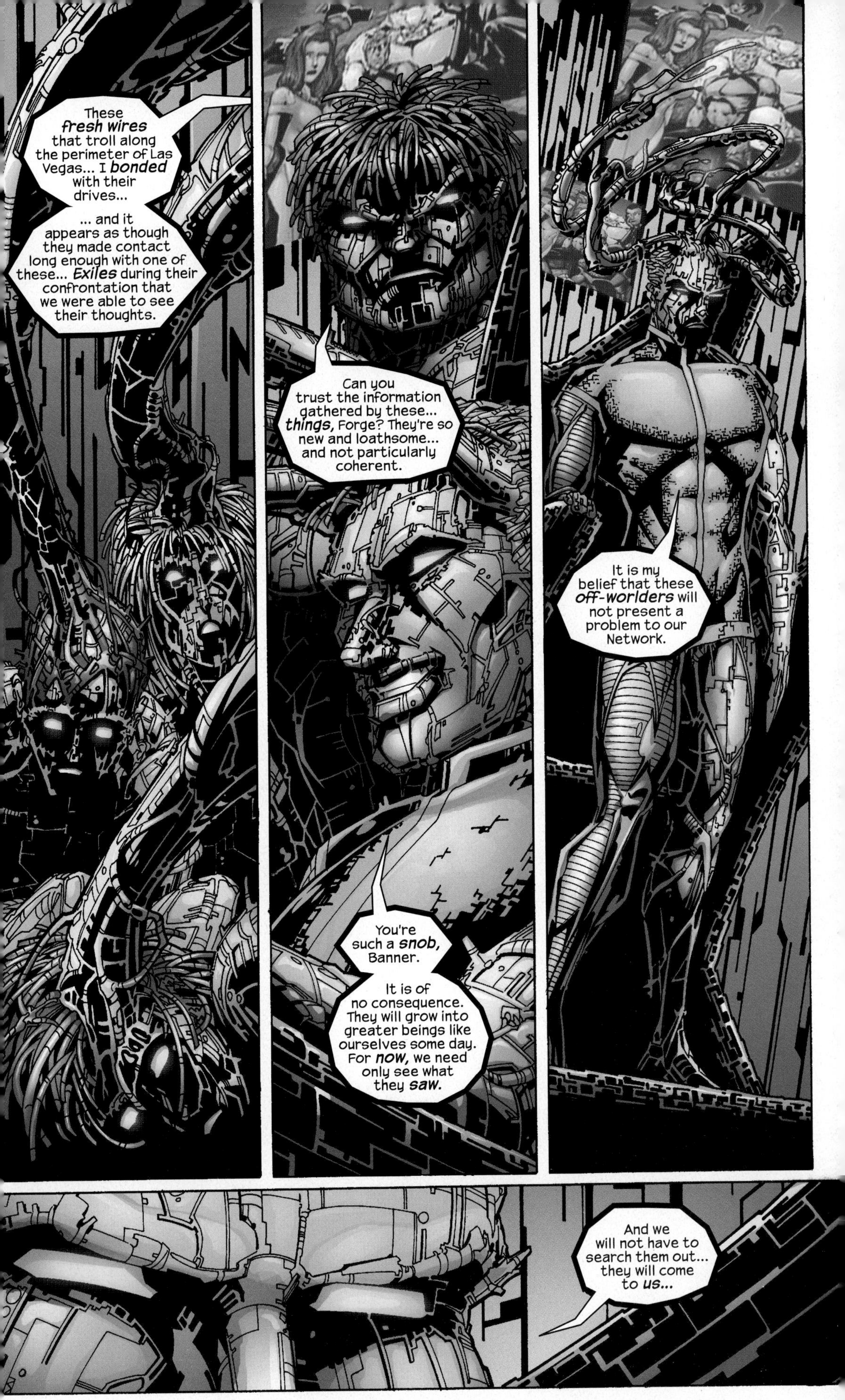
These fresh wires that troll along the perimeter of Las Vegas... I bonded with their drives...
... and it appears as though they made contact long enough with one of these... Exiles during their confrontation that we were able to see their thoughts.
Can you trust the information gathered by these... things, Forge? They're so new and loathsome... and not particularly coherent.
You're such a snob, Banner.
It is of no consequence. They will grow into greater beings like ourselves some day. For now, we need only see what they saw.
It is my belief that these off-worlders will not present a problem to our Network.
And we will not have to search them out... they will come to us...

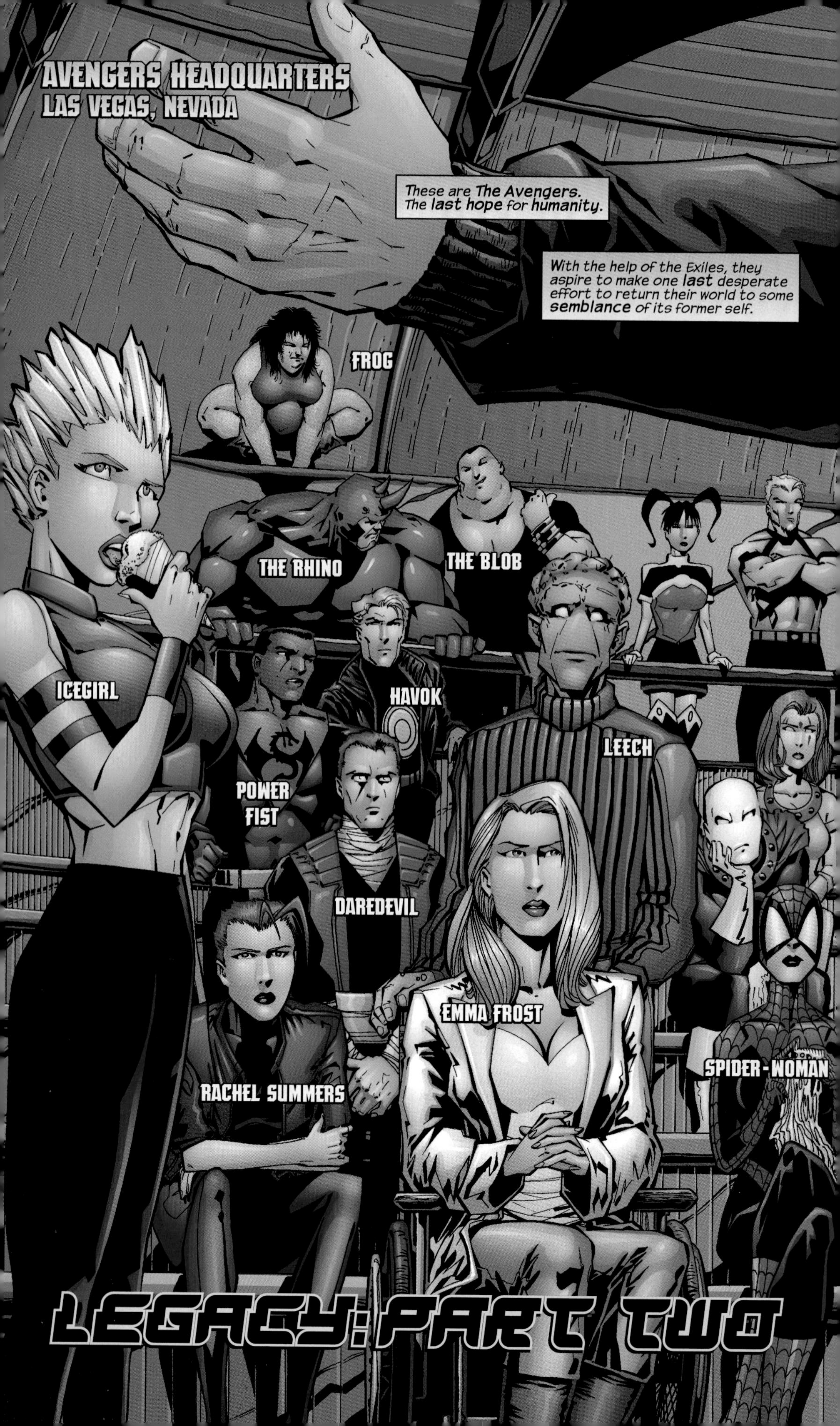
AVENGERS HEADQUARTERS
LAS VEGAS, NEVADA
These are The Avengers. The last hope for humanity.
With the help of the Exiles, they aspire to make one last desperate effort to return their world to some semblance of its former self.
FROG
THE RHINO
THE BLOB
ICEGIRL
HAVOK
LEECH
POWER FIST
DAREDEVIL
EMMA FROST
SPIDER-WOMAN
RACHEL SUMMERS
LEGACY: PART TWO

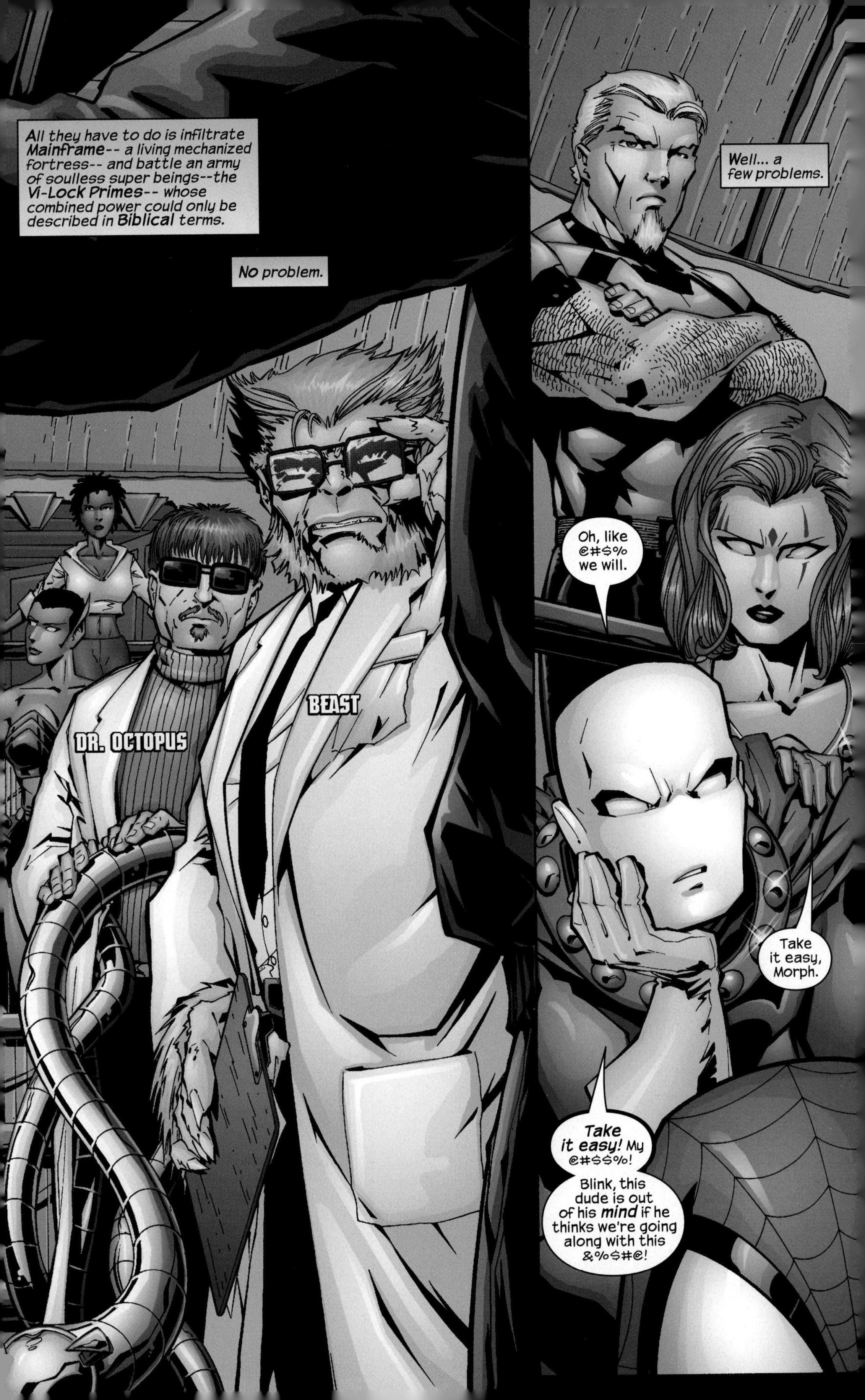

All they have to do is infiltrate Mainframe-- a living mechanized fortress-- and battle an army of soulless super beings--the Vi-Lock Primes-- whose combined power could only be described in Biblical terms.
No problem.
Well... a few problems.
BEAST
DR. OCTOPUS
Oh, like @#$% we will.
Take it easy, Morph.
Take it easy! My @#$$%!
Blink, this dude is out of his mind if he thinks we're going along with this &%$#@!

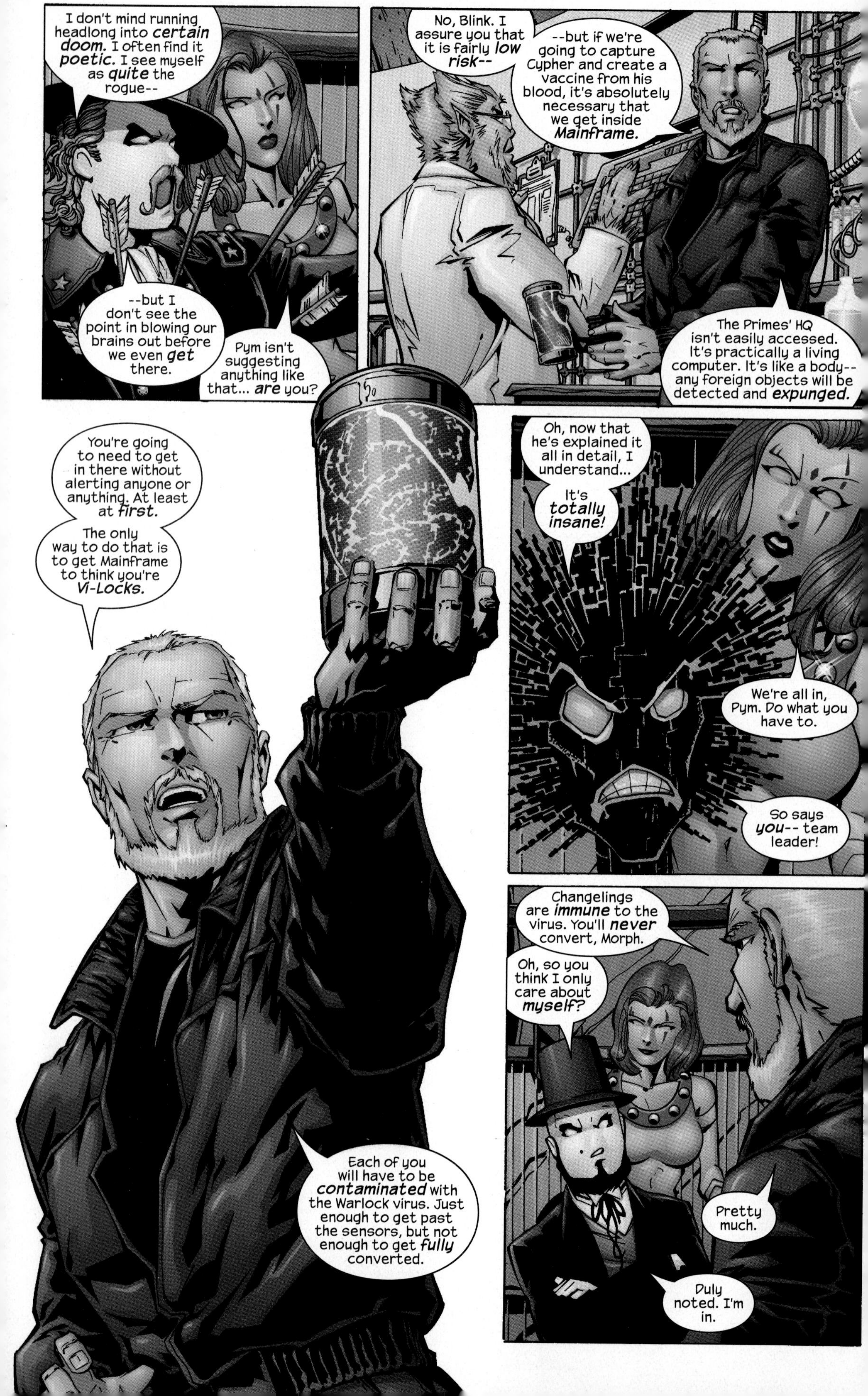
I don't mind running headlong into *certain doom.* I often find it *poetic.* I see myself as *quite* the rogue--
--but I don't see the point in blowing our brains out before we even *get* there.
Pym isn't suggesting anything like that... *are* you?
No, Blink. I assure you that it is fairly *low risk*--
--but if we're going to capture Cypher and create a vaccine from his blood, it's absolutely necessary that we get inside *Mainframe.*
The Primes' HQ isn't easily accessed. It's practically a living computer. It's like a body--any foreign objects will be detected and *expunged.*
You're going to need to get in there without alerting anyone or anything. At least at *first.*
The only way to do that is to get Mainframe to think you're *Vi-Locks.*
Each of you will have to be *contaminated* with the Warlock virus. Just enough to get past the sensors, but not enough to get *fully* converted.
Oh, now that he's explained it all in detail, I understand...
It's *totally insane!*
We're all in, Pym. Do what you have to.
So says *you*-- team leader!
Changelings are *immune* to the virus. You'll *never* convert, Morph.
Oh, so you think I only care about *myself?*
Pretty much.
Duly noted. I'm in.

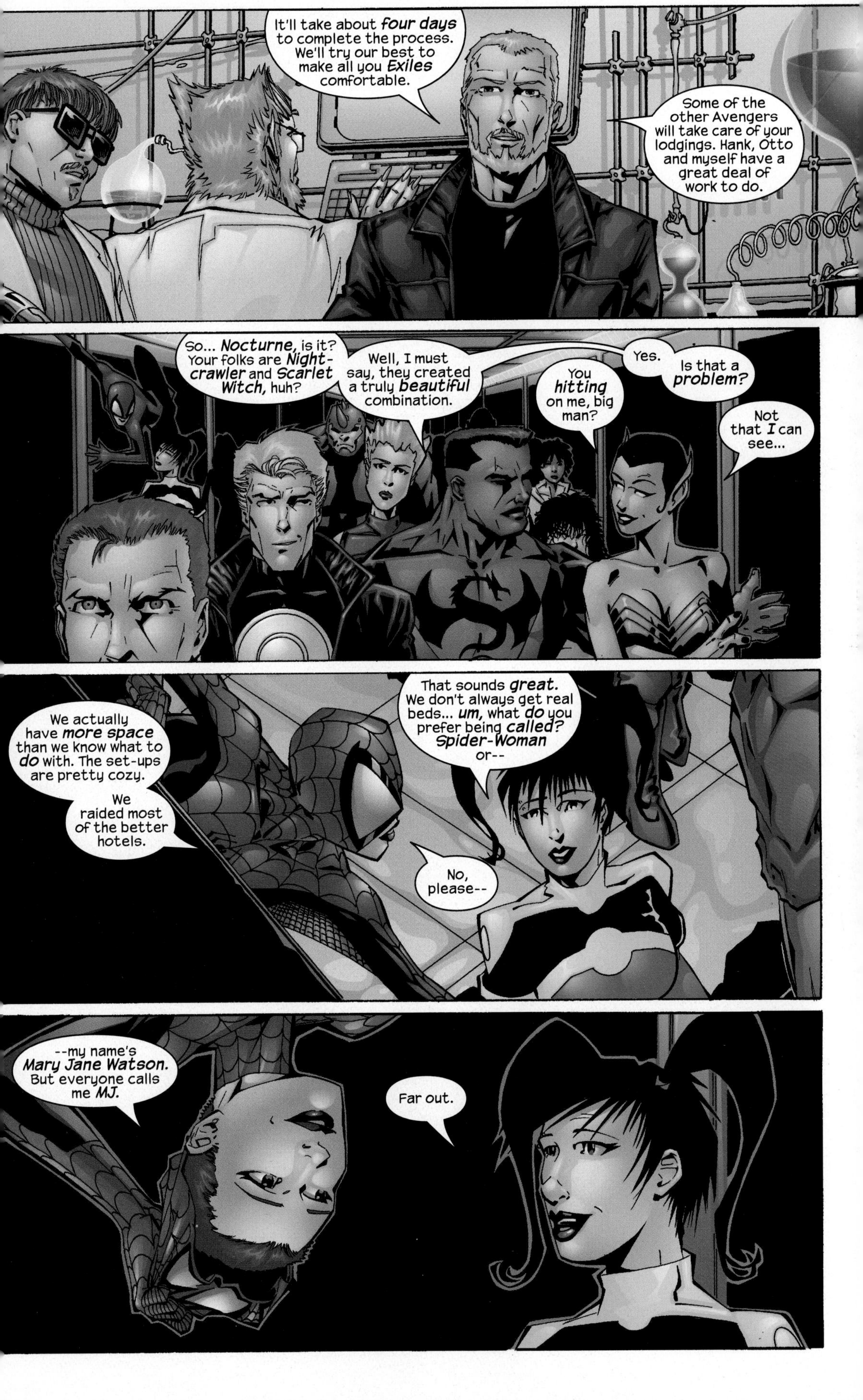
It'll take about four days to complete the process. We'll try our best to make all you Exiles comfortable.
Some of the other Avengers will take care of your lodgings. Hank, Otto and myself have a great deal of work to do.
So... Nocturne, is it? Your folks are Night-crawler and Scarlet Witch, huh?
Yes.
Well, I must say, they created a truly beautiful combination.
You hitting on me, big man?
Is that a problem?
Not that I can see...
We actually have more space than we know what to do with. The set-ups are pretty cozy.
We raided most of the better hotels.
That sounds great. We don't always get real beds... um, what do you prefer being called? Spider-Woman or--
No, please--
--my name's Mary Jane Watson. But everyone calls me MJ.
Far out.

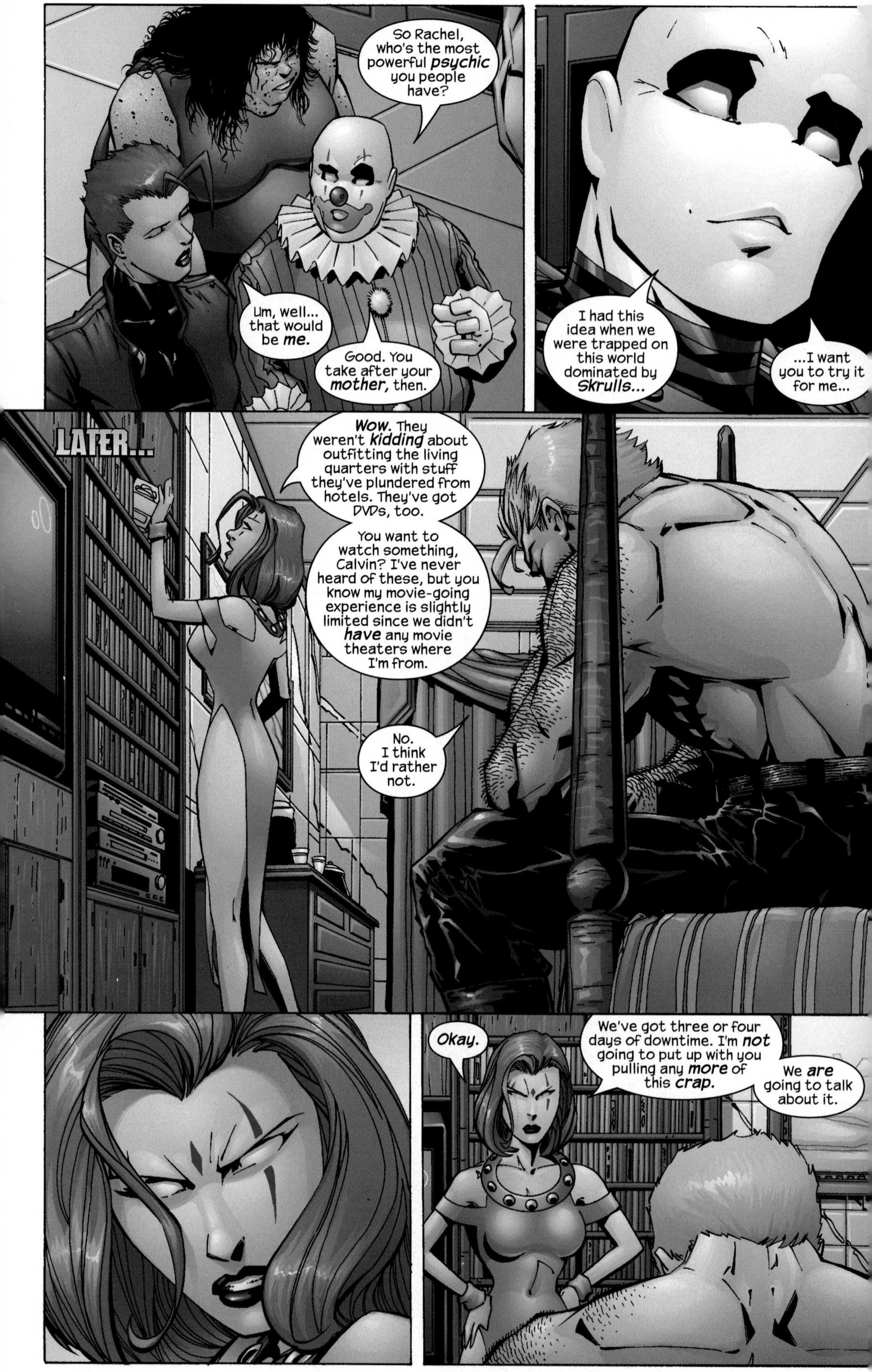
So Rachel, who's the most powerful *psychic* you people have?
Um, well... that would be *me.*
Good. You take after your *mother,* then.
I had this idea when we were trapped on this world dominated by *Skrulls...*
...I want you to try it for me...
LATER...
Wow. They weren't *kidding* about outfitting the living quarters with stuff they've plundered from hotels. They've got DVDs, too.
You want to watch something, Calvin? I've never heard of these, but you know my movie-going experience is slightly limited since we didn't *have* any movie theaters where I'm from.
No. I think I'd rather not.
Okay.
We've got three or four days of downtime. I'm *not* going to put up with you pulling any *more* of this *crap.*
We *are* going to talk about it.

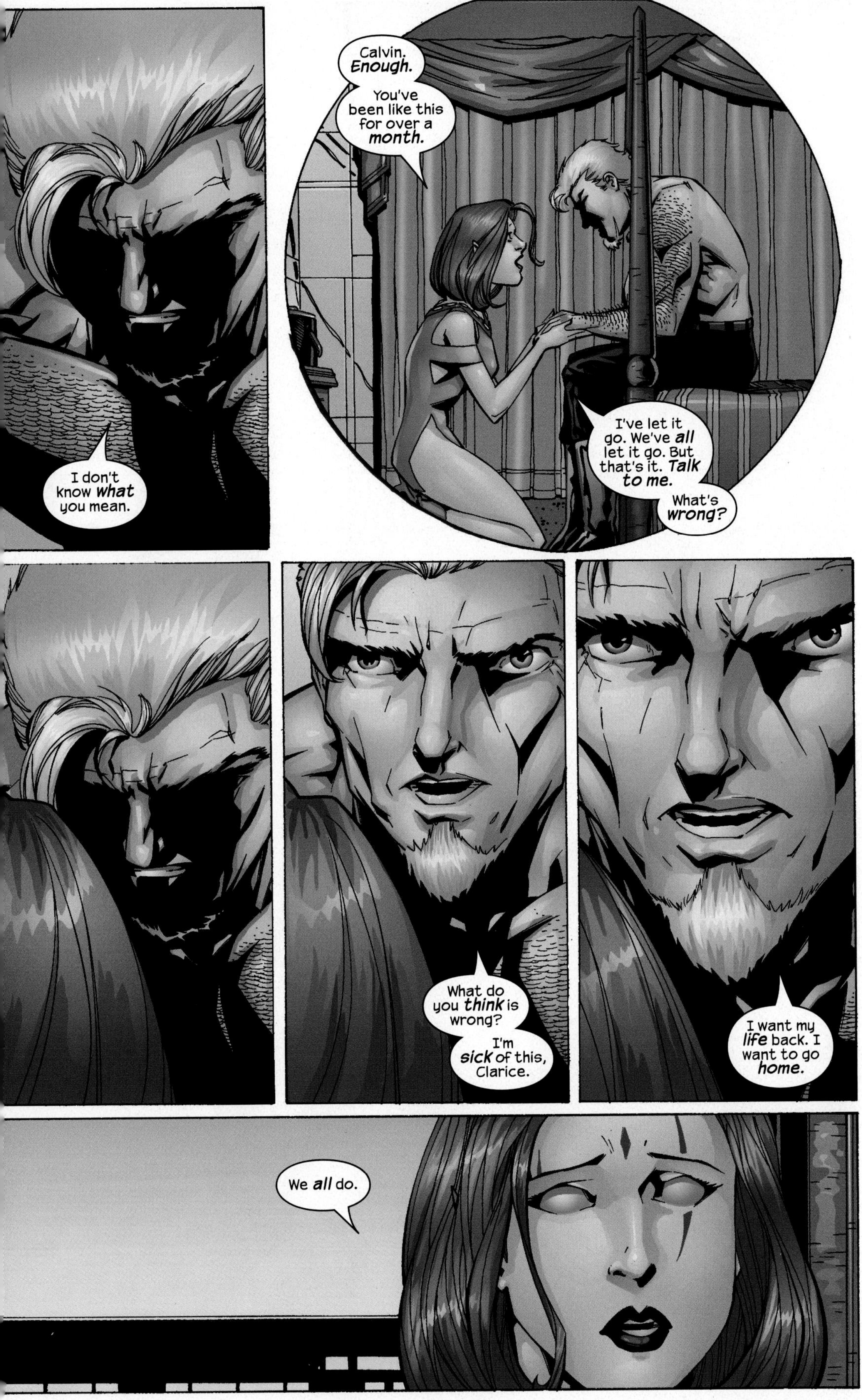

Calvin. Enough.
You've been like this for over a month.
I don't know what you mean.
I've let it go. We've all let it go. But that's it. Talk to me.
What's wrong?
What do you think is wrong?
I'm sick of this, Clarice.
I want my life back. I want to go home.
We all do.

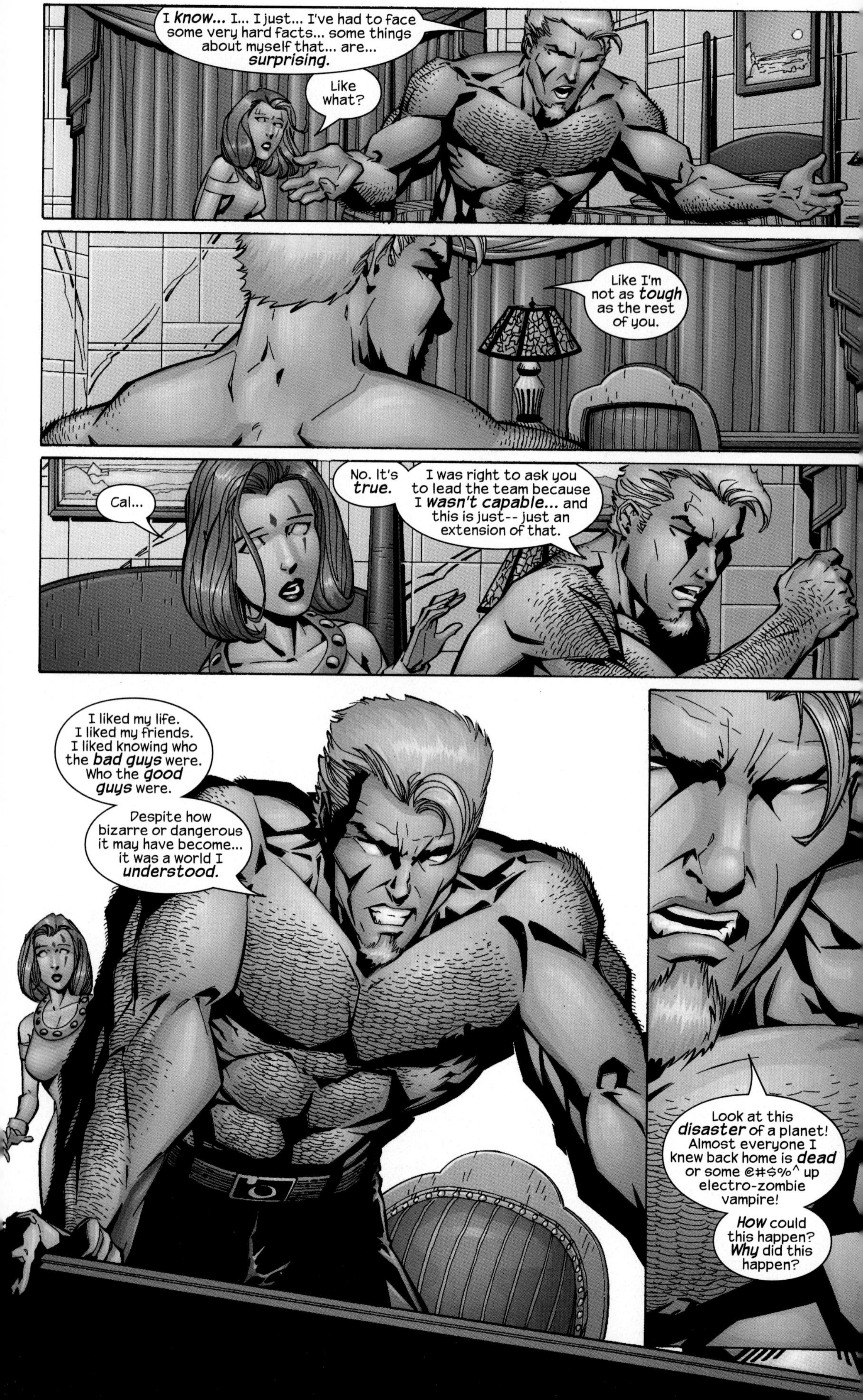

I know... I... I just... I've had to face some very hard facts... some things about myself that... are... surprising.
Like what?
Like I'm not as tough as the rest of you.
Cal...
No. It's true.
I was right to ask you to lead the team because I wasn't capable... and this is just-- just an extension of that.
I liked my life. I liked my friends. I liked knowing who the bad guys were. Who the good guys were.
Despite how bizarre or dangerous it may have become... it was a world I understood.
Look at this disaster of a planet! Almost everyone I knew back home is dead or some @#$%^ up electro-zombie vampire!
How could this happen? Why did this happen?

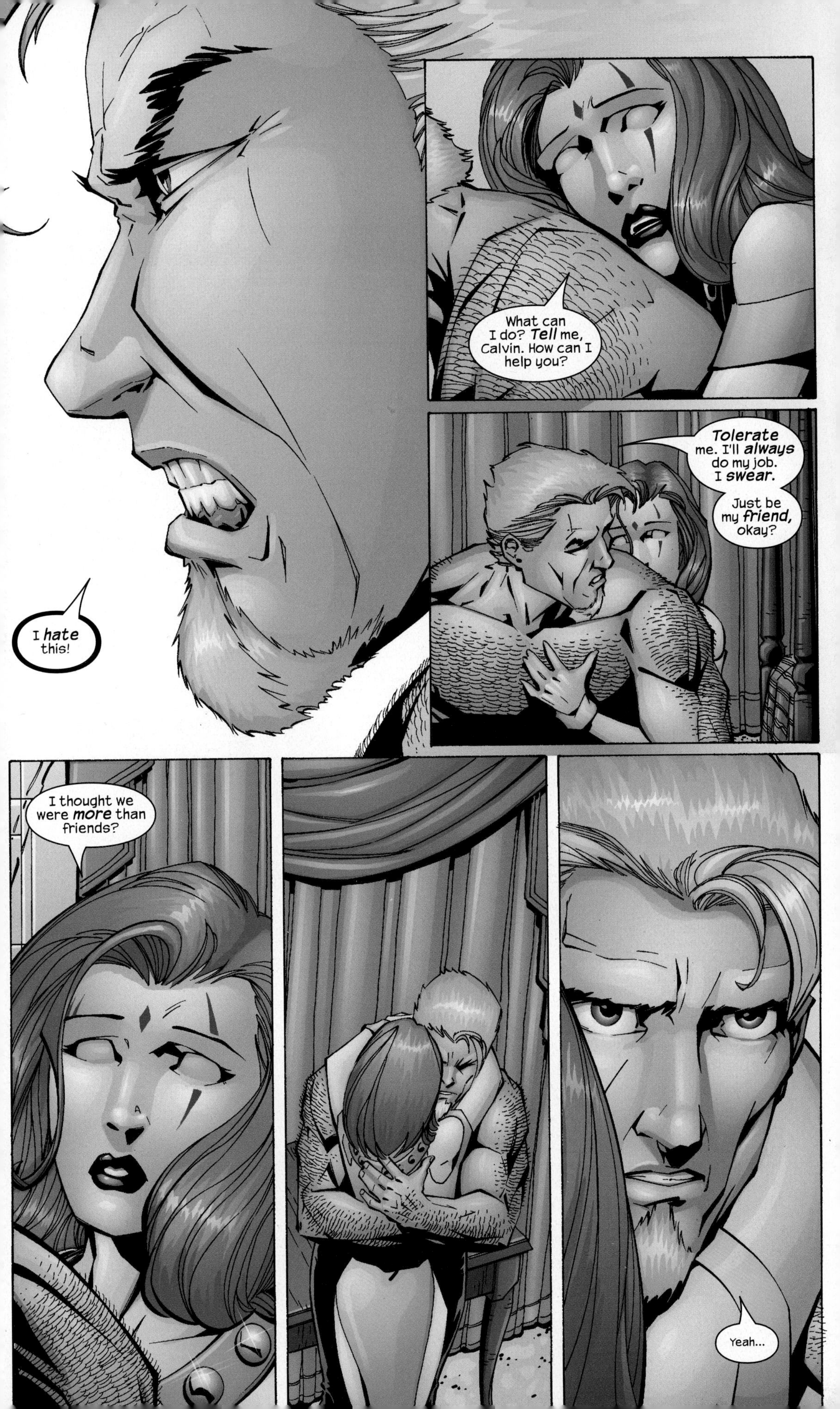
I *hate* this!
What can I do? *Tell* me, Calvin. How can I help you?
Tolerate me. I'll *always* do my job. I *swear.*
Just be my *friend,* okay?
I thought we were *more* than friends?
Yeah...

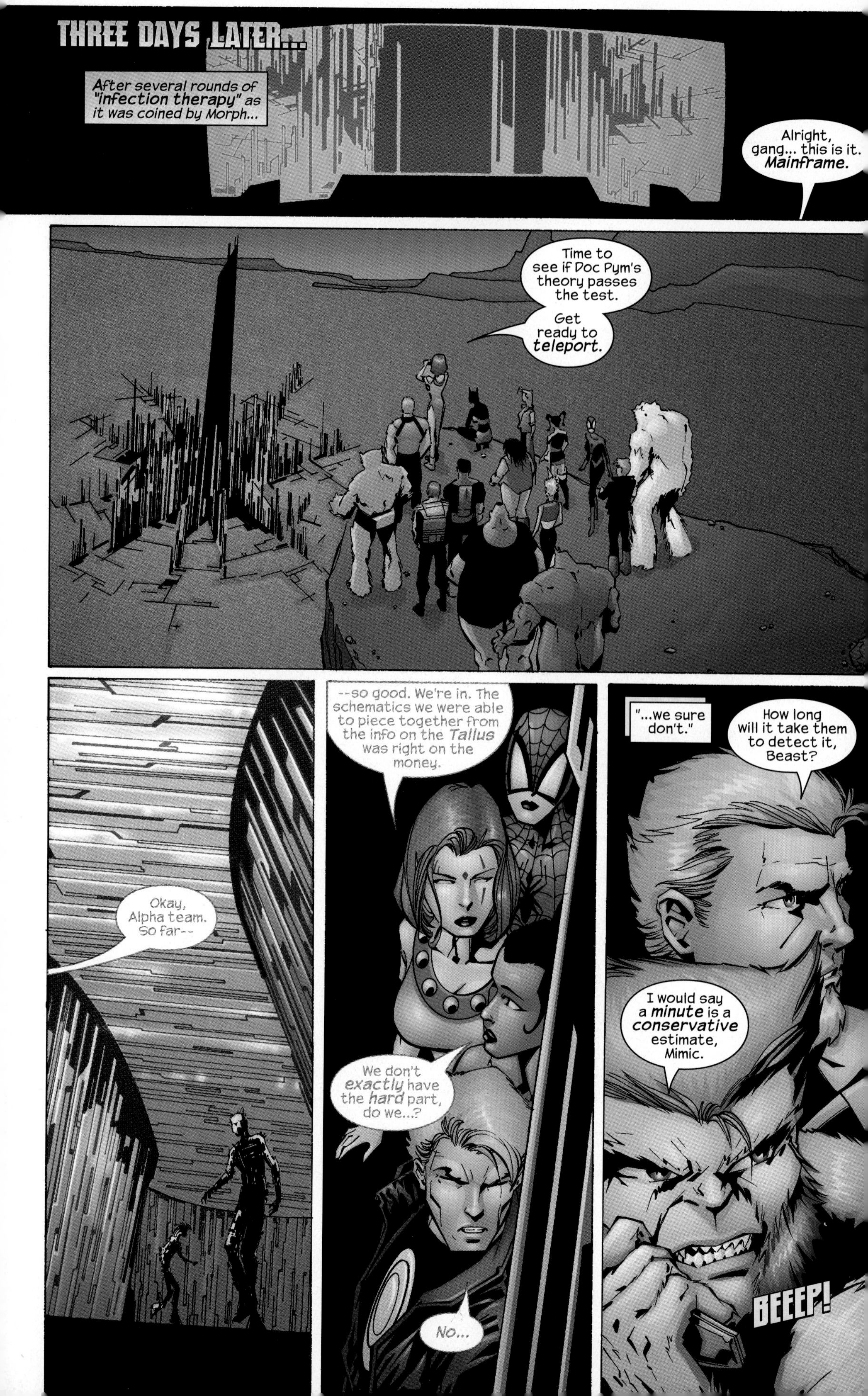
THREE DAYS LATER...
After several rounds of "infection therapy" as it was coined by Morph...
Alright, gang... this is it. Mainframe.
Time to see if Doc Pym's theory passes the test.
Get ready to teleport.
Okay, Alpha team. So far--
--so good. We're in. The schematics we were able to piece together from the info on the Tallus was right on the money.
We don't exactly have the hard part, do we...?
No...
"...we sure don't."
How long will it take them to detect it, Beast?
I would say a minute is a conservative estimate, Mimic.
BEEEP!

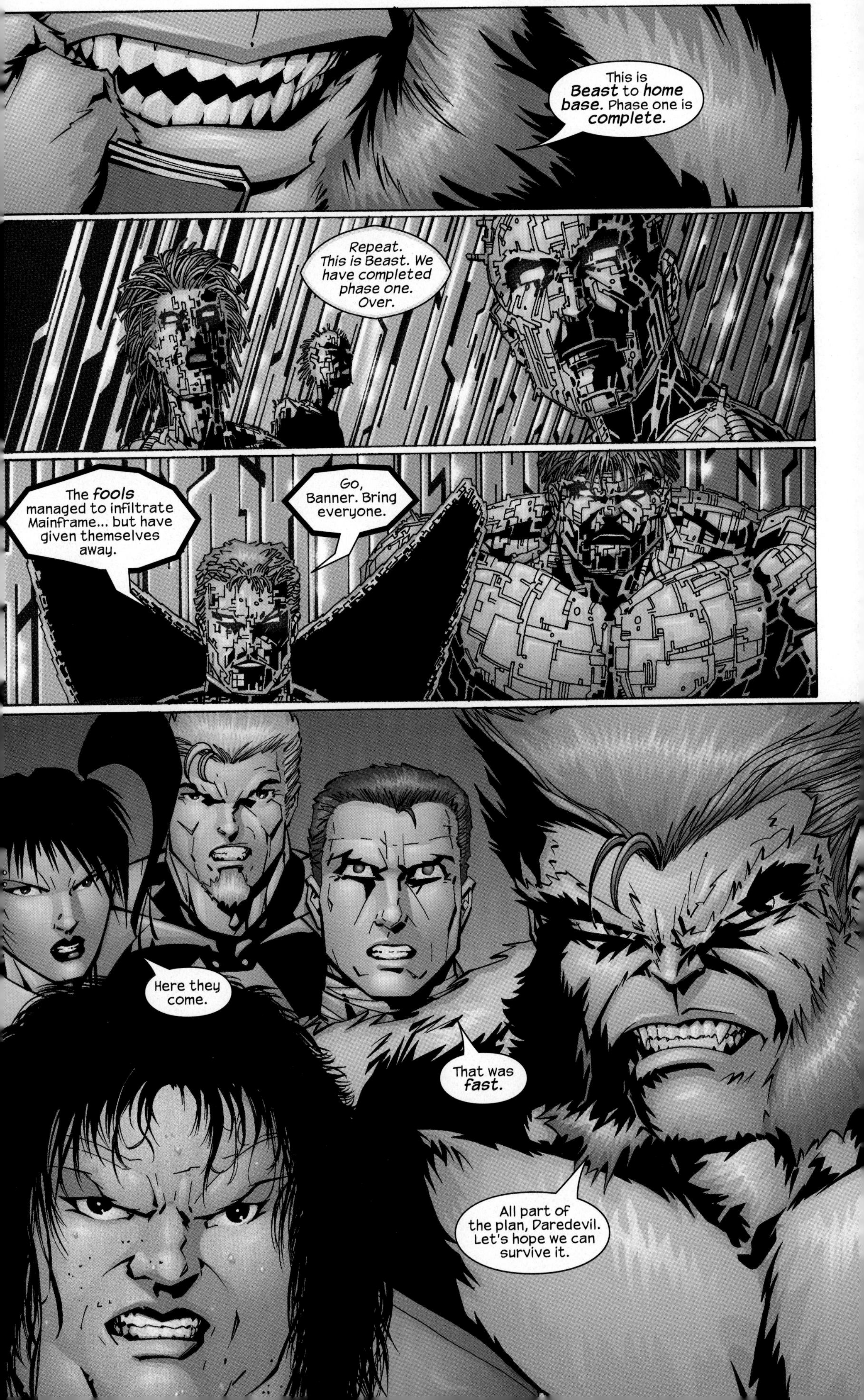
This is Beast to home base. Phase one is complete.
Repeat. This is Beast. We have completed phase one. Over.
The fools managed to infiltrate Mainframe... but have given themselves away.
Go, Banner. Bring everyone.
Here they come.
That was fast.
All part of the plan, Daredevil. Let's hope we can survive it.

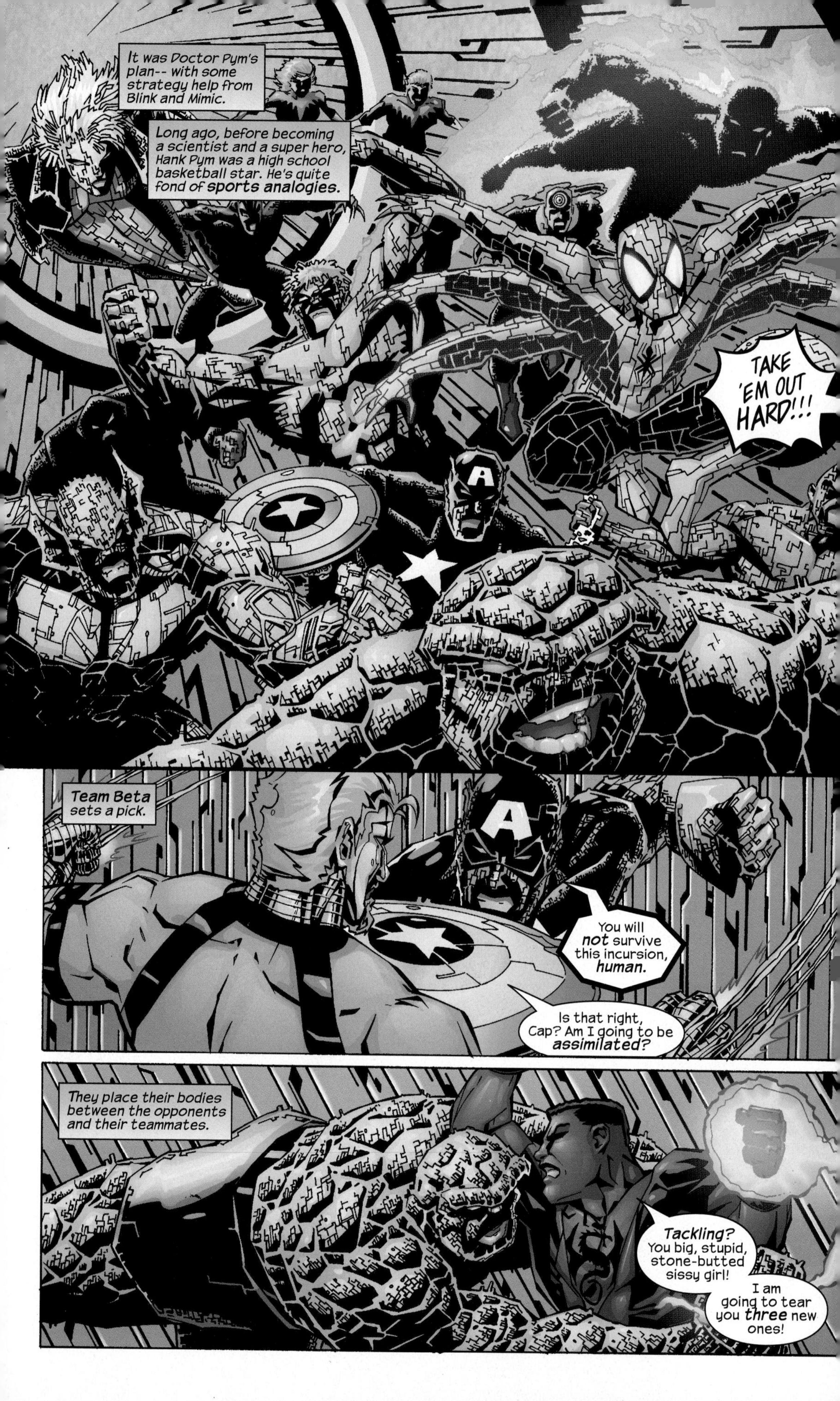

It was Doctor Pym's plan-- with some strategy help from Blink and Mimic.
Long ago, before becoming a scientist and a super hero, Hank Pym was a high school basketball star. He's quite fond of **sports analogies.**
TAKE 'EM OUT HARD!!!
Team Beta sets a pick.
You will **not** survive this incursion, **human.**
Is that right, Cap? Am I going to be **assimilated?**
They place their bodies between the opponents and their teammates.
Tackling? You big, stupid, stone-butted sissy girl!
I am going to tear you **three** new ones!

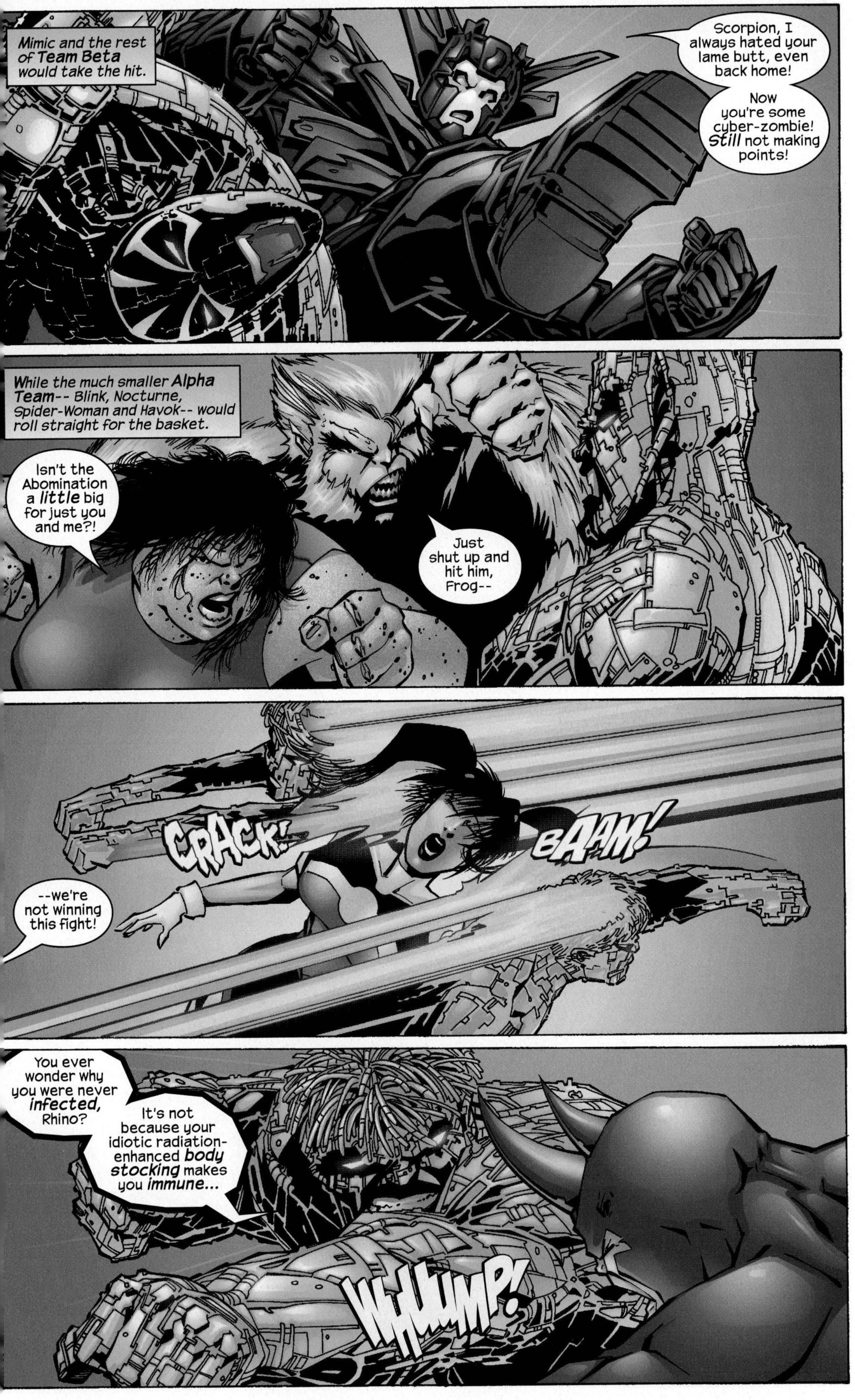

Mimic and the rest of Team Beta would take the hit.
Scorpion, I always hated your lame butt, even back home!
Now you're some cyber-zombie! Still not making points!
While the much smaller Alpha Team-- Blink, Nocturne, Spider-Woman and Havok-- would roll straight for the basket.
Isn't the Abomination a little big for just you and me?!
Just shut up and hit him, Frog--
CRACK!
BAAM!
--we're not winning this fight!
You ever wonder why you were never infected, Rhino?
It's not because your idiotic radiation-enhanced body stocking makes you immune...
WHUUMP!

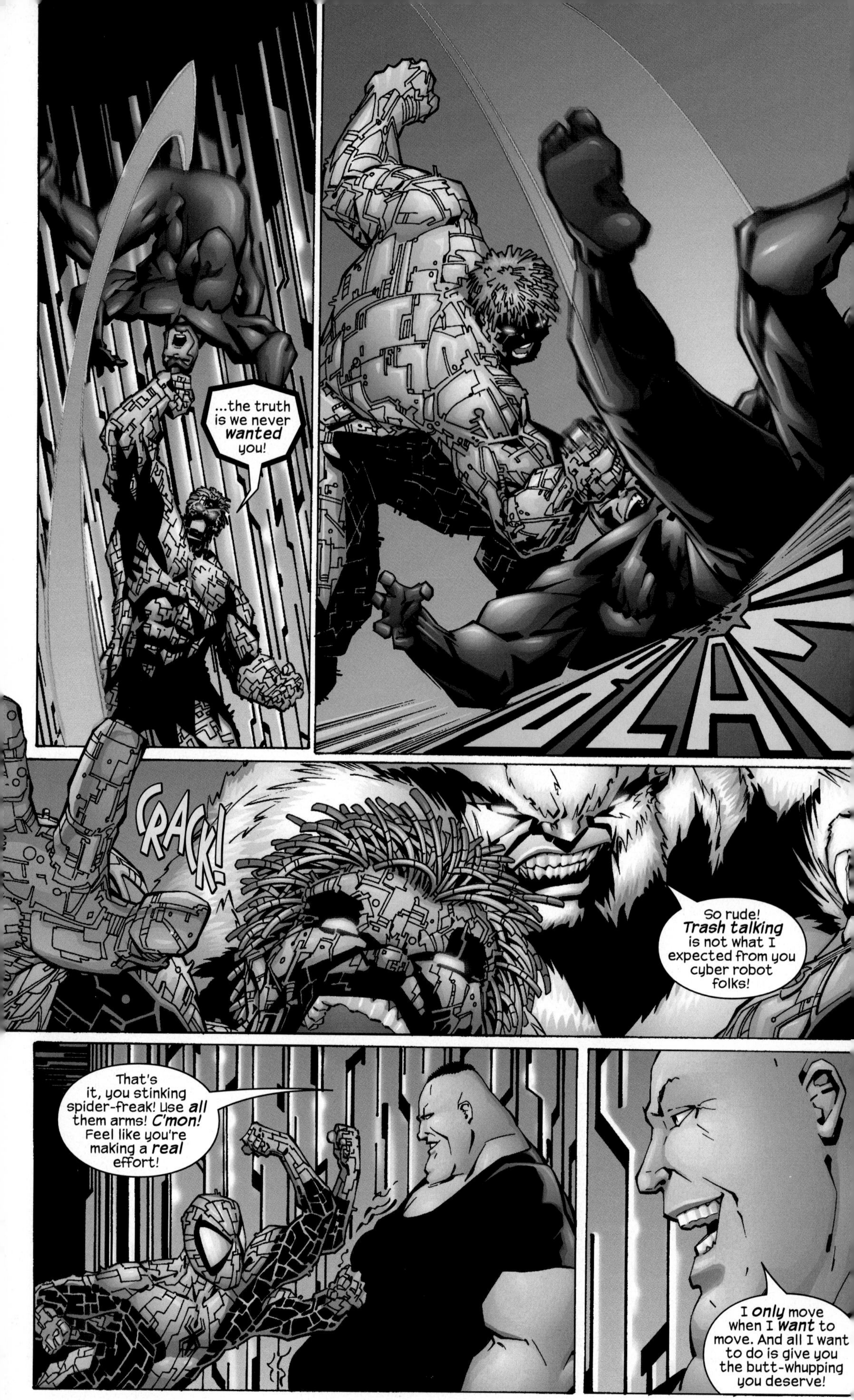
...the truth is we never *wanted* you!
BLAM
CRACK!
So rude! *Trash talking* is not what I expected from you cyber robot folks!
That's it, you stinking spider-freak! Use *all* them arms! *C'mon!* Feel like you're making a *real* effort!
I *only* move when I *want* to move. And all I want to do is give you the butt-whupping you deserve!

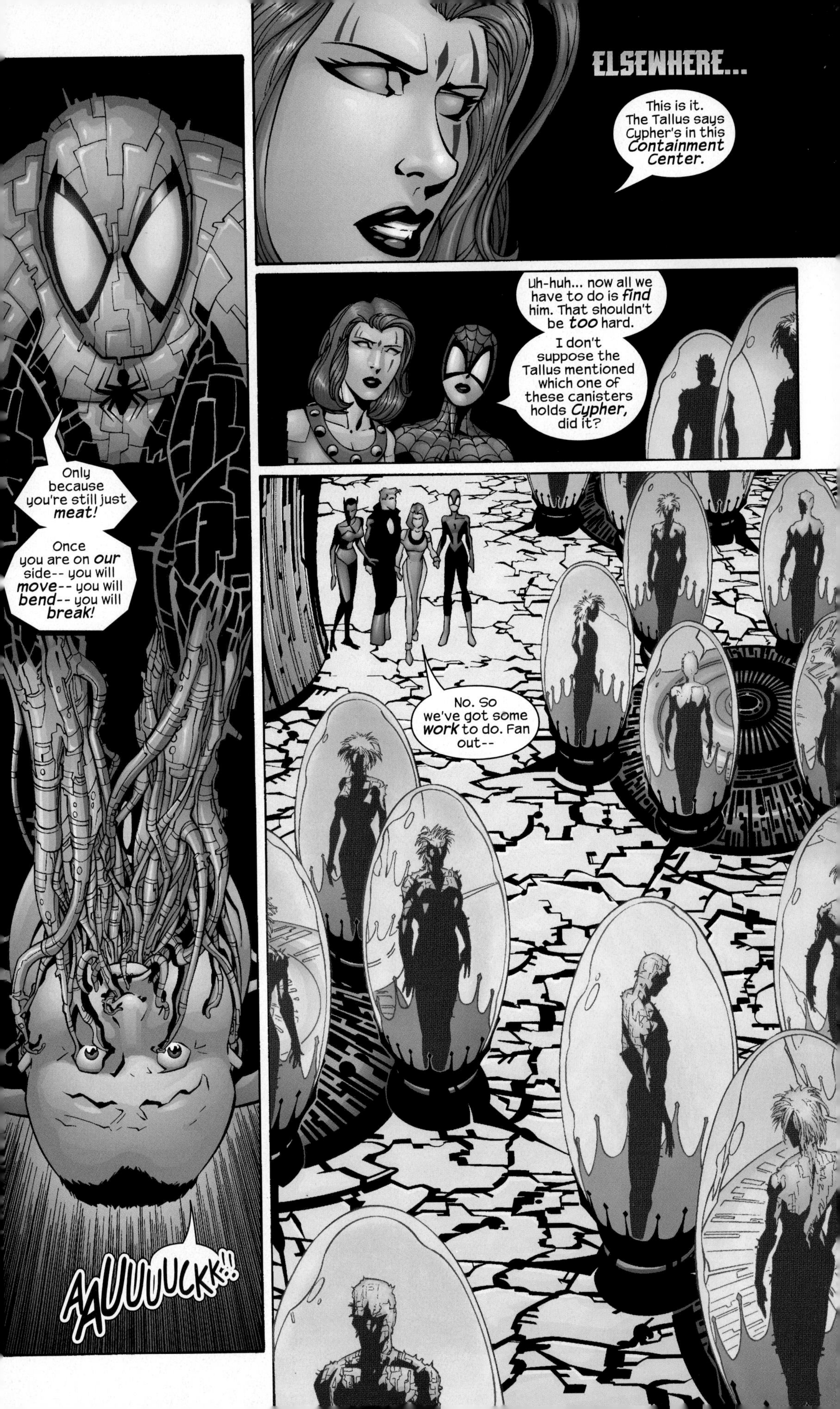
Only because you're still just *meat!*
Once you are on *our* side-- you will *move*-- you will *bend*-- you will *break!*
AAUUUUCKK!!
ELSEWHERE...
This is it. The Tallus says Cypher's in this *Containment Center.*
Uh-huh... now all we have to do is *find* him. That shouldn't be *too* hard.
I don't suppose the Tallus mentioned which one of these canisters holds *Cypher,* did it?
No. So we've got some *work* to do. Fan out--

"--we don't have a lot of time."

This is *all* wrong.

Why would they be so dim as to transmit over the air *inside* Mainframe?

No. They *wouldn't* be.

What *else* is going on inside my complex? *Show me.*

Let me see *every* corner... every *room*... every...

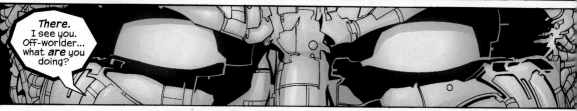

There. I see you. Off-worlder... what *are* you doing?

Time for you to meet the *master* of the house.

This *isn't* Cypher.

How can you be sure? The age looks right.

Because those are *breasts*. And in my experience they usually belong on the *women* folk.

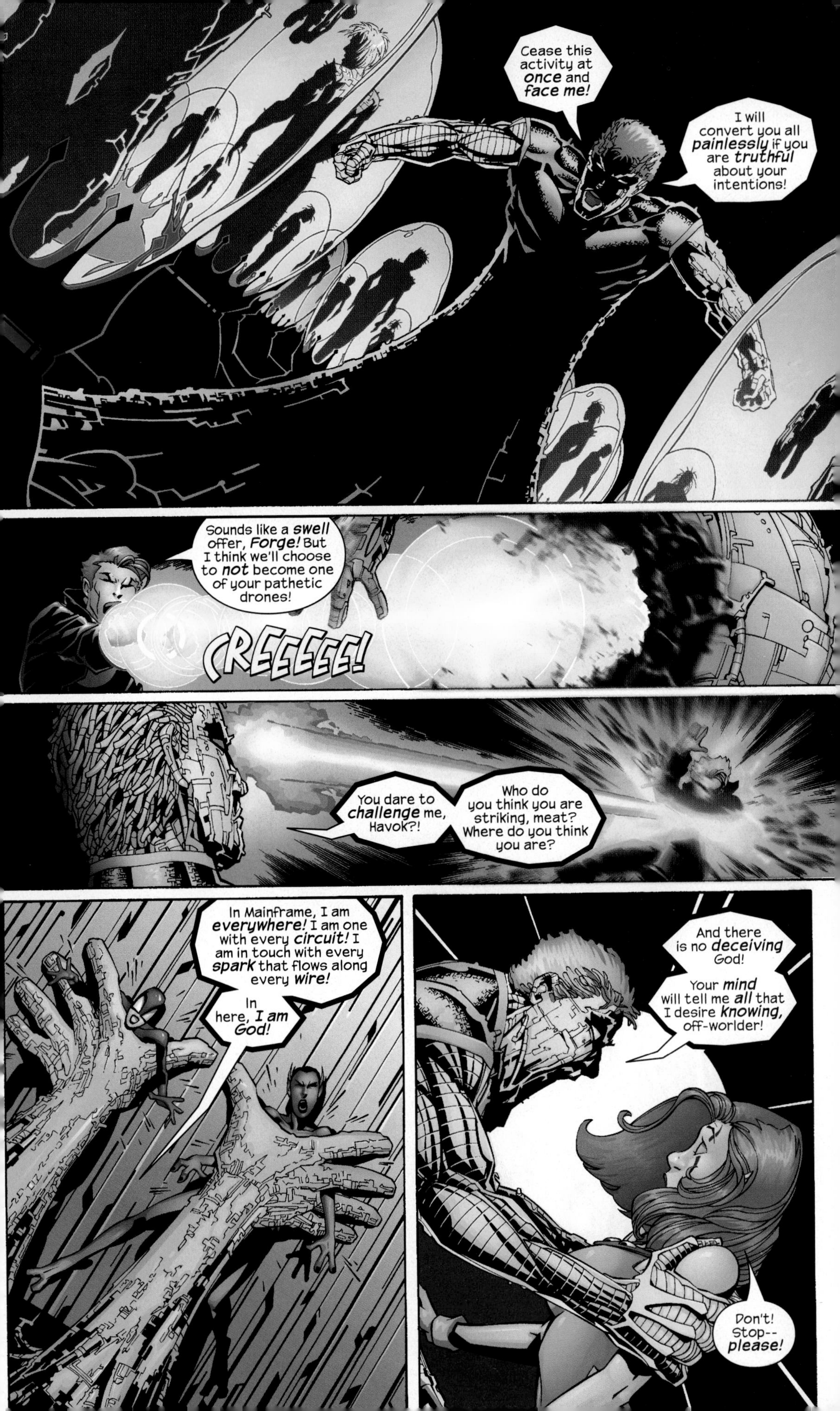
Cease this activity at *once* and *face me!*
I will convert you all *painlessly* if you are *truthful* about your intentions!
Sounds like a *swell* offer, *Forge!* But I think we'll choose to *not* become one of your pathetic drones!
CREEEEEE!
You dare to *challenge* me, Havok?!
Who do you think you are striking, meat? Where do you think you are?
In Mainframe, I am *everywhere!* I am one with every *circuit!* I am in touch with every *spark* that flows along every *wire!*
In here, *I am God!*
And there is no *deceiving* God!
Your *mind* will tell me *all* that I desire *knowing,* off-worlder!
Don't! Stop-- *please!*

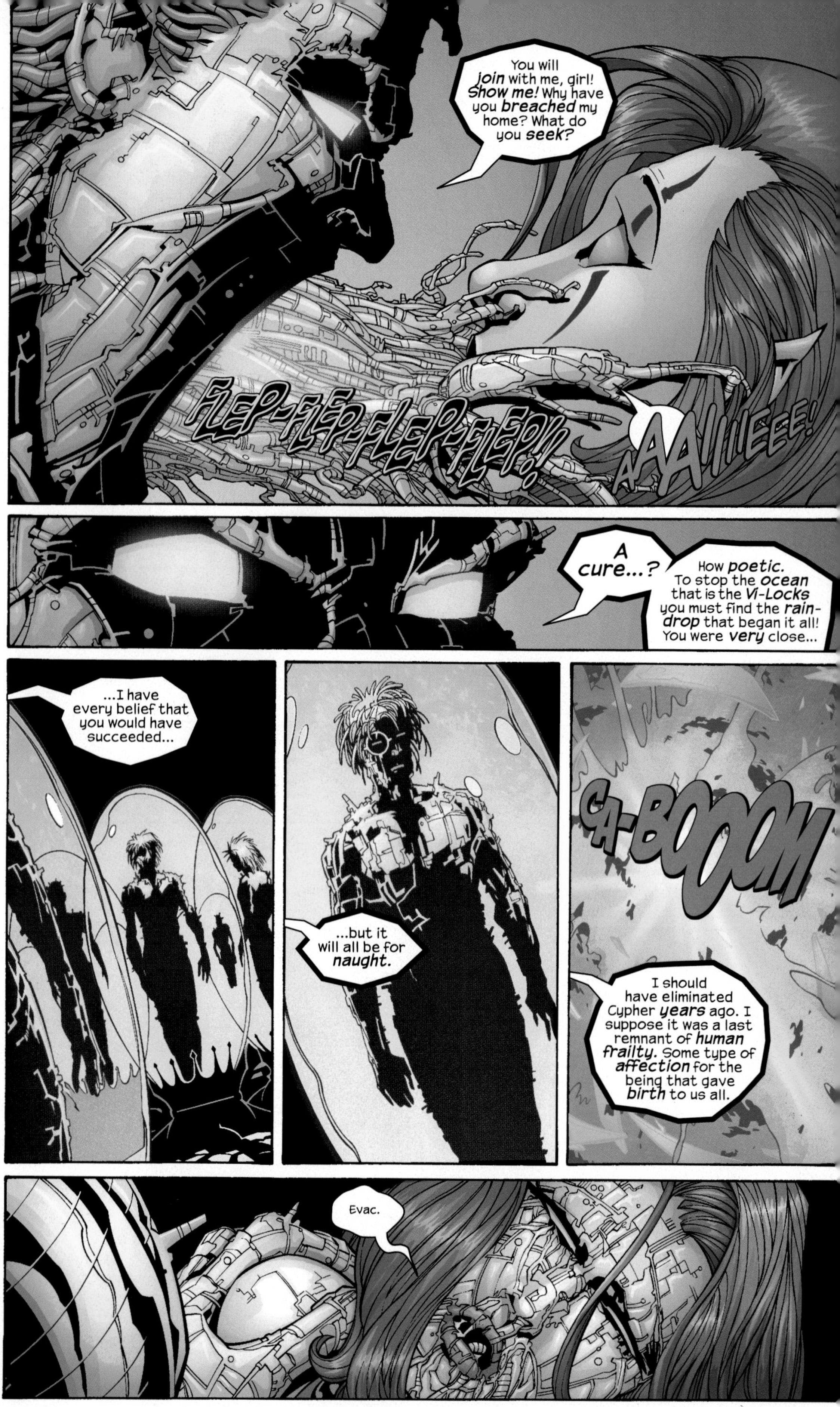
You will join with me, girl! Show me! Why have you breached my home? What do you seek?
FLEP-FLEP-FLEP-FLEP!!
AAAIIIIEEEE!
A cure...?
How poetic. To stop the ocean that is the Vi-Locks you must find the rain-drop that began it all! You were very close...
...I have every belief that you would have succeeded...
...but it will all be for naught.
CA-BOOOOM
I should have eliminated Cypher years ago. I suppose it was a last remnant of human frailty. Some type of affection for the being that gave birth to us all.
Evac.

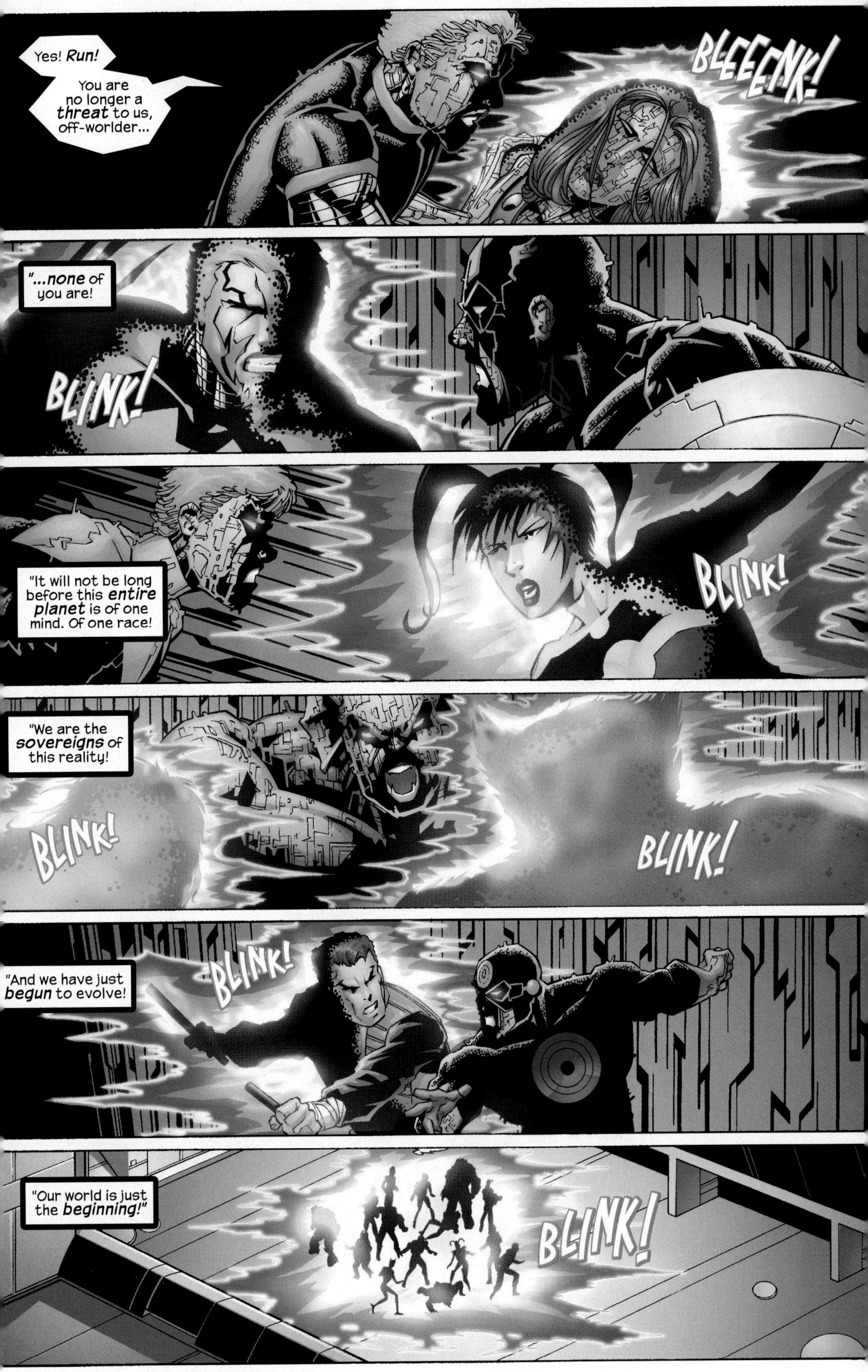
Yes! Run!
You are no longer a threat to us, off-worlder...
BLEEEINK!
"...none of you are!
BLINK!
"It will not be long before this entire planet is of one mind. Of one race!
BLINK!
"We are the sovereigns of this reality!
BLINK!
BLINK!
"And we have just begun to evolve!
BLINK!
"Our world is just the beginning!"
BLINK!

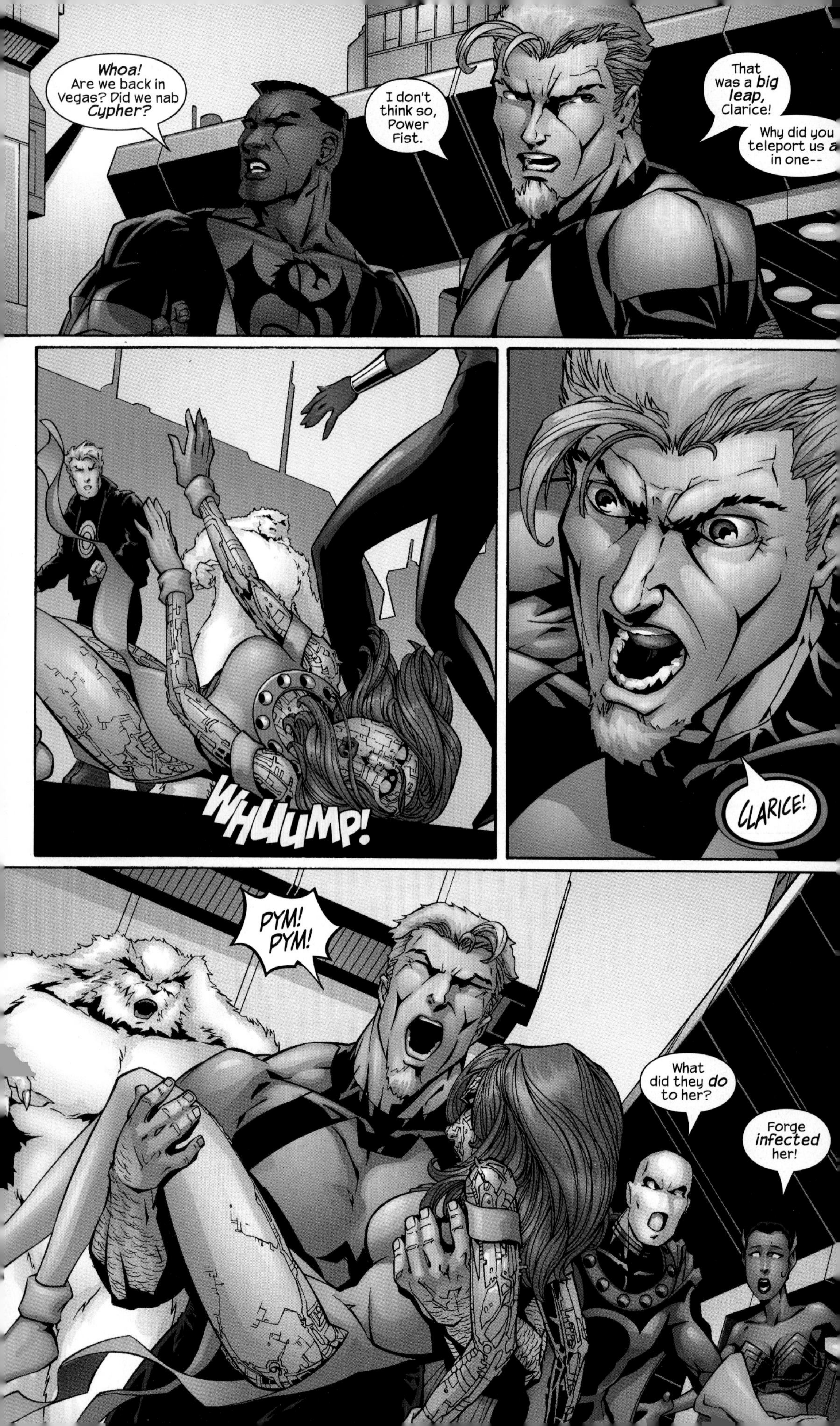

Whoa! Are we back in Vegas? Did we nab Cypher?
I don't think so, Power Fist.
That was a big leap, Clarice!
Why did you teleport us a in one--
WHUUMP!
CLARICE!
PYM! PYM!
What did they do to her?
Forge infected her!

God Almighty! It *must* have been *Forge!* He's the only Vi-Lock that can cause this much transformation so quickly.

Get her to the *medi-lab!*

Where the *hell* do you think I'm going?! Get moving, man! She's--

Calvin... we're in... *trouble.*

It's *going* to be okay. We're going to get you *transfused* before this spreads.

I swear to God, Clarice-- we're *going* to get you through this.

No... you don't understand... the *Tallus...* it's telling me we *failed.*

We failed... without Cypher we have only... only *one* alternative...

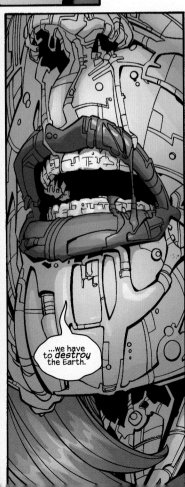

...we have to *destroy* the Earth.

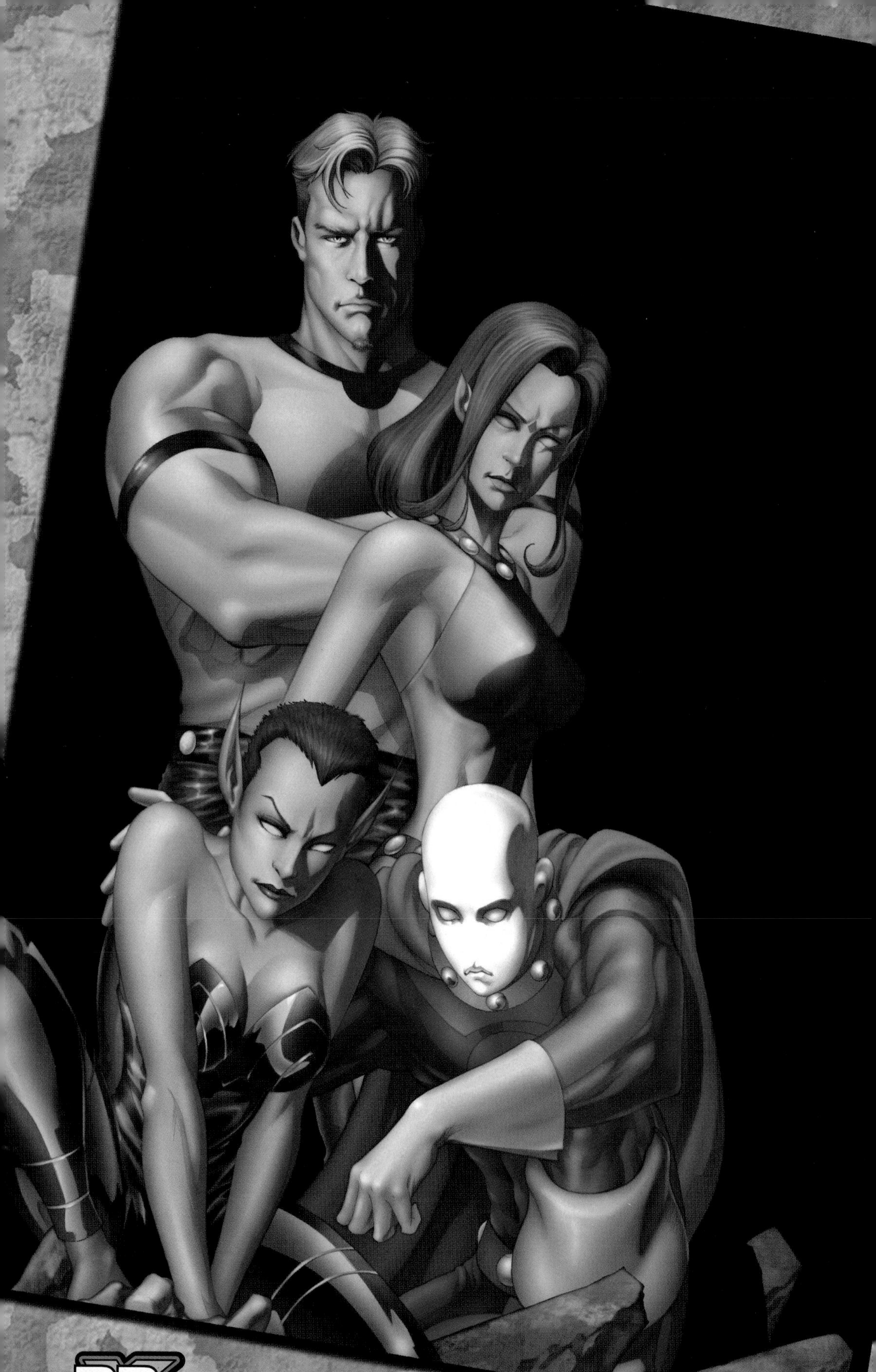

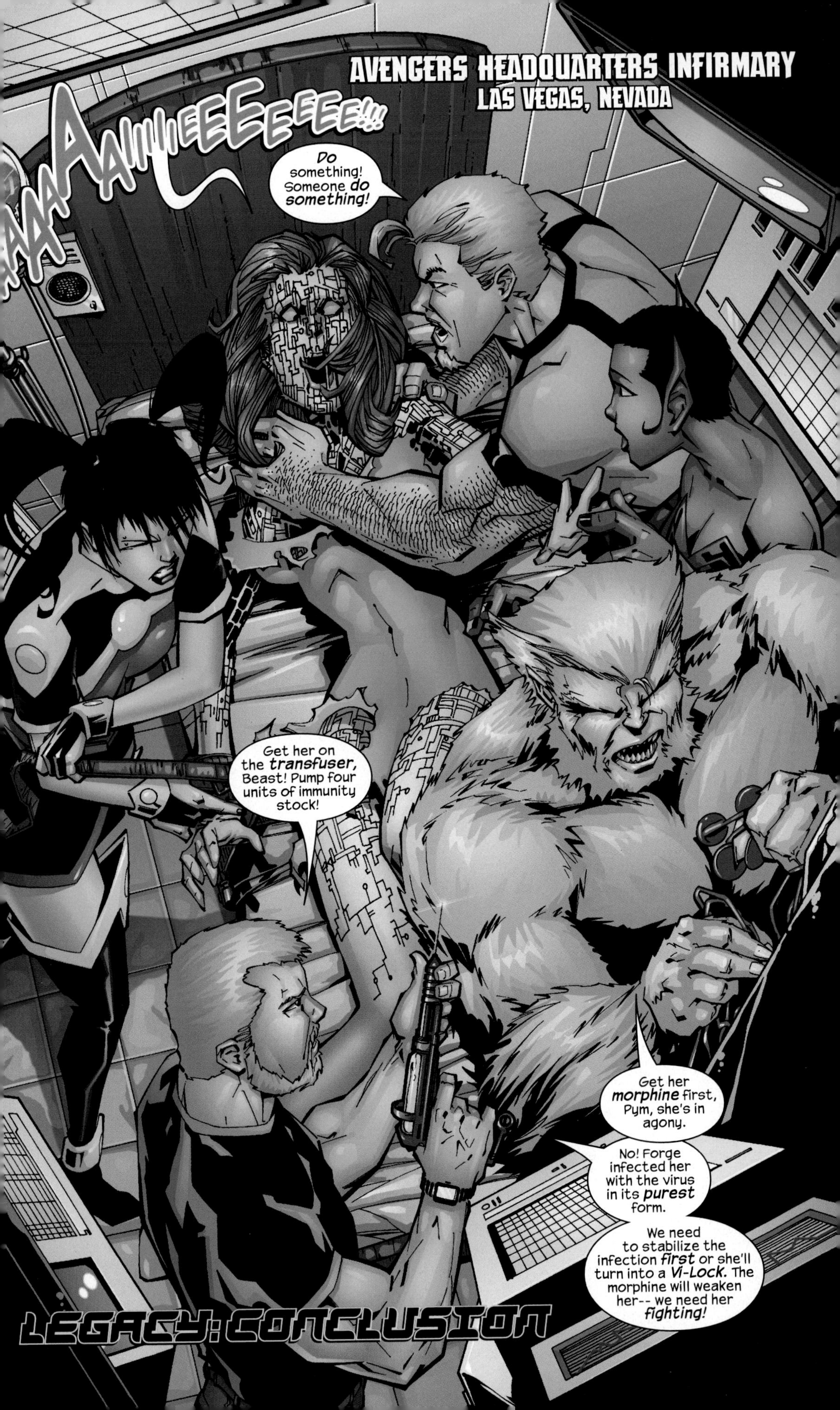

AVENGERS HEADQUARTERS INFIRMARY
LAS VEGAS, NEVADA
AAAAAAIIIIIEEEEEEEE!!!
Do something! Someone do something!
Get her on the transfuser, Beast! Pump four units of immunity stock!
Get her morphine first, Pym, she's in agony.
No! Forge infected her with the virus in its purest form.
We need to stabilize the infection first or she'll turn into a Vi-Lock. The morphine will weaken her-- we need her fighting!
LEGACY: CONCLUSION

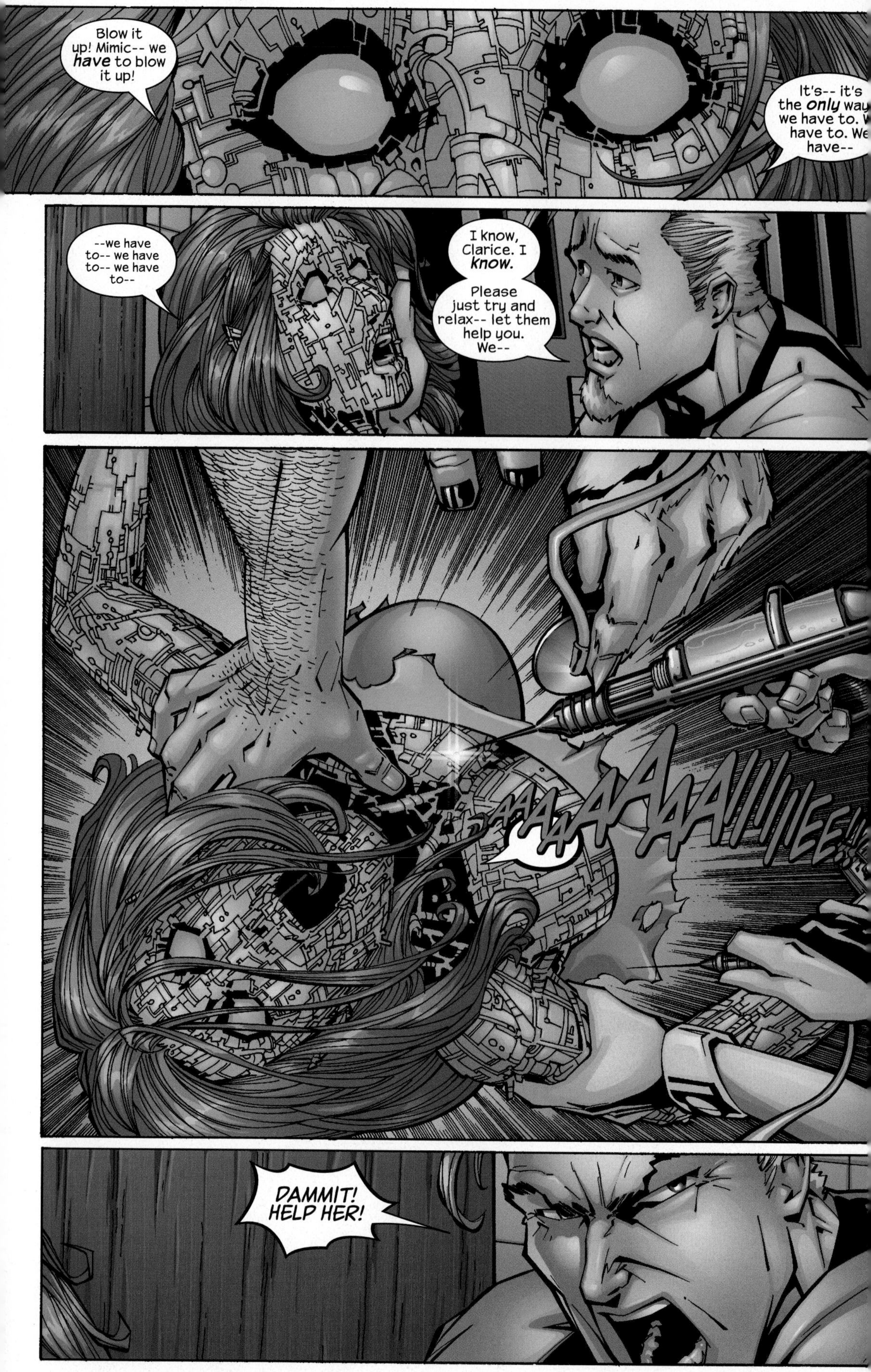
Blow it up! Mimic-- we *have* to blow it up!
It's-- it's the *only* way we have to. We have to. We have--
--we have to-- we have to-- we have to--
I know, Clarice. I *know.*
Please just try and relax-- let them help you. We--
AAAAAAAAIIIIIEEE!!
DAMMIT! HELP HER!

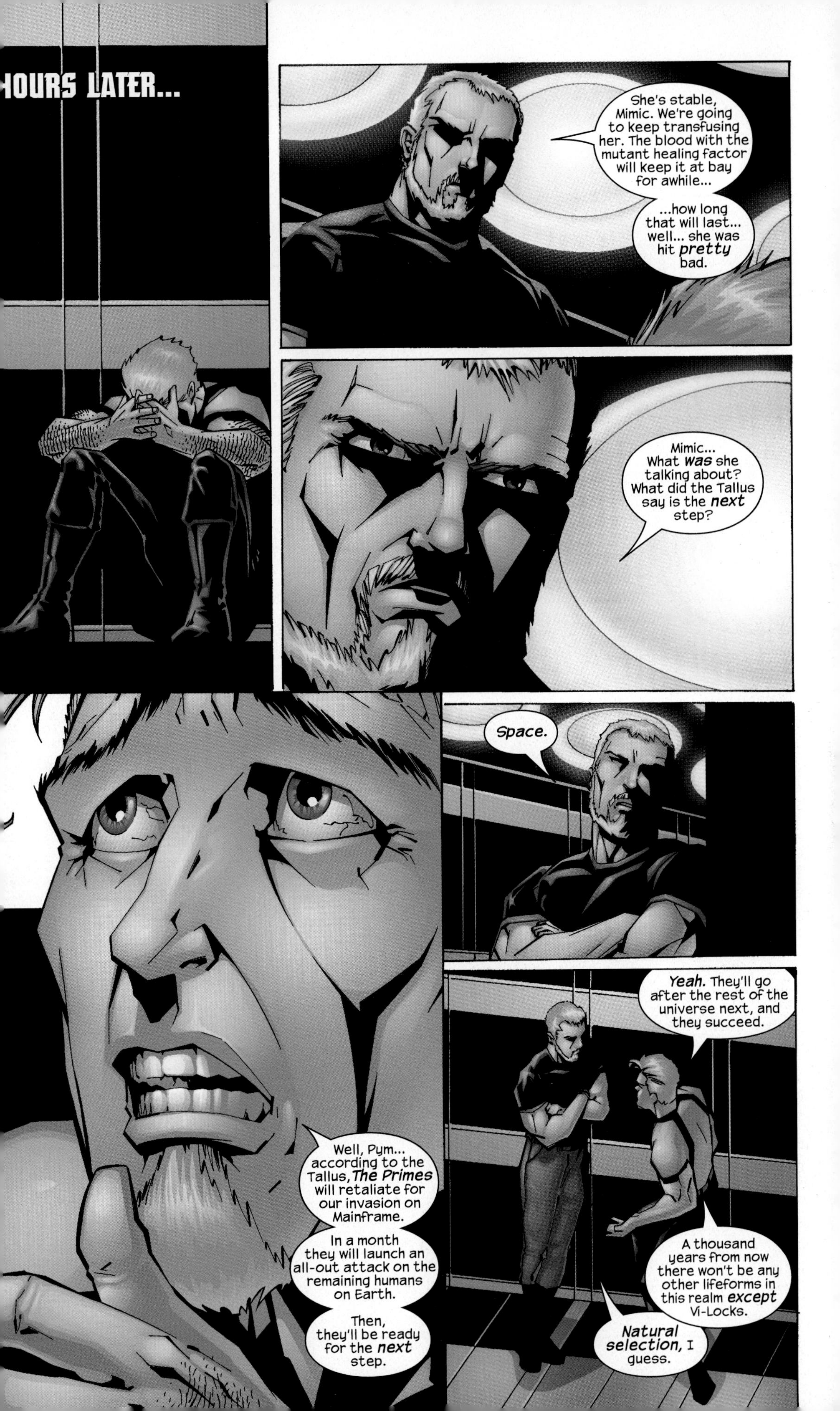
HOURS LATER...
She's stable, Mimic. We're going to keep transfusing her. The blood with the mutant healing factor will keep it at bay for awhile...
...how long that will last... well... she was hit *pretty* bad.
Mimic... What *was* she talking about? What did the Tallus say is the *next* step?
Well, Pym... according to the Tallus, *The Primes* will retaliate for our invasion on Mainframe.
In a month they will launch an all-out attack on the remaining humans on Earth.
Then, they'll be ready for the *next* step.
Space.
Yeah. They'll go after the rest of the universe next, and they succeed.
A thousand years from now there won't be any other lifeforms in this realm *except* Vi-Locks.
Natural selection, I guess.

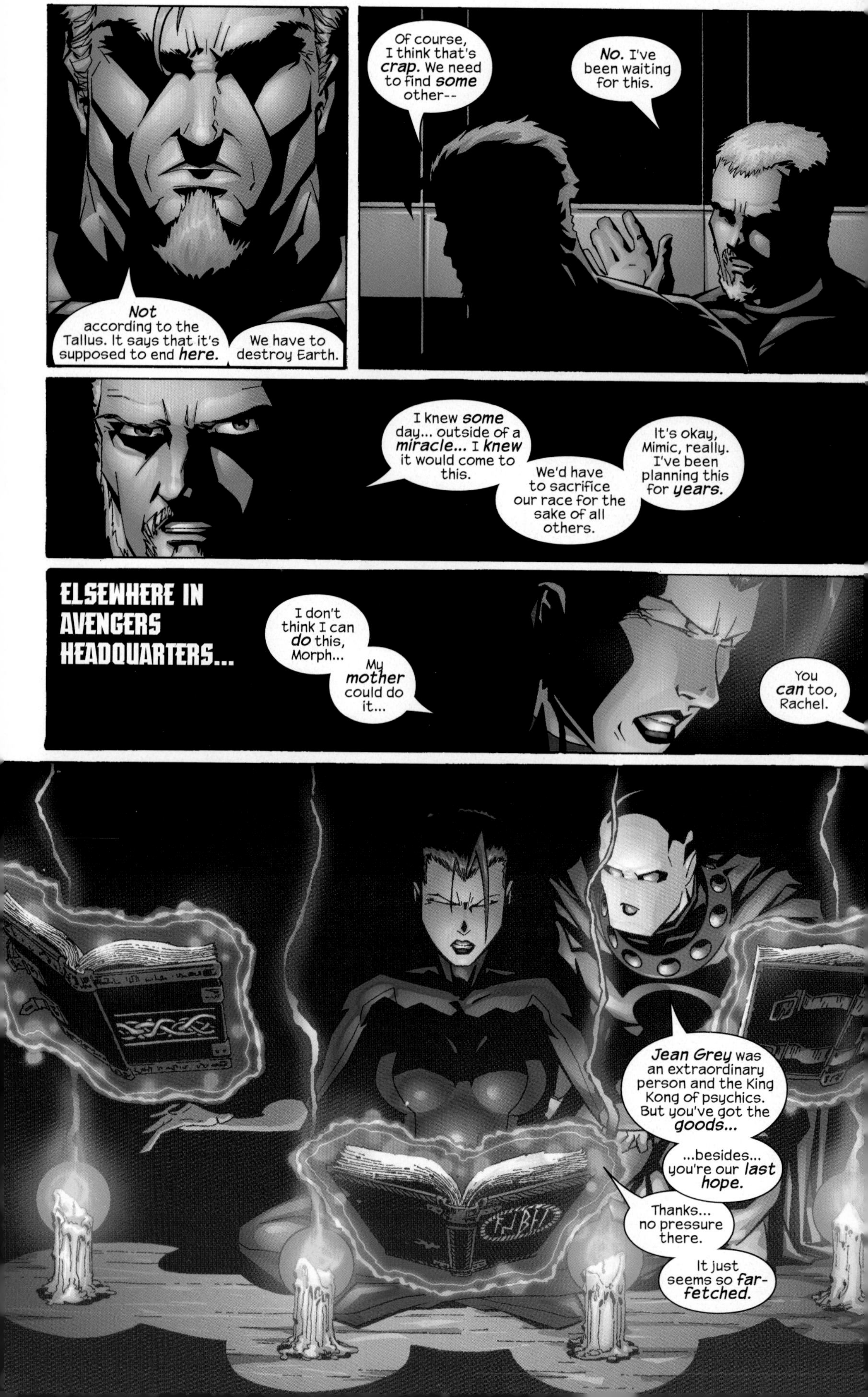

Not according to the Tallus. It says that it's supposed to end here.
We have to destroy Earth.
Of course, I think that's crap. We need to find some other--
No. I've been waiting for this.
I knew some day... outside of a miracle... I knew it would come to this.
We'd have to sacrifice our race for the sake of all others.
It's okay, Mimic, really. I've been planning this for years.
ELSEWHERE IN AVENGERS HEADQUARTERS...
I don't think I can do this, Morph...
My mother could do it...
You can too, Rachel.
Jean Grey was an extraordinary person and the King Kong of psychics. But you've got the goods...
...besides... you're our last hope.
Thanks... no pressure there.
It just seems so far-fetched.

Not where I come from. I've played *racquetball* with these guys!

Well, *more* like we fought Doctor Doom, the Kree army, and a few hundred other bad guys... but they *exist.*

And if what this planet needs is *pure blood* with *healing factors* to knock the spark plugs out of these dirt-bag robot, life-sucking scum...

...they're *just* the ticket.

Keep repeating the *incantation.* And visualize where you want to send it.

If they hear you... they'll come.

At least I hope so.

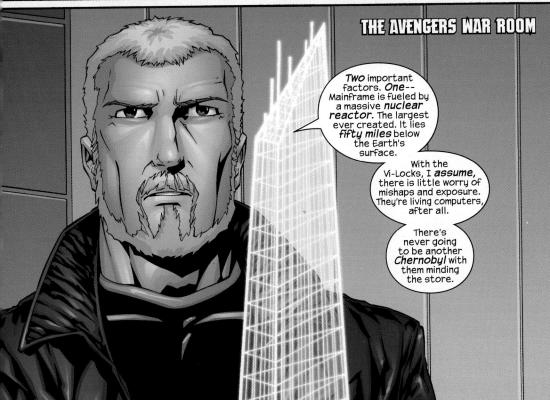

THE AVENGERS WAR ROOM

TWO important factors. One-- Mainframe is fueled by a massive *nuclear reactor.* The largest ever created. It lies *fifty miles* below the Earth's surface.

With the Vi-Locks, I *assume,* there is little worry of mishaps and exposure. They're living computers, after all.

There's never going to be another *Chernobyl* with them minding the store.

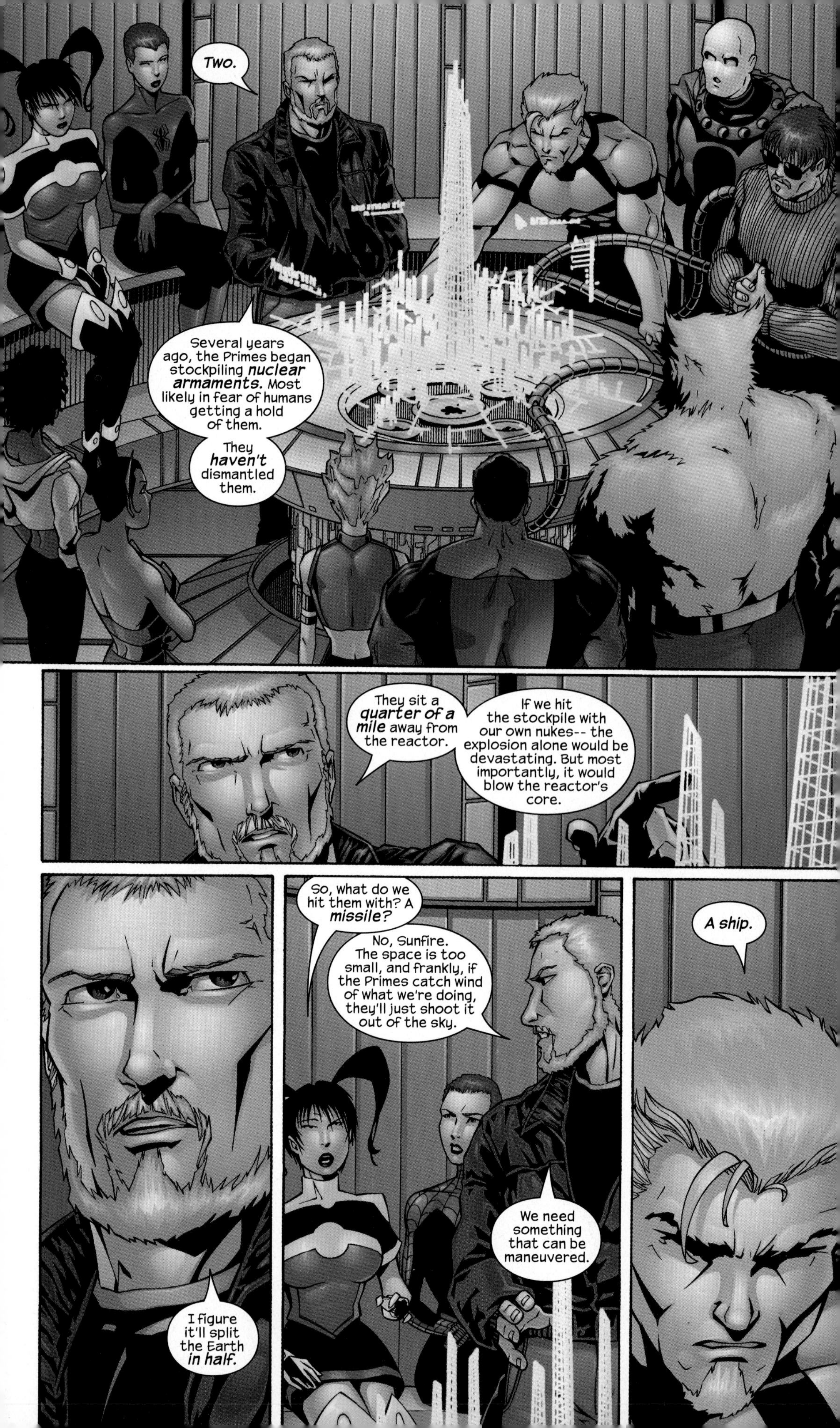
TWO.
Several years ago, the Primes began stockpiling nuclear armaments. Most likely in fear of humans getting a hold of them.
They haven't dismantled them.
They sit a quarter of a mile away from the reactor.
If we hit the stockpile with our own nukes-- the explosion alone would be devastating. But most importantly, it would blow the reactor's core.
I figure it'll split the Earth in half.
So, what do we hit them with? A missile?
No, Sunfire. The space is too small, and frankly, if the Primes catch wind of what we're doing, they'll just shoot it out of the sky.
We need something that can be maneuvered.
A ship.

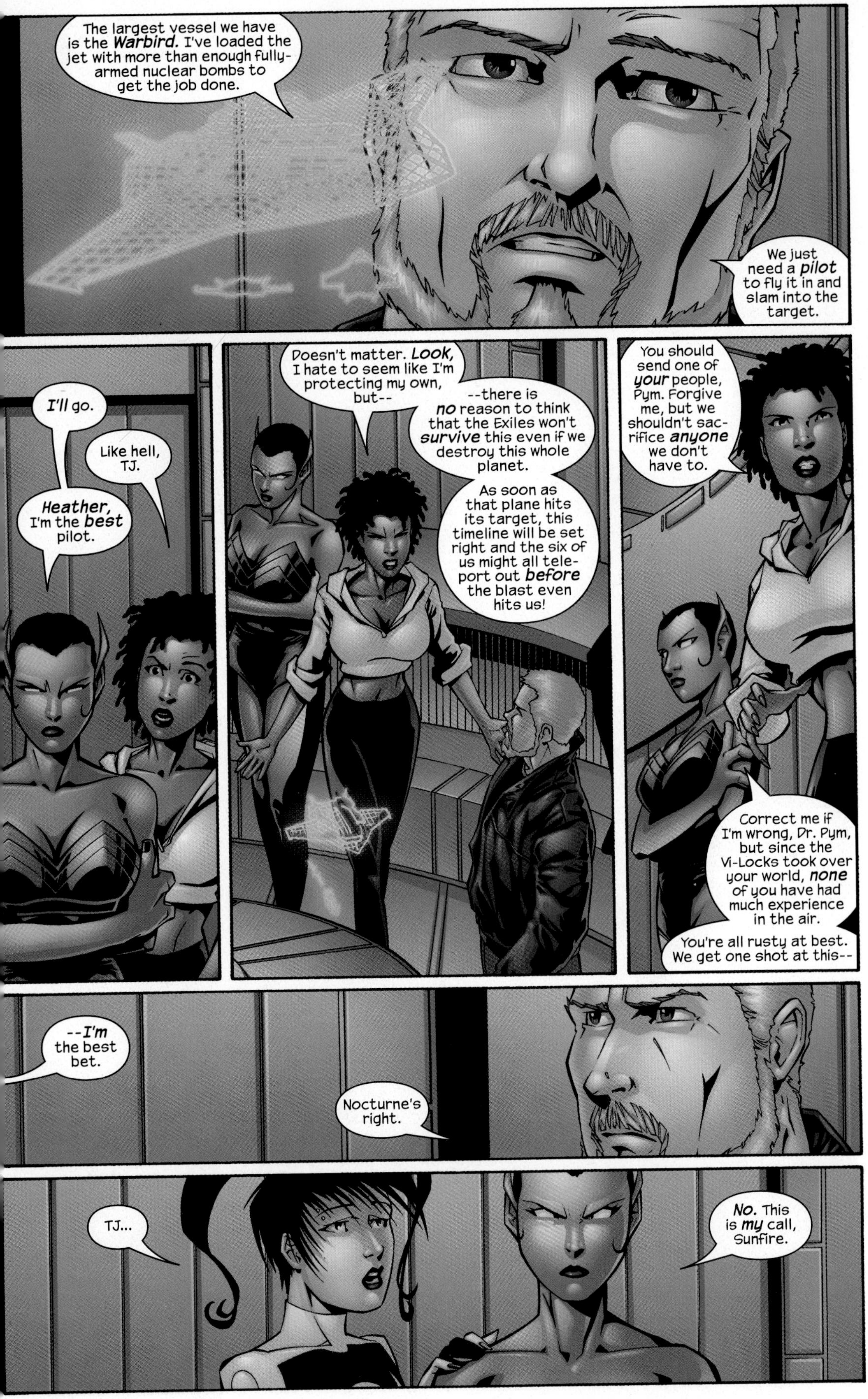
The largest vessel we have is the *Warbird*. I've loaded the jet with more than enough fully-armed nuclear bombs to get the job done.
We just need a *pilot* to fly it in and slam into the target.
I'll go.
Like hell, TJ.
Heather, I'm the *best* pilot.
Doesn't matter. *Look*, I hate to seem like I'm protecting my own, but--
--there is *no* reason to think that the Exiles won't *survive* this even if we destroy this whole planet.
As soon as that plane hits its target, this timeline will be set right and the six of us might all teleport out *before* the blast even hits us!
You should send one of *your* people, Pym. Forgive me, but we shouldn't sacrifice *anyone* we don't have to.
Correct me if I'm wrong, Dr. Pym, but since the Vi-Locks took over your world, *none* of you have had much experience in the air.
You're all rusty at best. We get one shot at this--
--*I'm* the best bet.
Nocturne's right.
TJ...
No. This is *my* call, Sunfire.

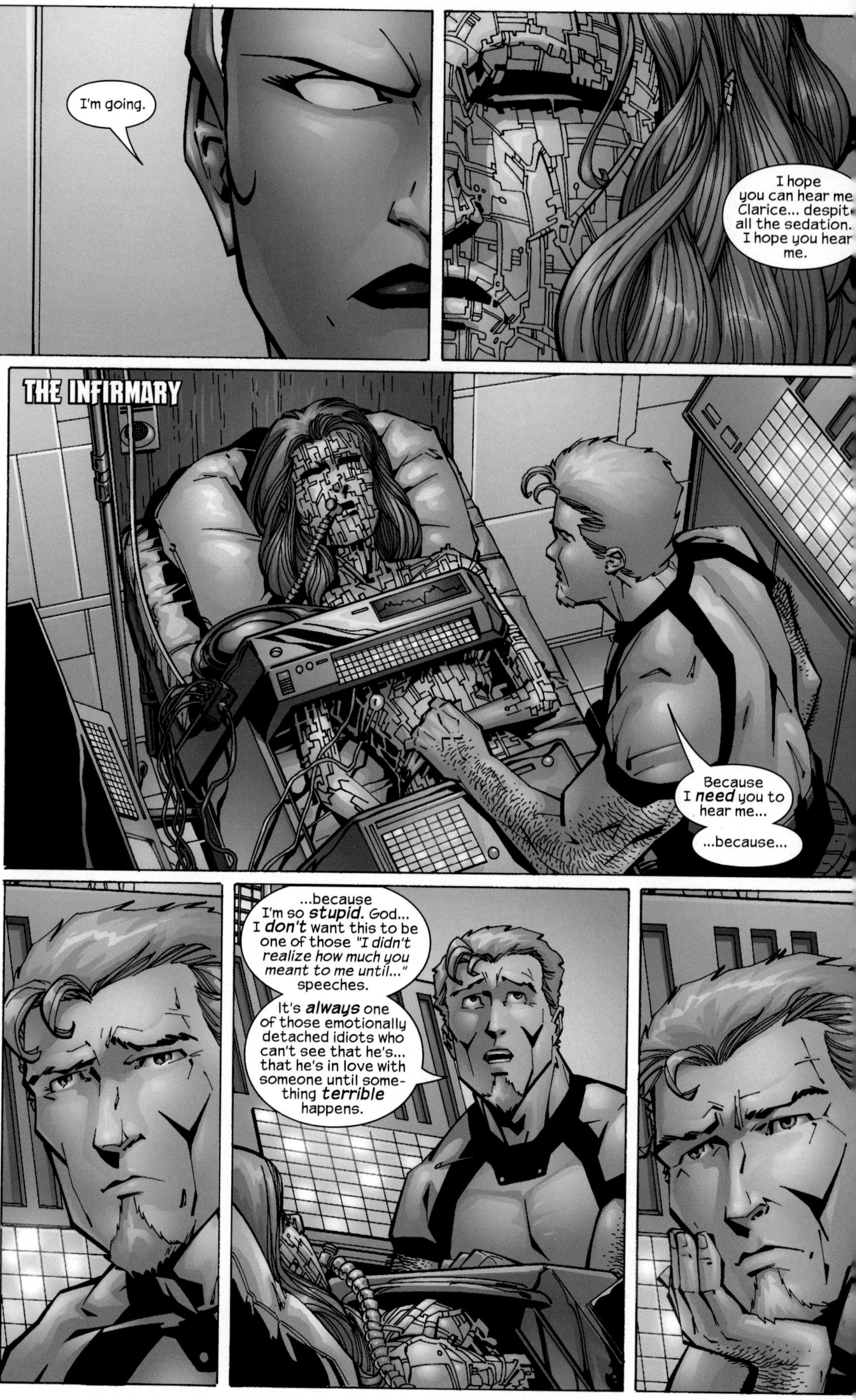
I'm going.
I hope you can hear me Clarice... despit all the sedation. I hope you hear me.
THE INFIRMARY
Because I need you to hear me...
...because...
...because I'm so stupid. God... I don't want this to be one of those "I didn't realize how much you meant to me until..." speeches.
It's always one of those emotionally detached idiots who can't see that he's... that he's in love with someone until some-thing terrible happens.

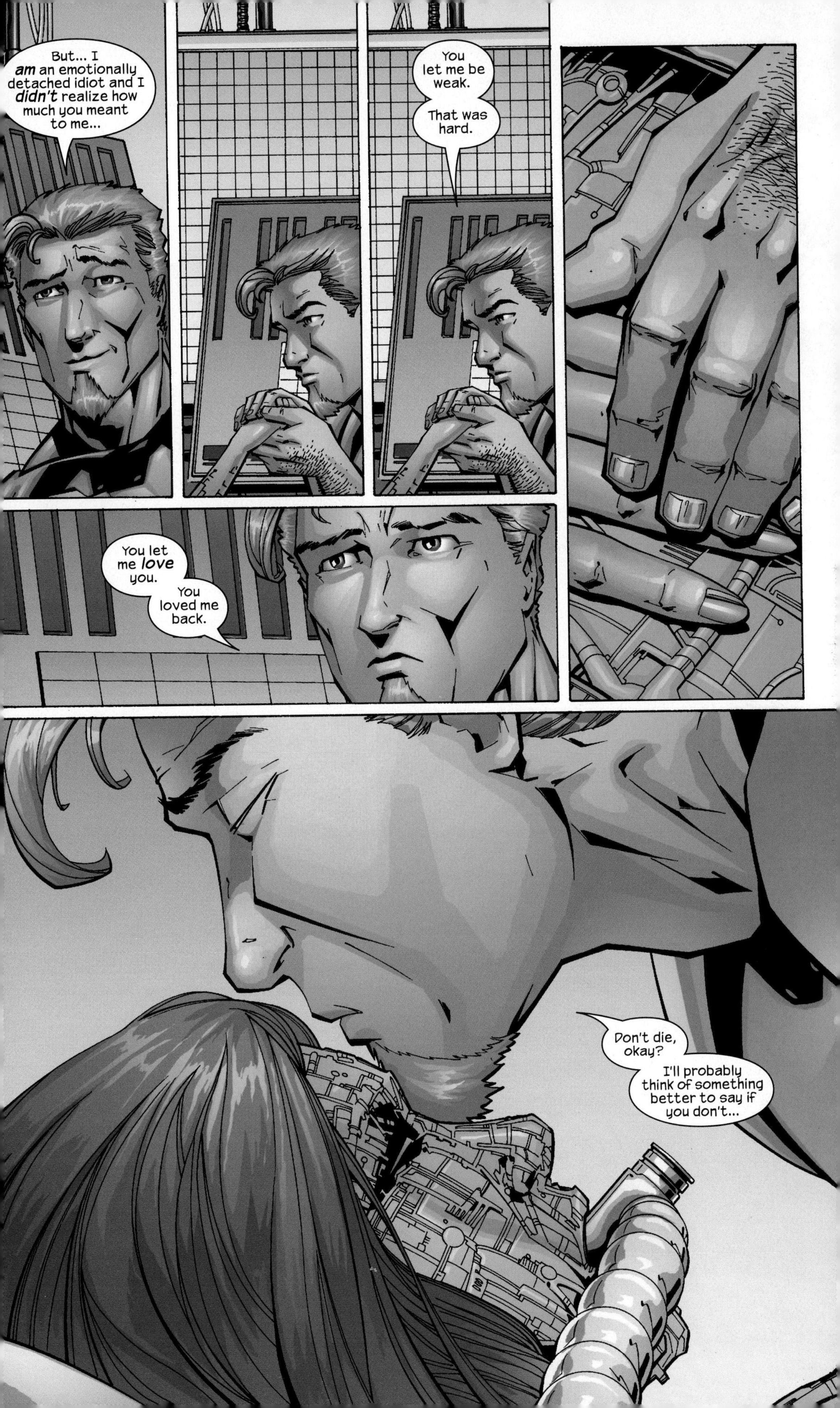
But... I *am* an emotionally detached idiot and I *didn't* realize how much you meant to me...
You let me be weak.
That was hard.
You let me *love* you.
You loved me back.
Don't die, okay?
I'll probably think of something better to say if you don't...

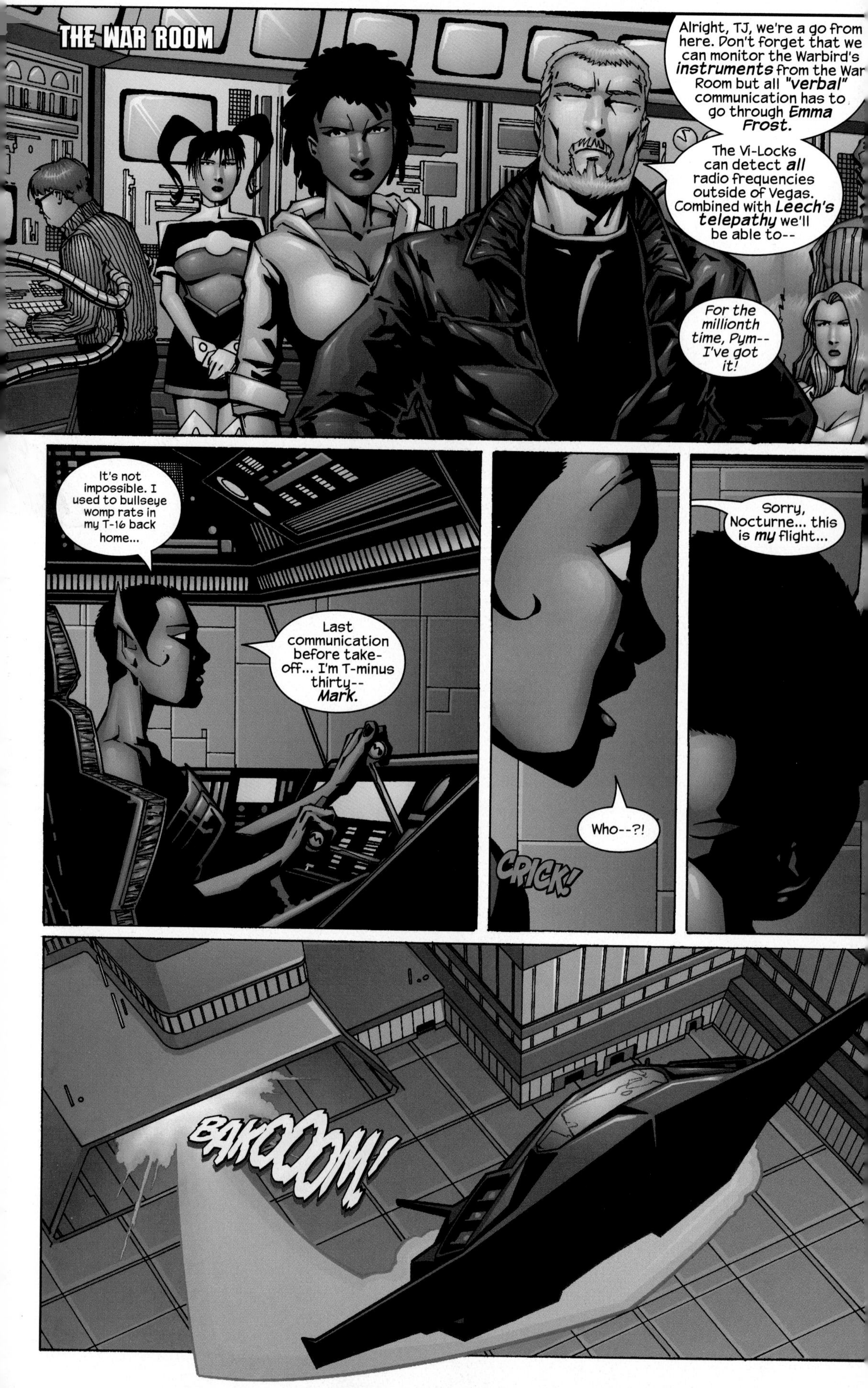
THE WAR ROOM
Alright, TJ, we're a go from here. Don't forget that we can monitor the Warbird's instruments from the War Room but all "verbal" communication has to go through Emma Frost.
The Vi-Locks can detect all radio frequencies outside of Vegas. Combined with Leech's telepathy we'll be able to--
For the millionth time, Pym-- I've got it!
It's not impossible. I used to bullseye womp rats in my T-16 back home...
Last communication before take-off... I'm T-minus thirty-- Mark.
Who--?!
CRICK!
Sorry, Nocturne... this is my flight...
BAKOOOM!

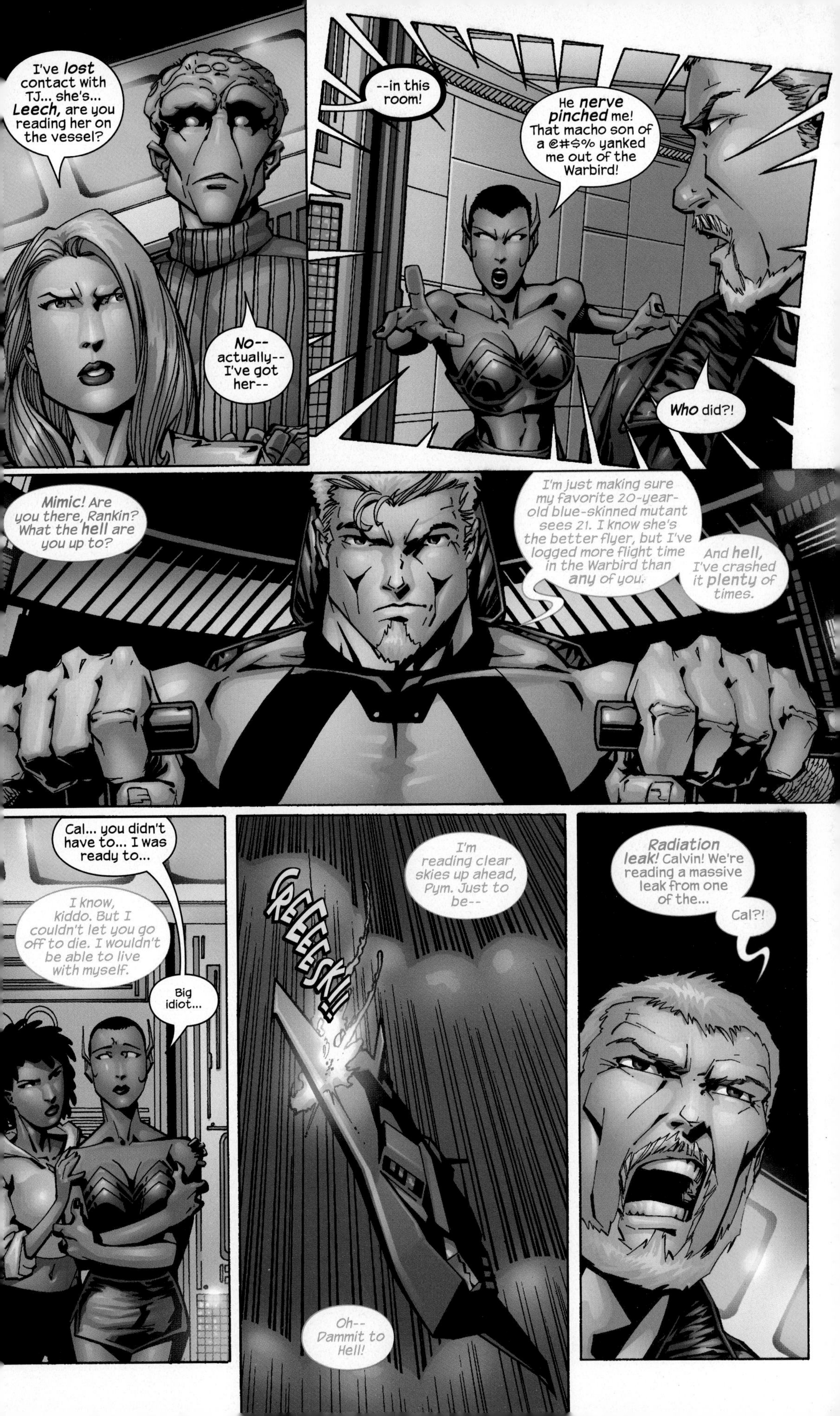
I've lost contact with TJ... she's... Leech, are you reading her on the vessel?
No-- actually-- I've got her--
--in this room!
He nerve pinched me! That macho son of a @#$% yanked me out of the Warbird!
Who did?!
Mimic! Are you there, Rankin? What the hell are you up to?
I'm just making sure my favorite 20-year-old blue-skinned mutant sees 21. I know she's the better flyer, but I've logged more flight time in the Warbird than any of you.
And hell, I've crashed it plenty of times.
Cal... you didn't have to... I was ready to...
I know, kiddo. But I couldn't let you go off to die. I wouldn't be able to live with myself.
Big idiot...
I'm reading clear skies up ahead, Pym. Just to be--
CREEESK!!
Oh-- Dammit to Hell!
Radiation leak! Calvin! We're reading a massive leak from one of the...
Cal?!

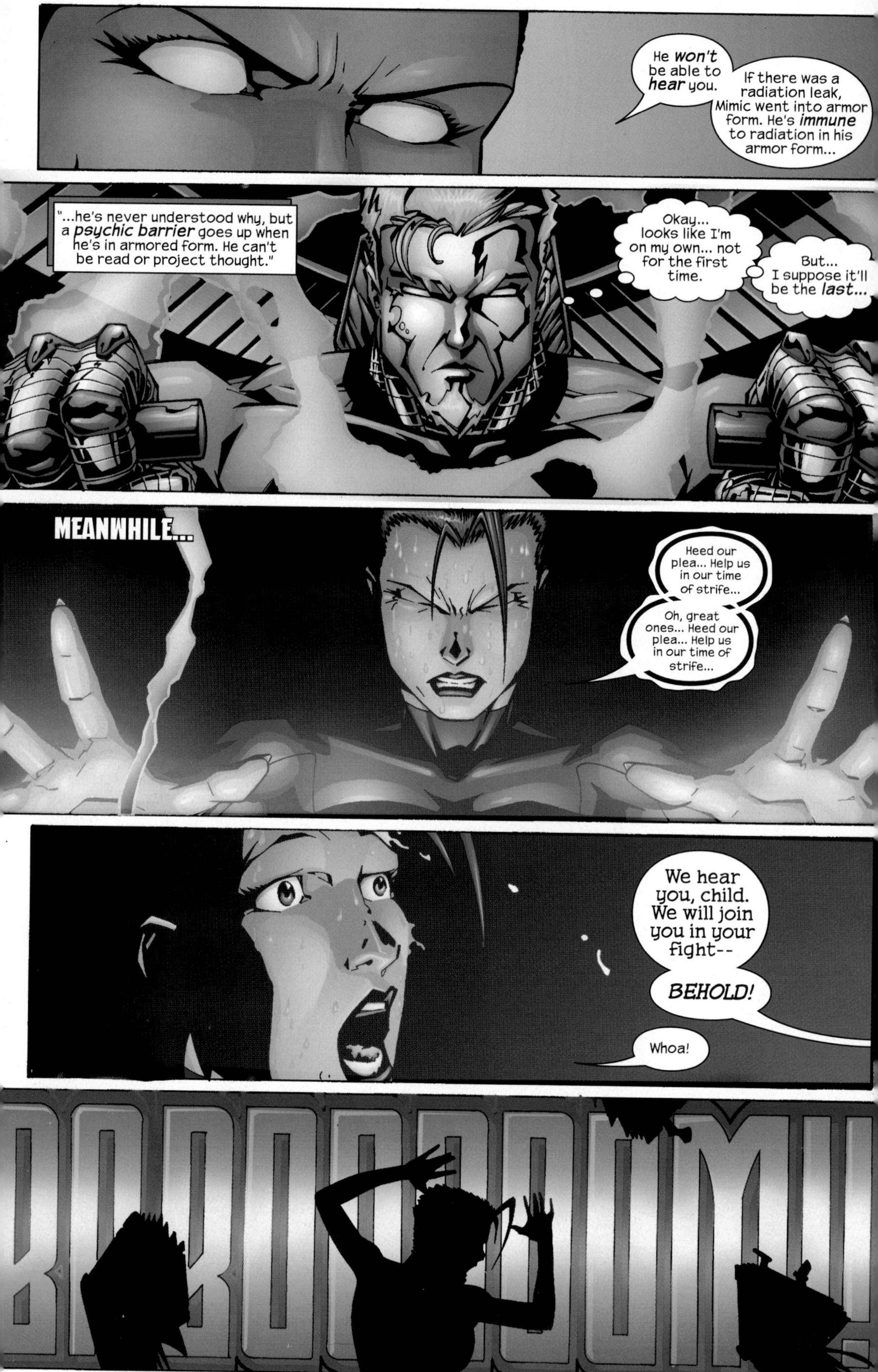
He won't be able to hear you.
If there was a radiation leak, Mimic went into armor form. He's immune to radiation in his armor form...
"...he's never understood why, but a psychic barrier goes up when he's in armored form. He can't be read or project thought."
Okay... looks like I'm on my own... not for the first time.
But... I suppose it'll be the last...
MEANWHILE...
Heed our plea... Help us in our time of strife...
Oh, great ones... Heed our plea... Help us in our time of strife...
We hear you, child. We will join you in your fight--
BEHOLD!
Whoa!
BOOOOOOM!!

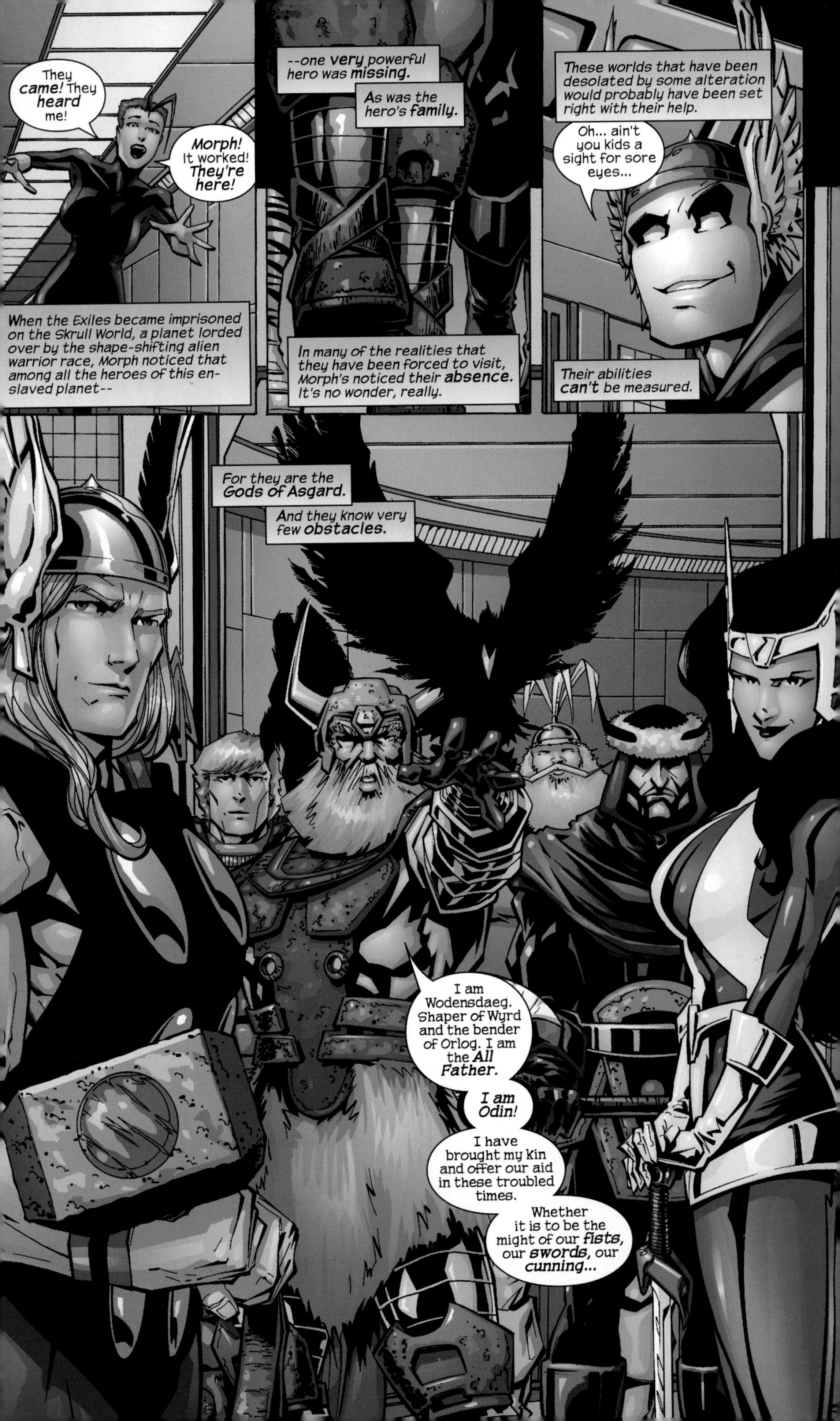

They came! They heard me!
Morph! It worked! They're here!
When the Exiles became imprisoned on the Skrull World, a planet lorded over by the shape-shifting alien warrior race, Morph noticed that among all the heroes of this enslaved planet--
--one very powerful hero was missing.
As was the hero's family.
In many of the realities that they have been forced to visit, Morph's noticed their absence. It's no wonder, really.
These worlds that have been desolated by some alteration would probably have been set right with their help.
Oh... ain't you kids a sight for sore eyes...
Their abilities can't be measured.
For they are the Gods of Asgard.
And they know very few obstacles.
I am Wodensdaeg. Shaper of Wyrd and the bender of Orlog. I am the All Father.
I am Odin!
I have brought my kin and offer our aid in these troubled times.
Whether it is to be the might of our fists, our swords, our cunning...

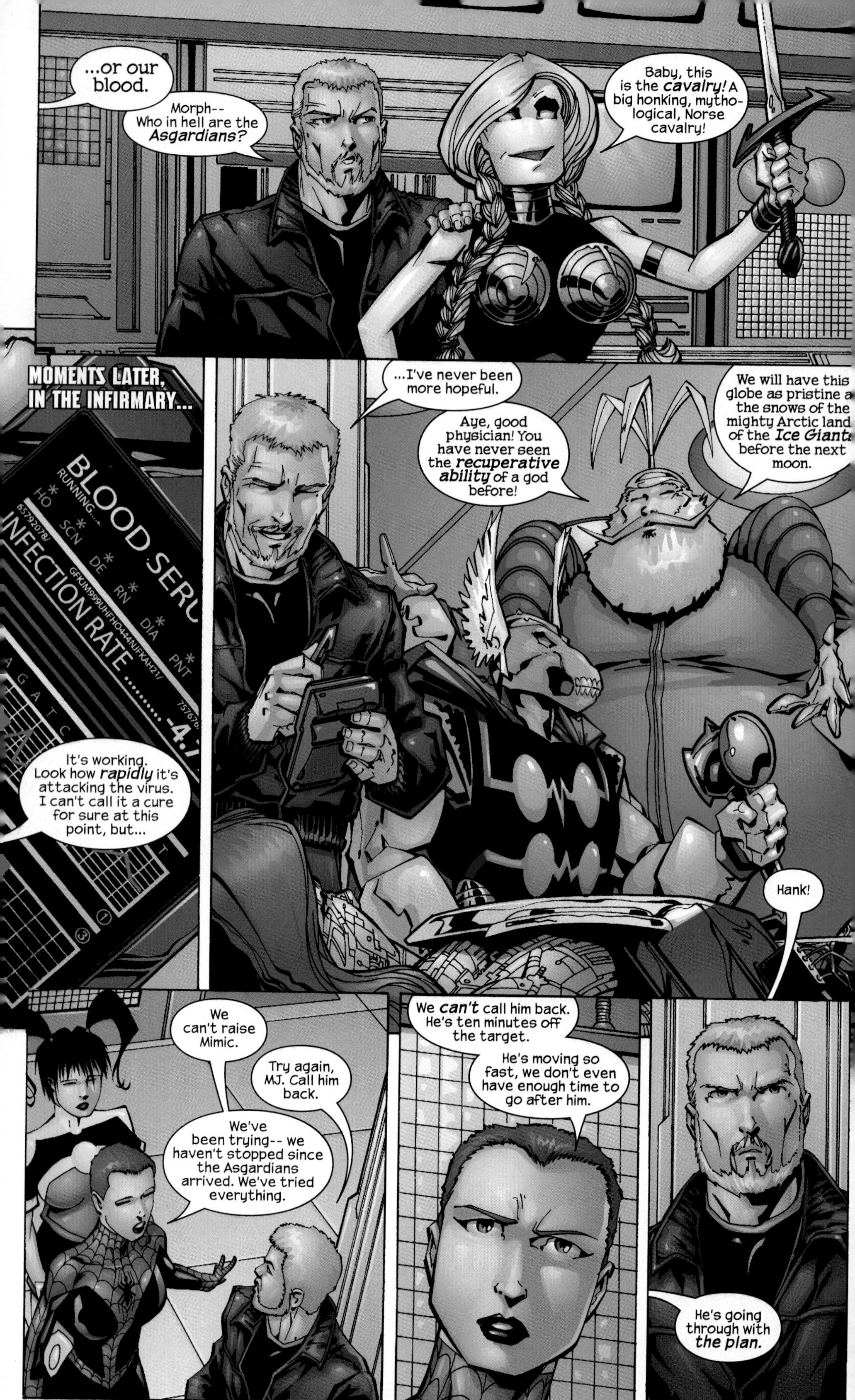
...or our blood.
Morph-- Who in hell are the *Asgardians?*
Baby, this is the *cavalry!* A big honking, mytho-logical, Norse cavalry!
MOMENTS LATER, IN THE INFIRMARY...
BLOOD SERU
RUNNING....
INFECTION RATE
It's working. Look how *rapidly* it's attacking the virus. I can't call it a cure for sure at this point, but...
...I've never been more hopeful.
Aye, good physician! You have never seen the *recuperative ability* of a god before!
We will have this globe as pristine a the snows of the mighty Arctic land of the *Ice Giant* before the next moon.
Hank!
We can't raise Mimic.
Try again, MJ. Call him back.
We've been trying-- we haven't stopped since the Asgardians arrived. We've tried everything.
We *can't* call him back. He's ten minutes off the target.
He's moving so fast, we don't even have enough time to go after him.
He's going through with *the plan.*

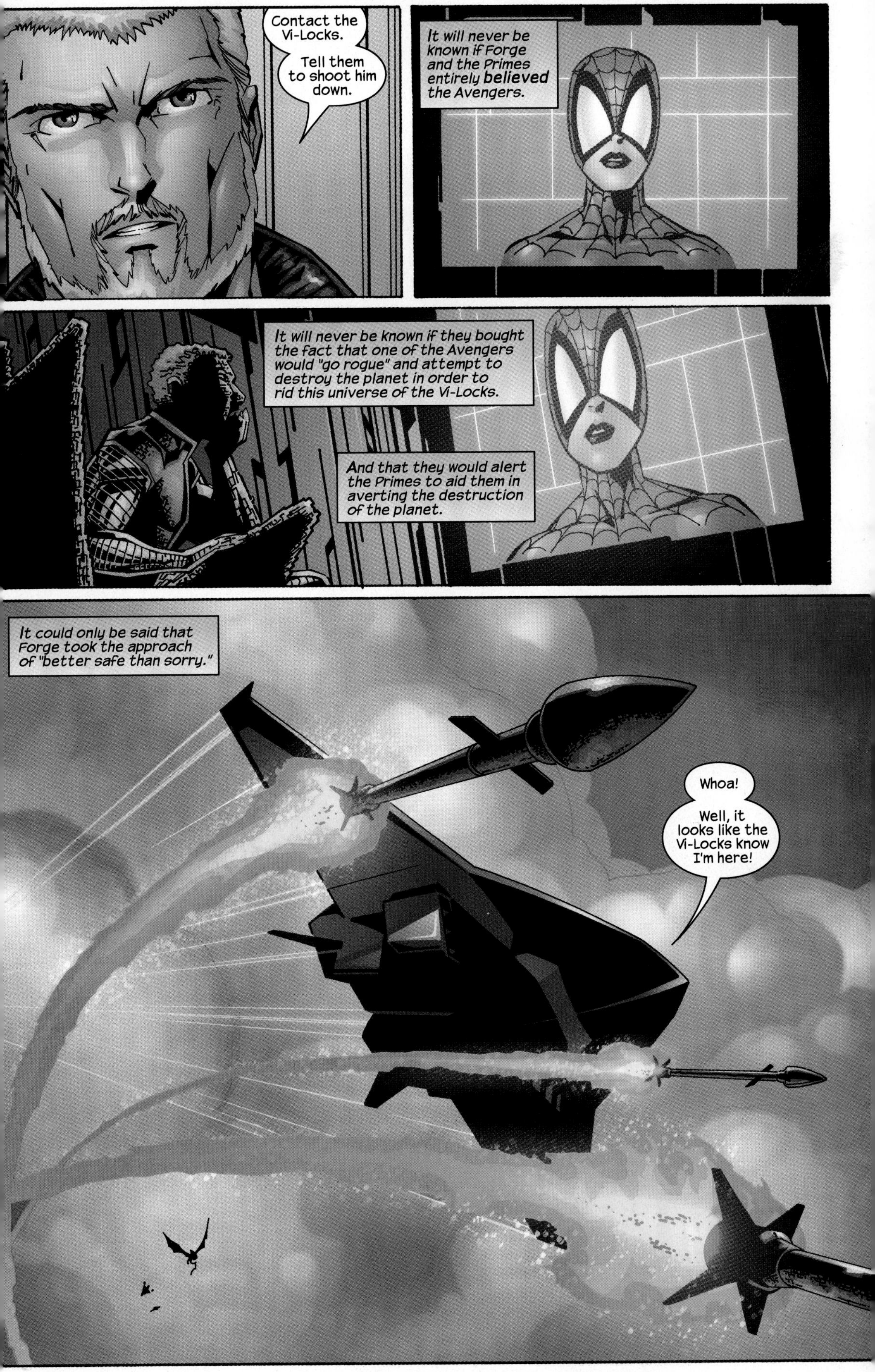
Contact the Vi-Locks.
Tell them to shoot him down.
It will never be known if Forge and the Primes entirely **believed** the Avengers.
It will never be known if they bought the fact that one of the Avengers would "go rogue" and attempt to destroy the planet in order to rid this universe of the Vi-Locks.
And that they would alert the Primes to aid them in averting the destruction of the planet.
It could only be said that Forge took the approach of "better safe than sorry."
Whoa!
Well, it looks like the Vi-Locks know I'm here!

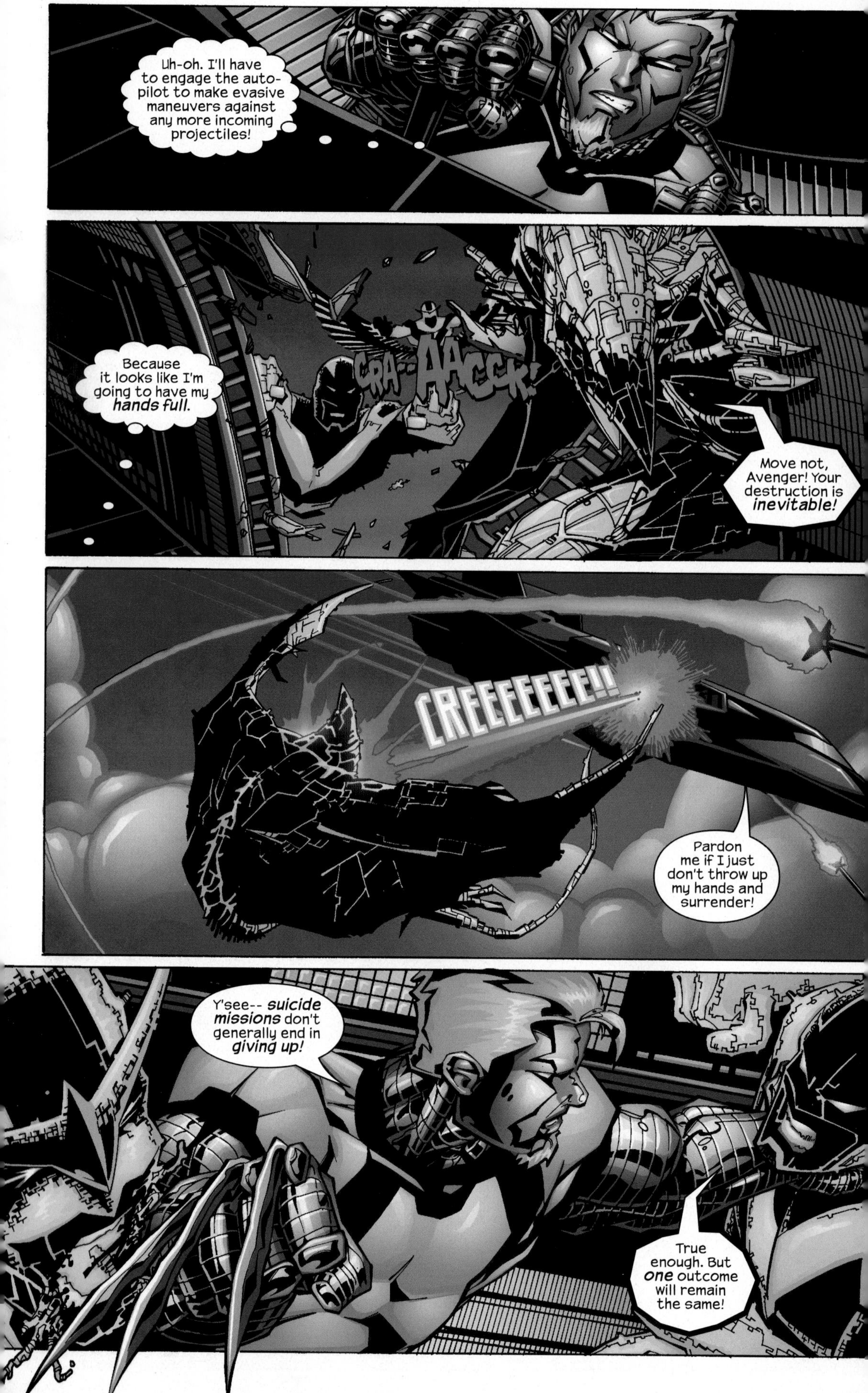

Uh-oh. I'll have to engage the auto-pilot to make evasive maneuvers against any more incoming projectiles!
Because it looks like I'm going to have my hands full.
CRA--AACCK!
Move not, Avenger! Your destruction is inevitable!
CREEEEEEE!!
Pardon me if I just don't throw up my hands and surrender!
Y'see-- suicide missions don't generally end in giving up!
True enough. But one outcome will remain the same!

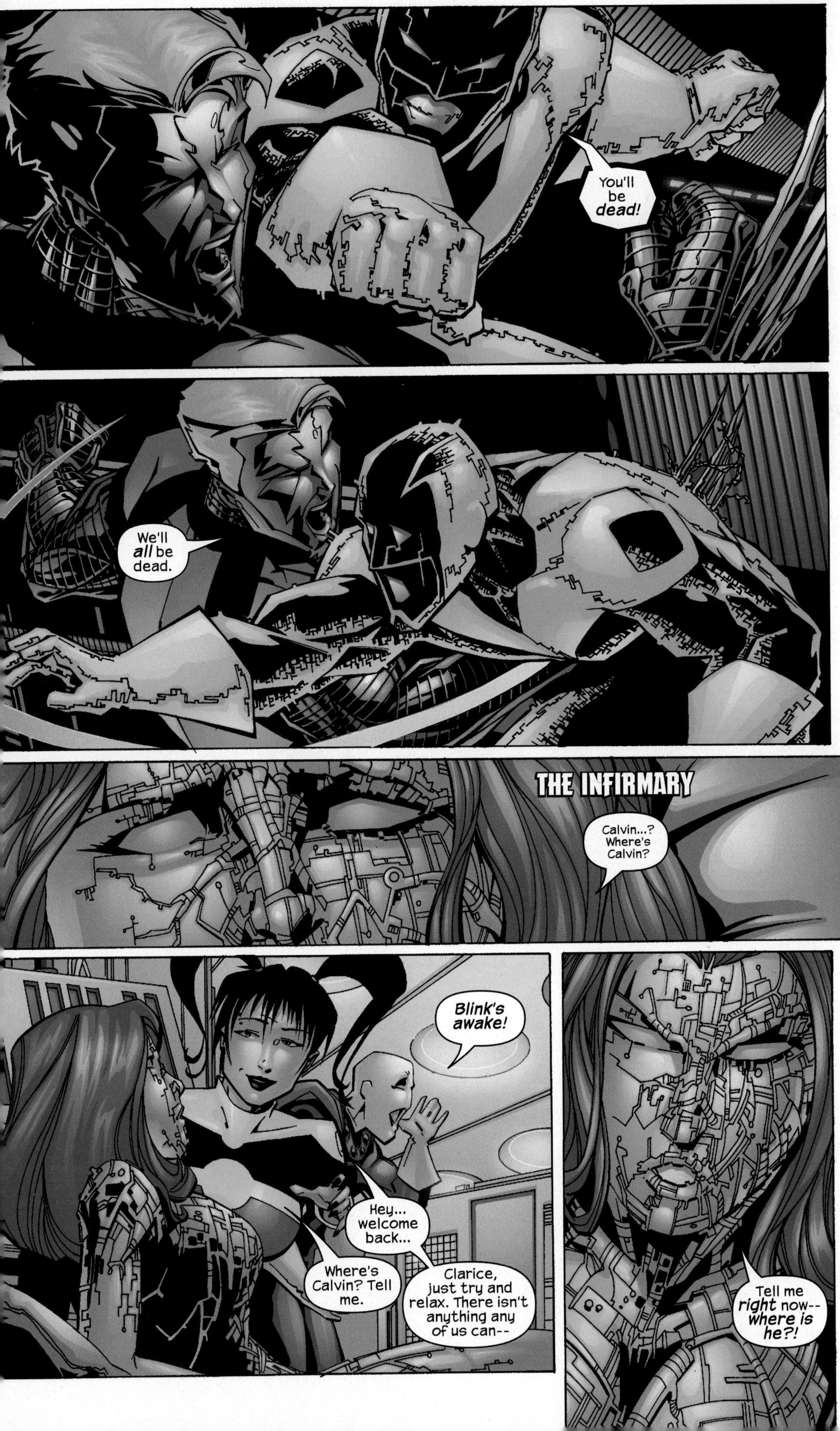

You'll be *dead!*
We'll *all* be dead.
THE INFIRMARY
Calvin...? Where's Calvin?
Blink's awake!
Hey... welcome back...
Where's Calvin? Tell me.
Clarice, just try and relax. There isn't anything any of us can--
Tell me *right* now-- *where is he?!*

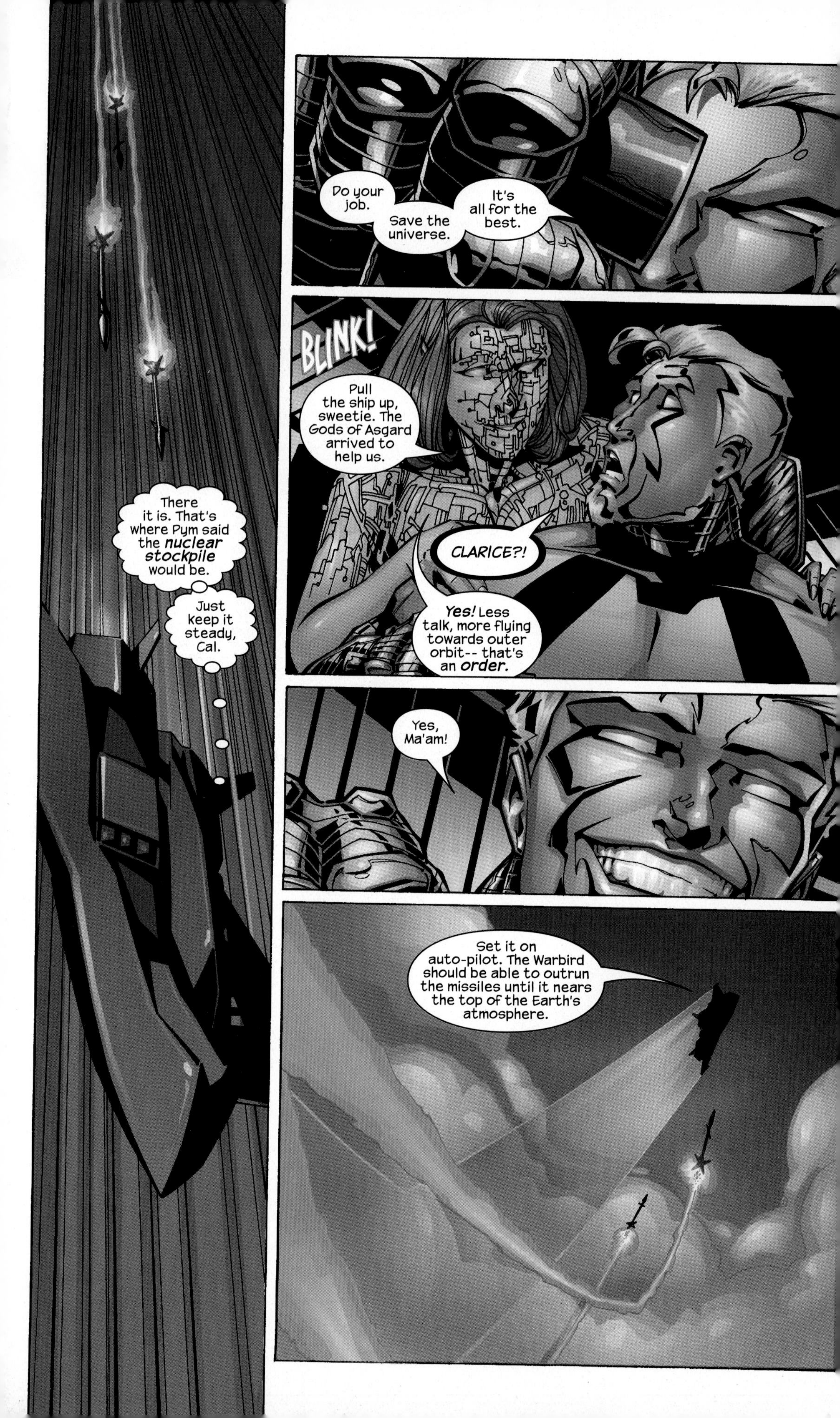

There it is. That's where Pym said the *nuclear stockpile* would be.
Just keep it steady, Cal.
Do your job.
Save the universe.
It's all for the best.
BLINK!
Pull the ship up, sweetie. The Gods of Asgard arrived to help us.
CLARICE?!
Yes! Less talk, more flying towards outer orbit-- that's an *order*.
Yes, Ma'am!
Set it on auto-pilot. The Warbird should be able to outrun the missiles until it nears the top of the Earth's atmosphere.

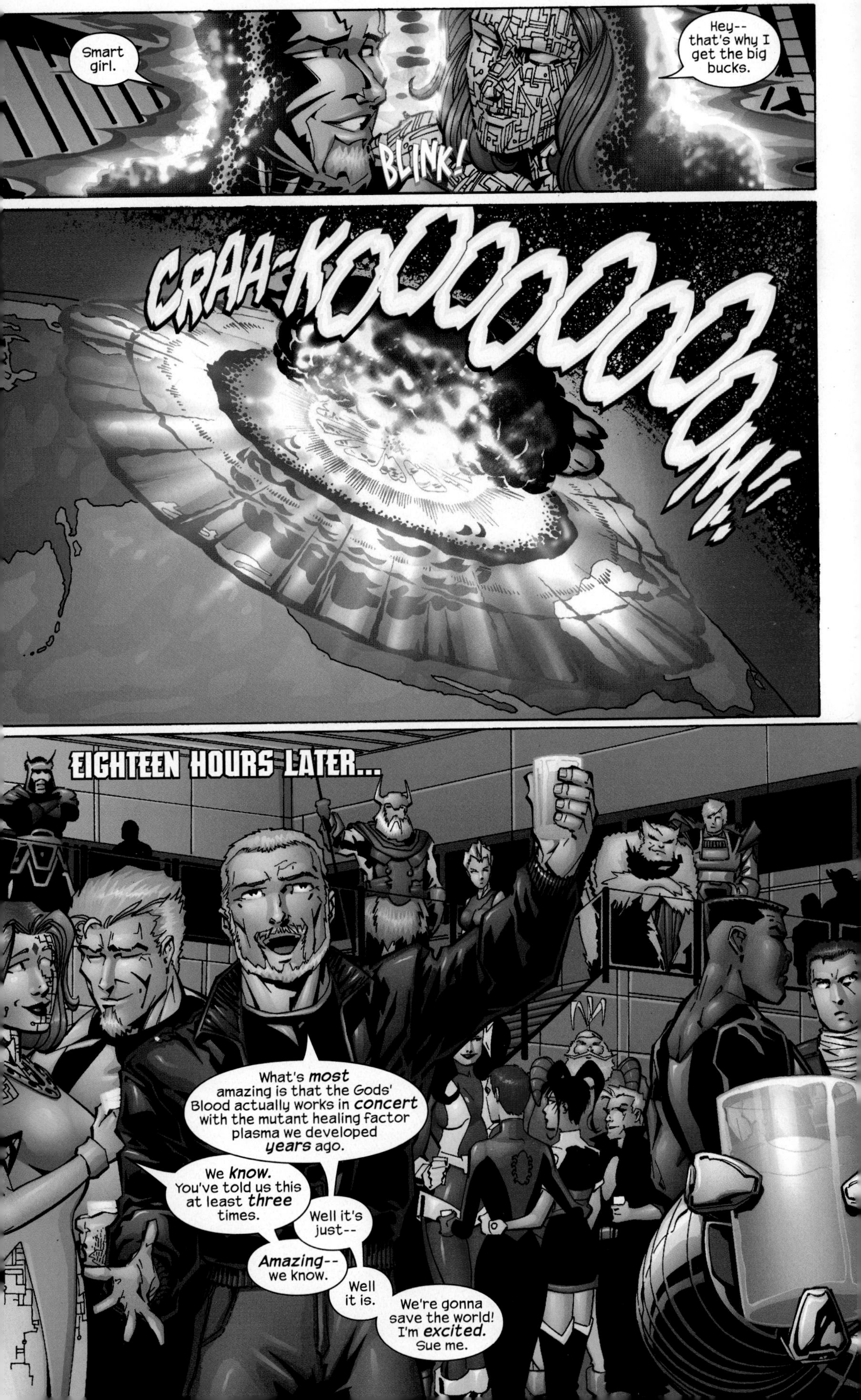
Smart girl.
Hey-- that's why I get the big bucks.
BLINK!
CRAA-KOOOOOOOOOM!!
EIGHTEEN HOURS LATER...
What's most amazing is that the Gods' Blood actually works in concert with the mutant healing factor plasma we developed years ago.
We know. You've told us this at least three times.
Well it's just--
Amazing-- we know.
Well it is.
We're gonna save the world! I'm excited. Sue me.

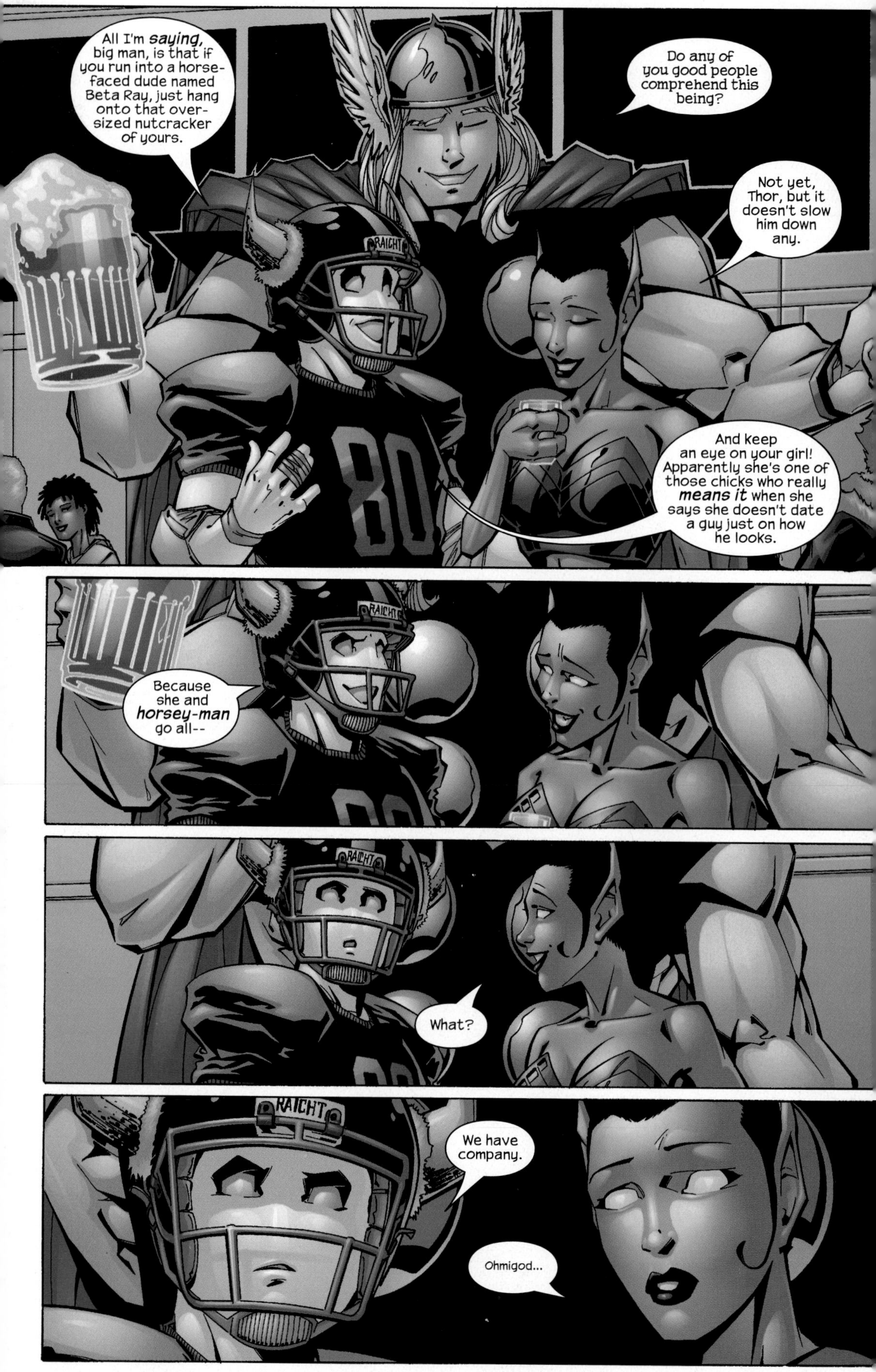

All I'm *saying,* big man, is that if you run into a horse-faced dude named Beta Ray, just hang onto that over-sized nutcracker of yours.
Do any of you good people comprehend this being?
Not yet, Thor, but it doesn't slow him down any.
And keep an eye on your girl! Apparently she's one of those chicks who really ***means it*** when she says she doesn't date a guy just on how he looks.
RAICHT
80
Because she and ***horsey-man*** go all--
What?
We have company.
Ohmigod...

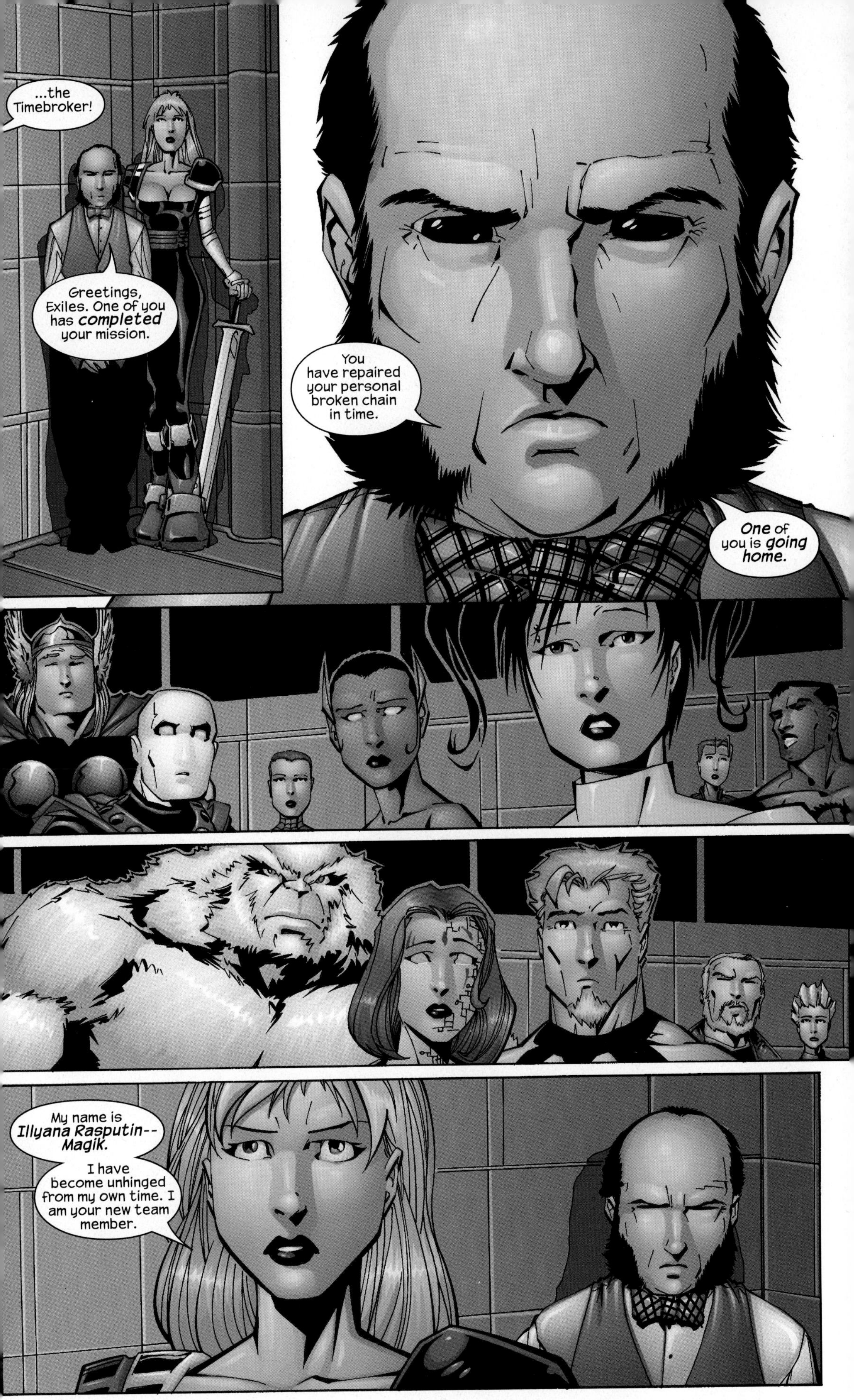

...the Timebroker!
Greetings, Exiles. One of you has *completed* your mission.
You have repaired your personal broken chain in time.
One of you is *going home.*
My name is *Illyana Rasputin-- Magik.*
I have become unhinged from my own time. I am your new team member.

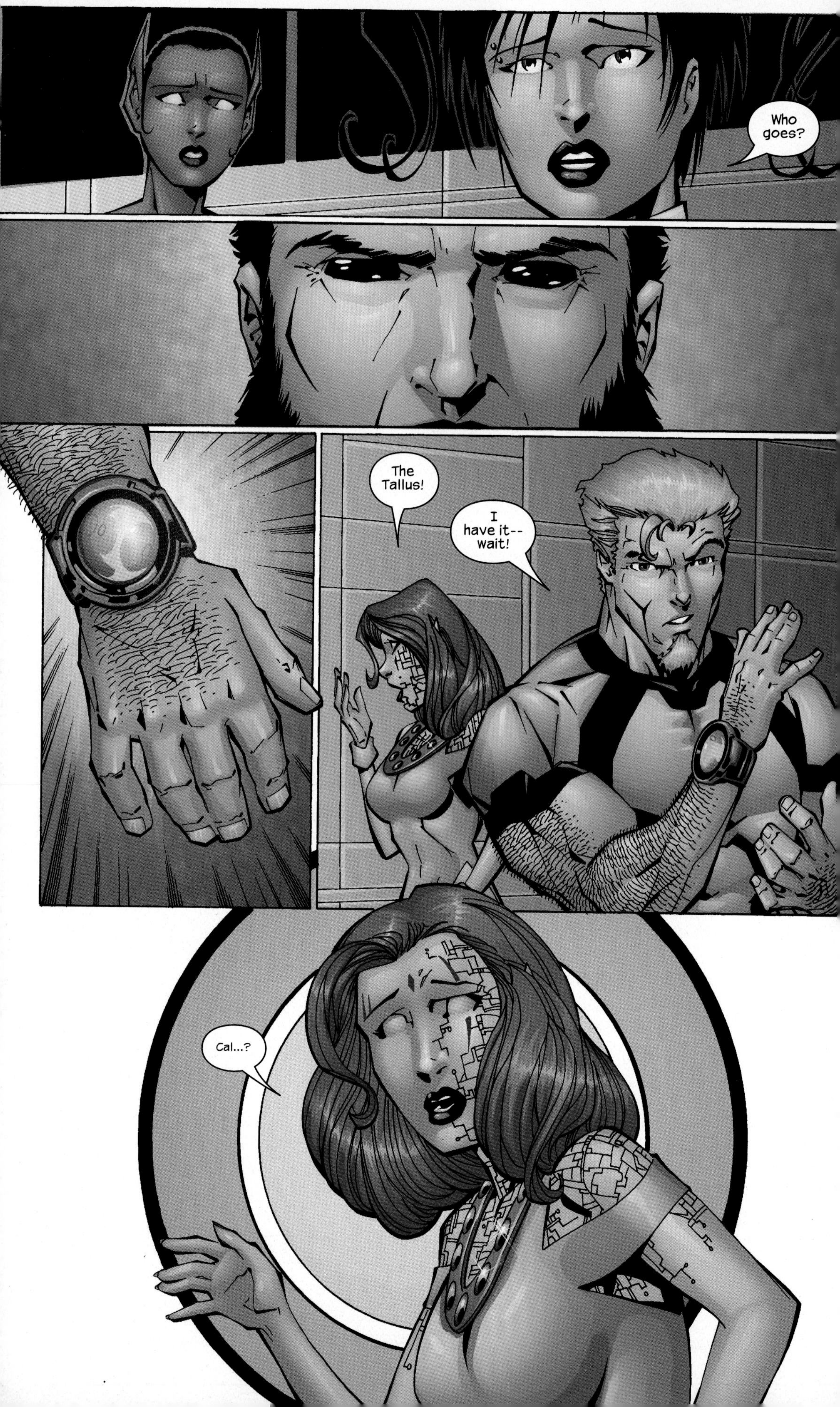
Who goes?
The Tallus!
I have it-- wait!
Cal...?

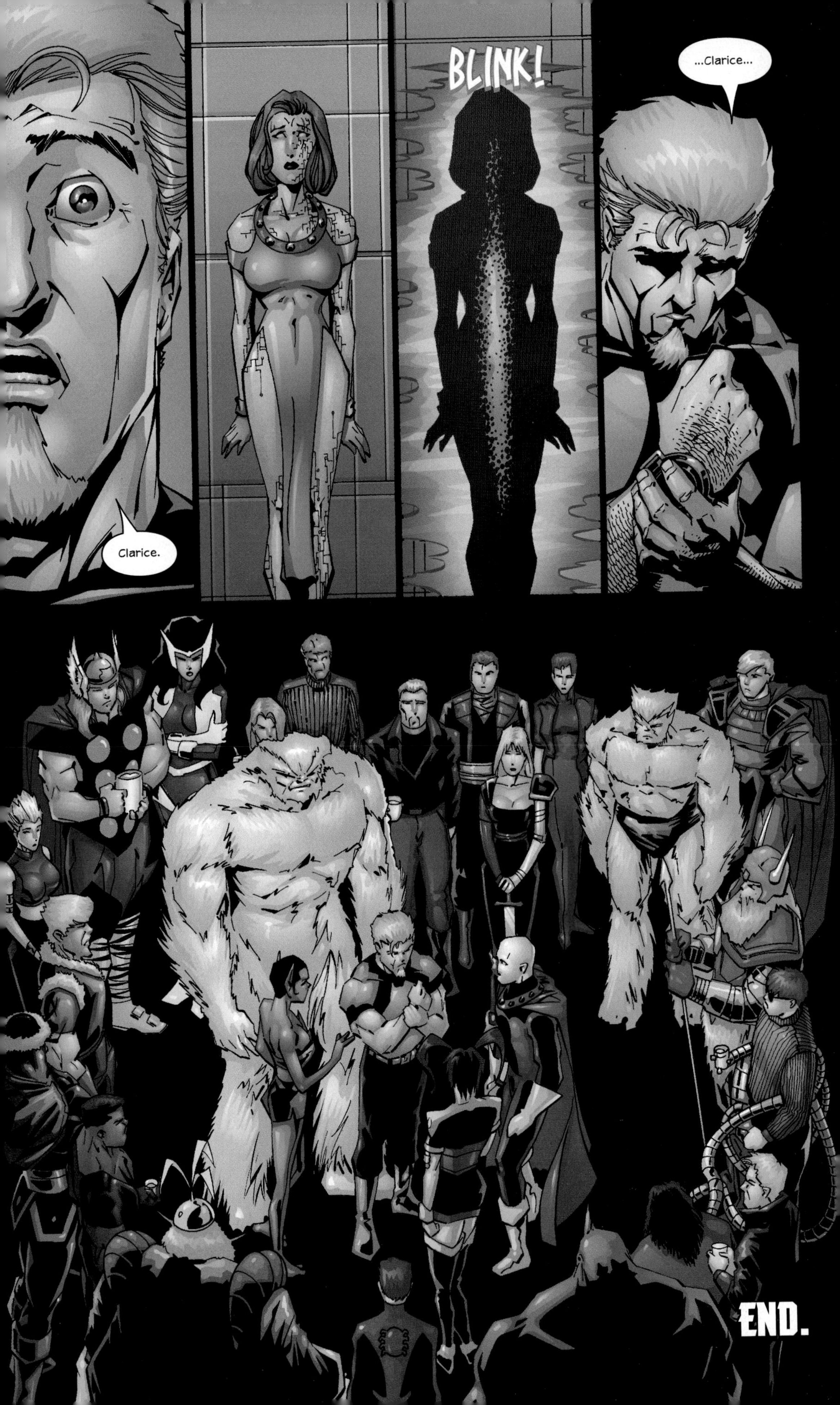

Clarice.
BLINK!
...Clarice...
END.

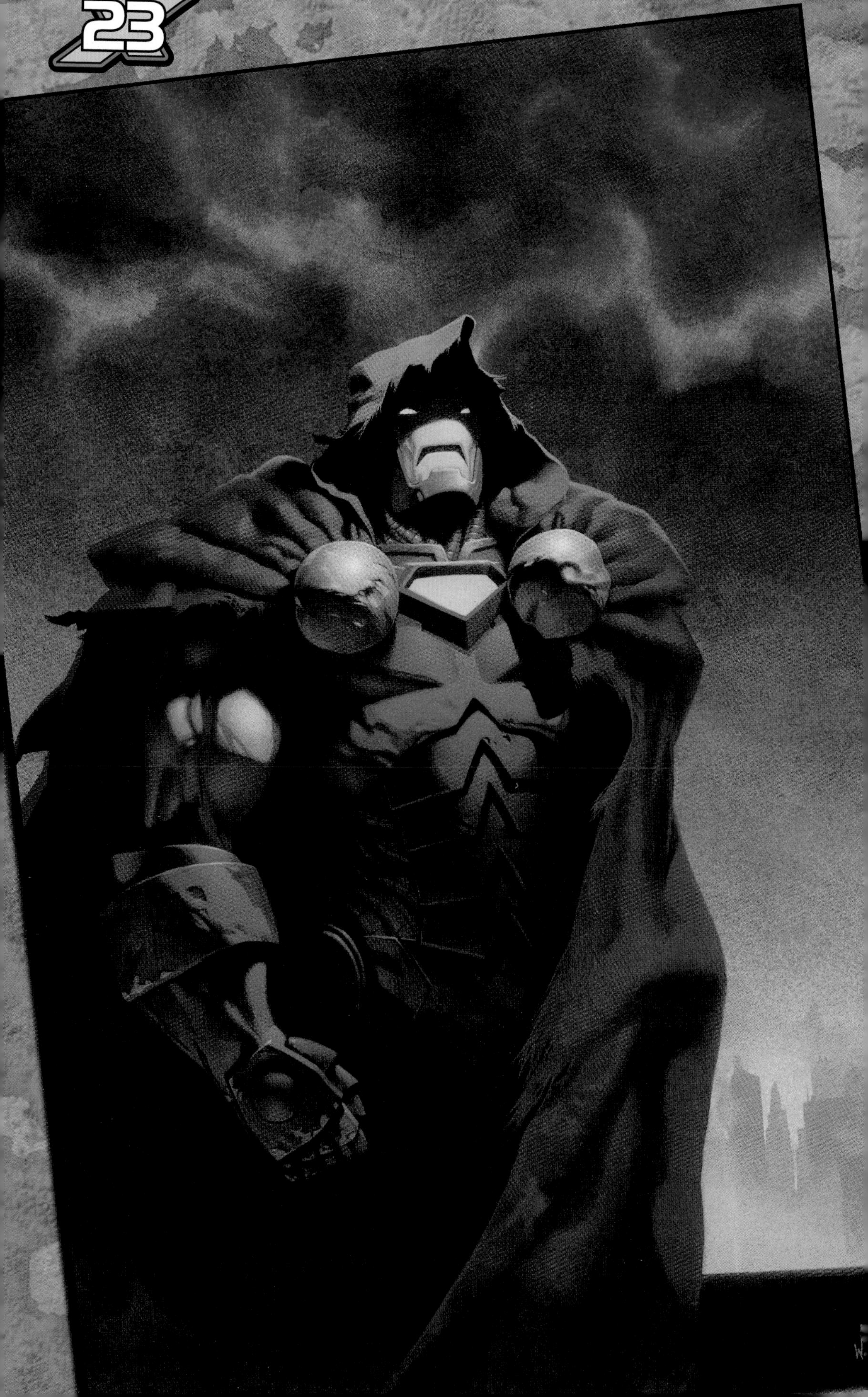

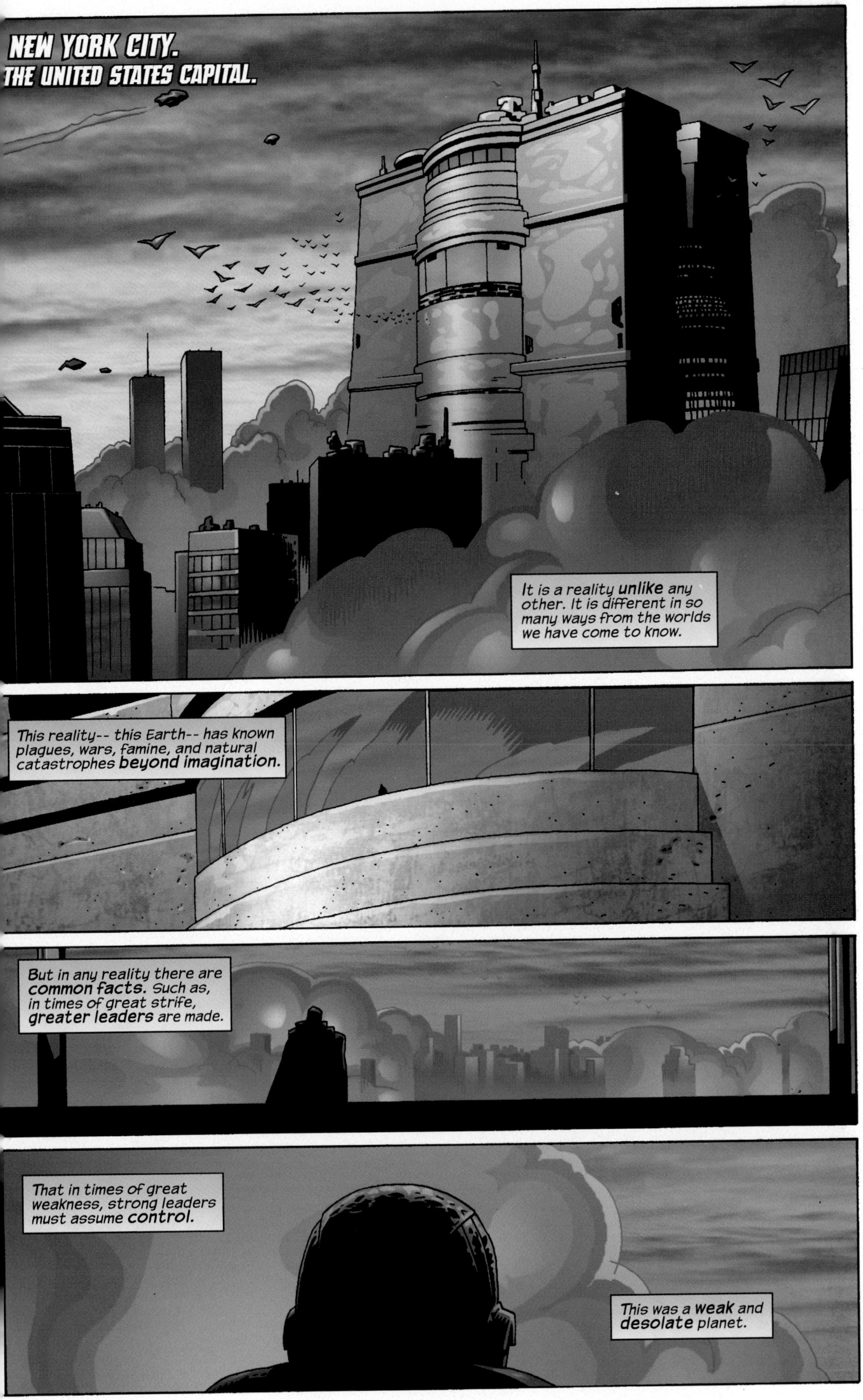
NEW YORK CITY.
THE UNITED STATES CAPITAL.
It is a reality unlike any other. It is different in so many ways from the worlds we have come to know.
This reality-- this Earth-- has known plagues, wars, famine, and natural catastrophes beyond imagination.
But in any reality there are common facts. Such as, in times of great strife, greater leaders are made.
That in times of great weakness, strong leaders must assume control.
This was a weak and desolate planet.

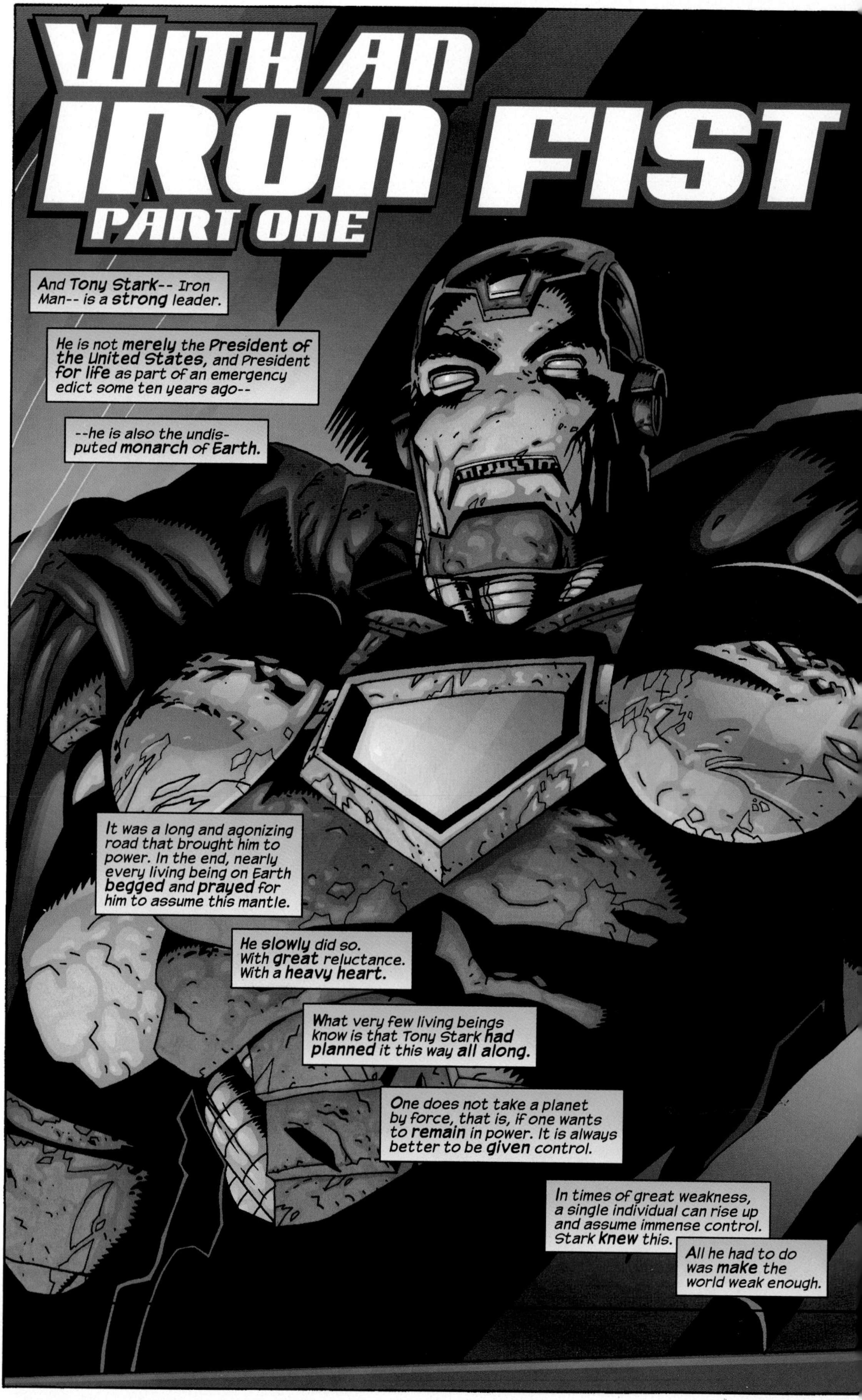
WITH AN IRON FIST
PART ONE
And Tony Stark-- Iron Man-- is a strong leader.
He is not merely the President of the United States, and President for life as part of an emergency edict some ten years ago--
--he is also the undisputed monarch of Earth.
It was a long and agonizing road that brought him to power. In the end, nearly every living being on Earth begged and prayed for him to assume this mantle.
He slowly did so. With great reluctance. With a heavy heart.
What very few living beings know is that Tony Stark had planned it this way all along.
One does not take a planet by force, that is, if one wants to remain in power. It is always better to be given control.
In times of great weakness, a single individual can rise up and assume immense control. Stark knew this.
All he had to do was make the world weak enough.

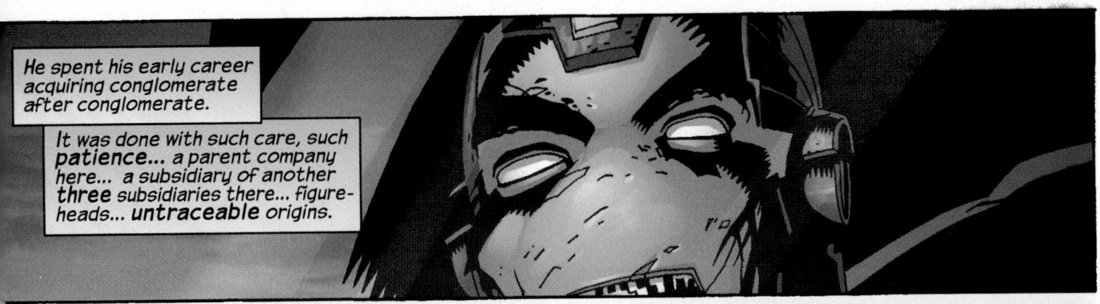

He spent his early career acquiring conglomerate after conglomerate.
It was done with such care, such patience... a parent company here... a subsidiary of another three subsidiaries there... figure-heads... untraceable origins.

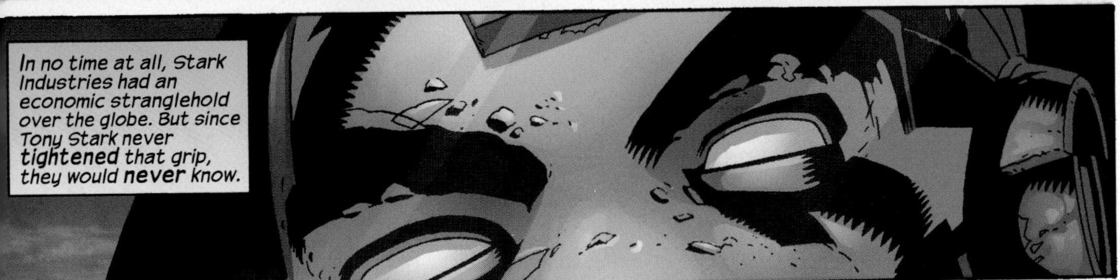

In no time at all, Stark Industries had an economic stranglehold over the globe. But since Tony Stark never tightened that grip, they would never know.

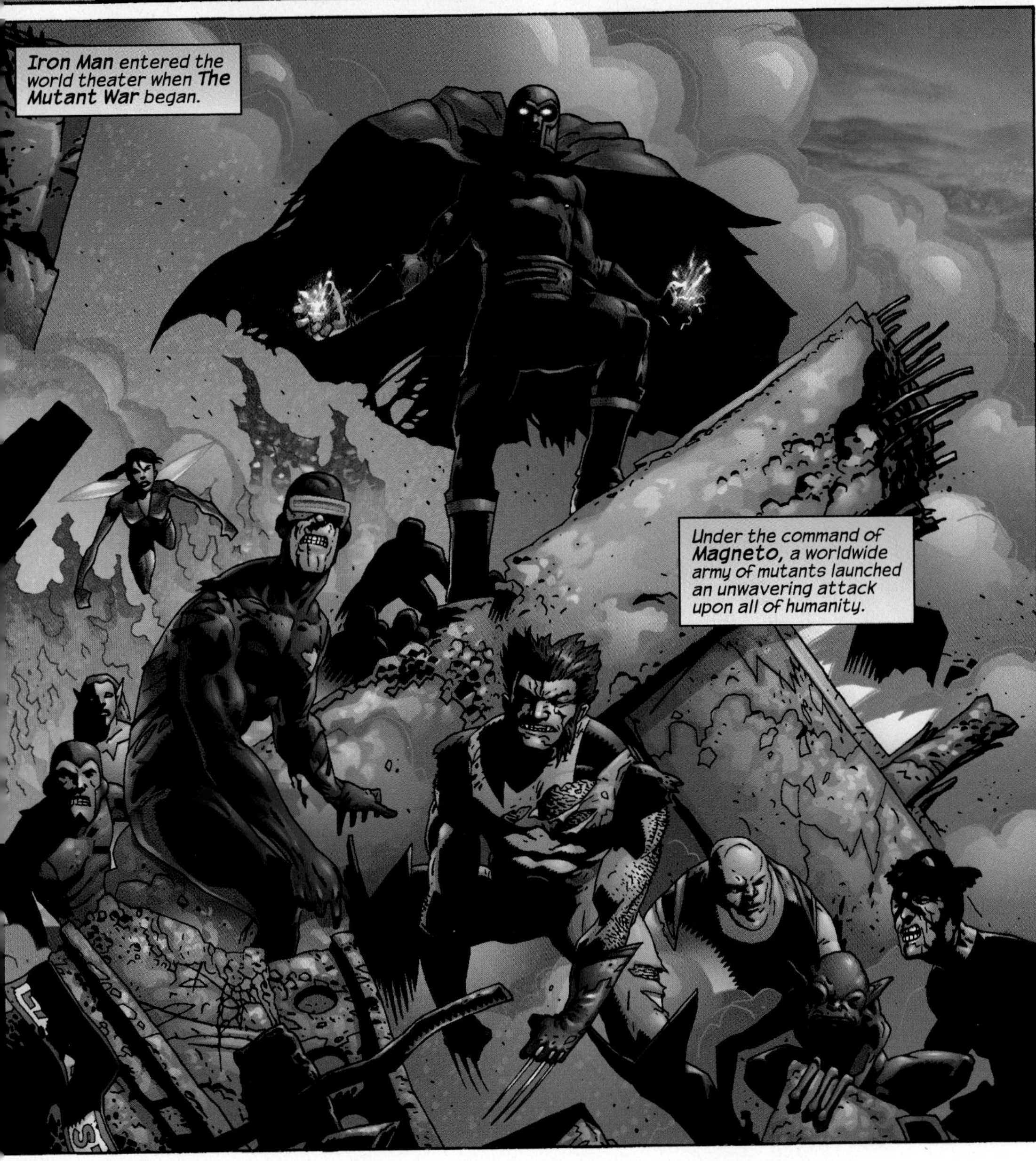

Iron Man entered the world theater when The Mutant War began.
Under the command of Magneto, a worldwide army of mutants launched an unwavering attack upon all of humanity.

It pitted **every** super being on the globe against the mutant soldiers of Magneto. There was terrorism on American soil the likes of which had **never** been conceived before.

Many were lost-- both hero **and** civilian.

But it was unknown-- to all but a few-- which secret individual actually **assisted** in creating this mutant army. Funding their **murderous** operations over and over again.

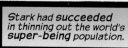

Stark had **succeeded** in thinning out the world's **super-being** population.

In return for his traitorous acts against his own race--

--Magneto promised Iron Man **leadership** of the remaining vestiges of humanity.

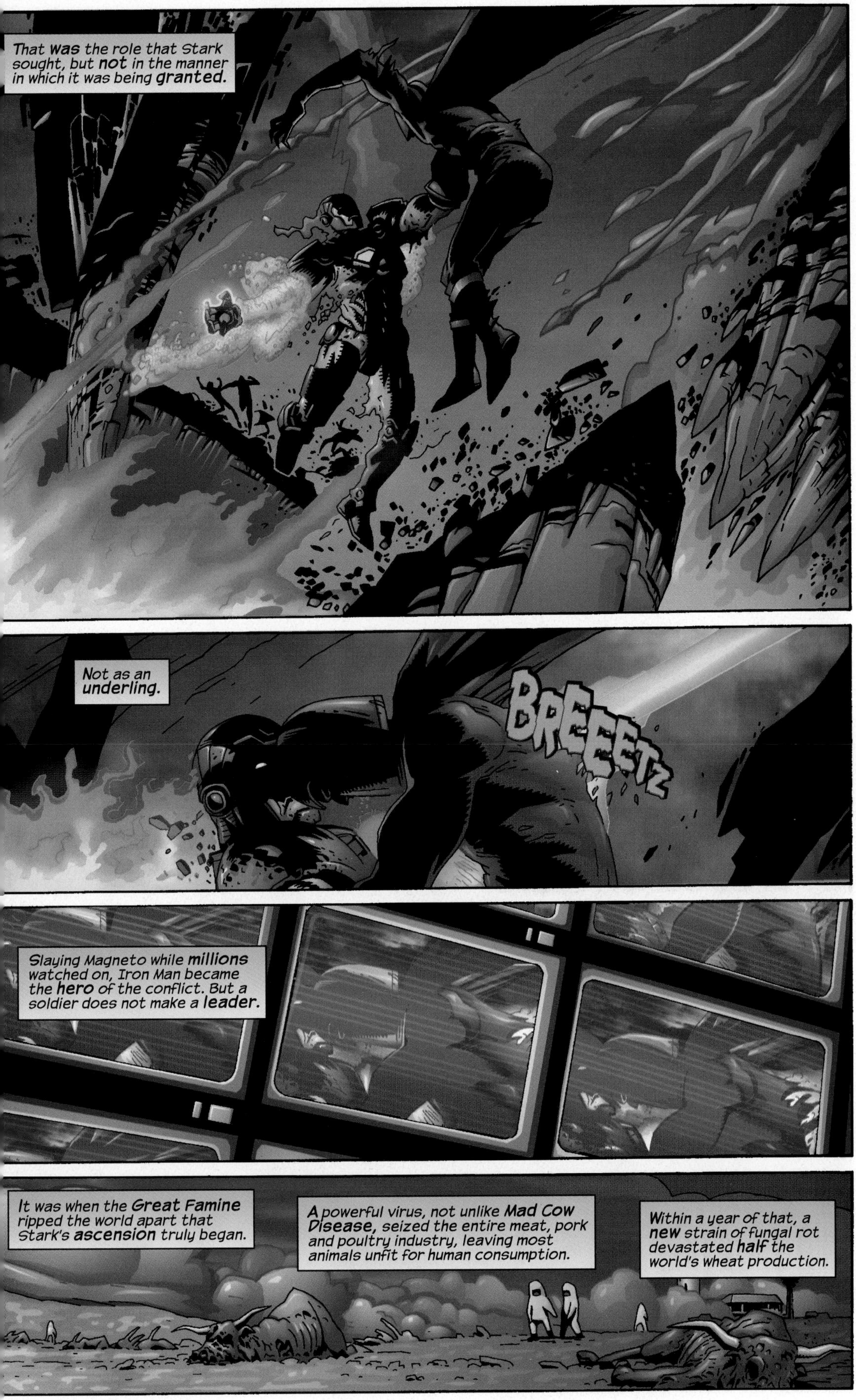

That was the role that Stark sought, but not in the manner in which it was being granted.
Not as an underling.
BREEETZ
Slaying Magneto while millions watched on, Iron Man became the hero of the conflict. But a soldier does not make a leader.
It was when the Great Famine ripped the world apart that Stark's ascension truly began.
A powerful virus, not unlike Mad Cow Disease, seized the entire meat, pork and poultry industry, leaving most animals unfit for human consumption.
Within a year of that, a new strain of fungal rot devastated half the world's wheat production.

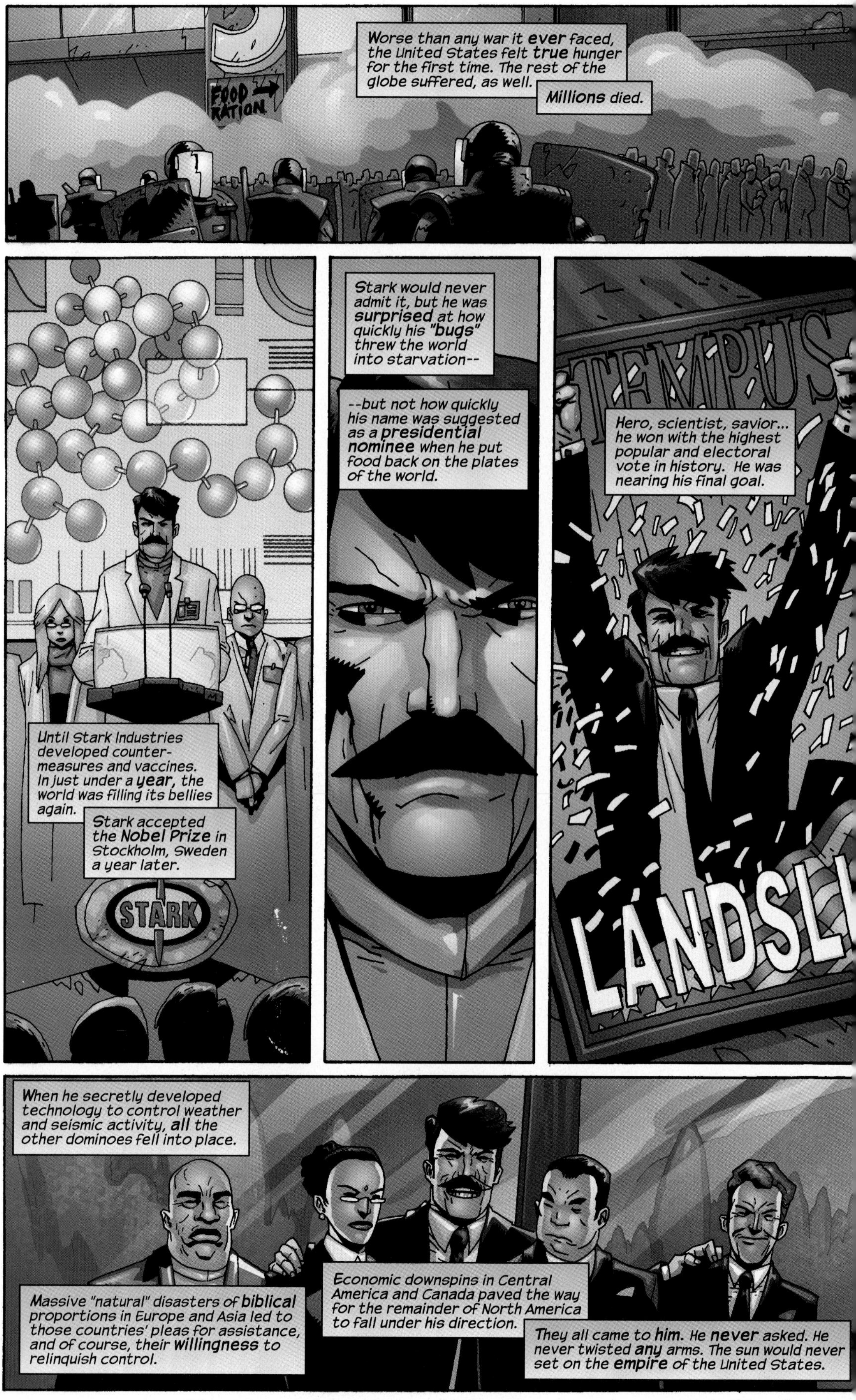
FOOD RATION
Worse than any war it ever faced, the United States felt true hunger for the first time. The rest of the globe suffered, as well.
Millions died.
Until Stark Industries developed counter-measures and vaccines. In just under a year, the world was filling its bellies again.
Stark accepted the Nobel Prize in Stockholm, Sweden a year later.
STARK
Stark would never admit it, but he was surprised at how quickly his "bugs" threw the world into starvation--
--but not how quickly his name was suggested as a presidential nominee when he put food back on the plates of the world.
TEMPUS
Hero, scientist, savior... he won with the highest popular and electoral vote in history. He was nearing his final goal.
LANDSLI
When he secretly developed technology to control weather and seismic activity, all the other dominoes fell into place.
Massive "natural" disasters of biblical proportions in Europe and Asia led to those countries' pleas for assistance, and of course, their willingness to relinquish control.
Economic downspins in Central America and Canada paved the way for the remainder of North America to fall under his direction.
They all came to him. He never asked. He never twisted any arms. The sun would never set on the empire of the United States.

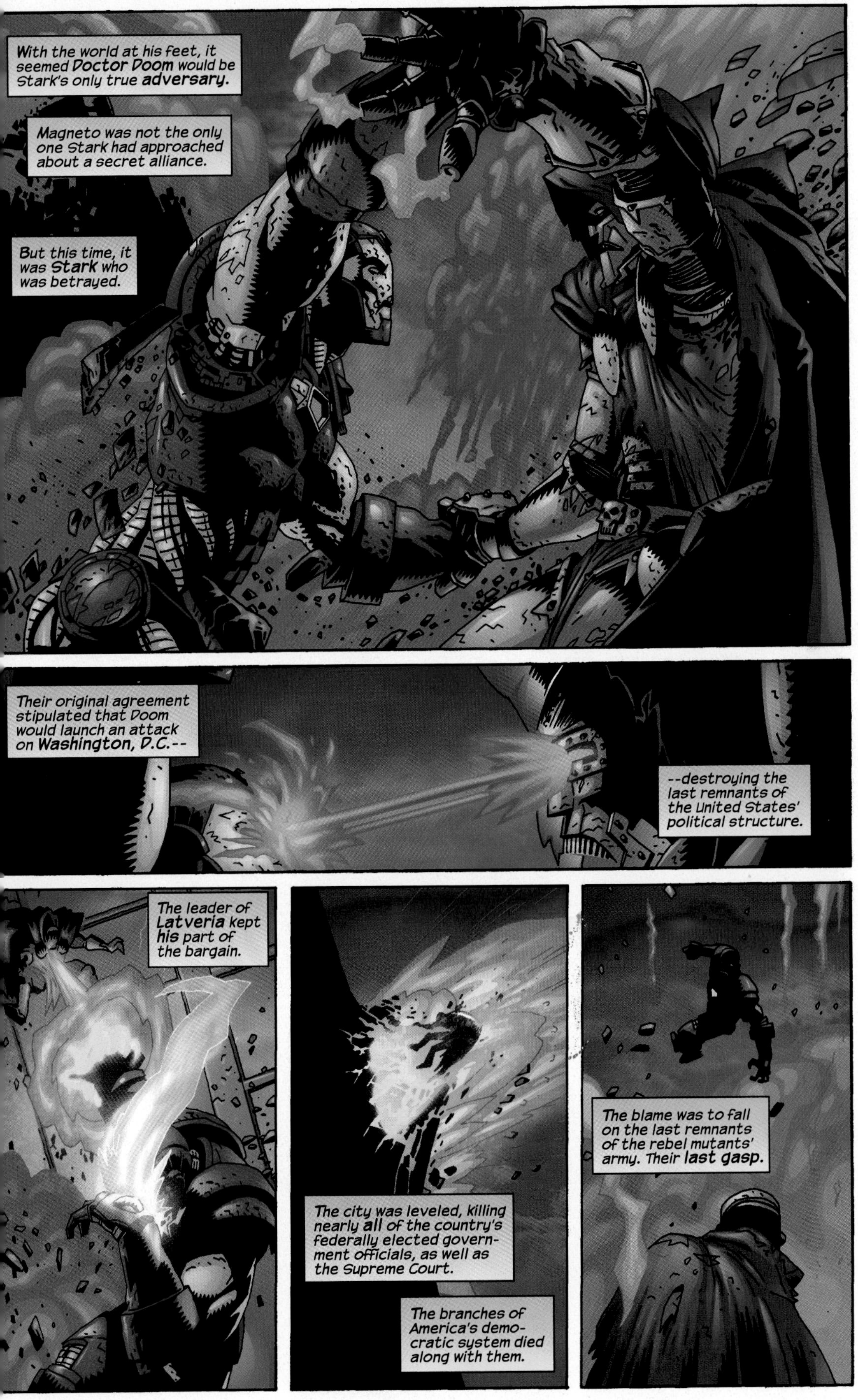

With the world at his feet, it seemed Doctor Doom would be Stark's only true adversary.
Magneto was not the only one Stark had approached about a secret alliance.
But this time, it was Stark who was betrayed.
Their original agreement stipulated that Doom would launch an attack on Washington, D.C.--
--destroying the last remnants of the United States' political structure.
The leader of Latveria kept his part of the bargain.
The city was leveled, killing nearly all of the country's federally elected government officials, as well as the Supreme Court.
The branches of America's democratic system died along with them.
The blame was to fall on the last remnants of the rebel mutants' army. Their last gasp.

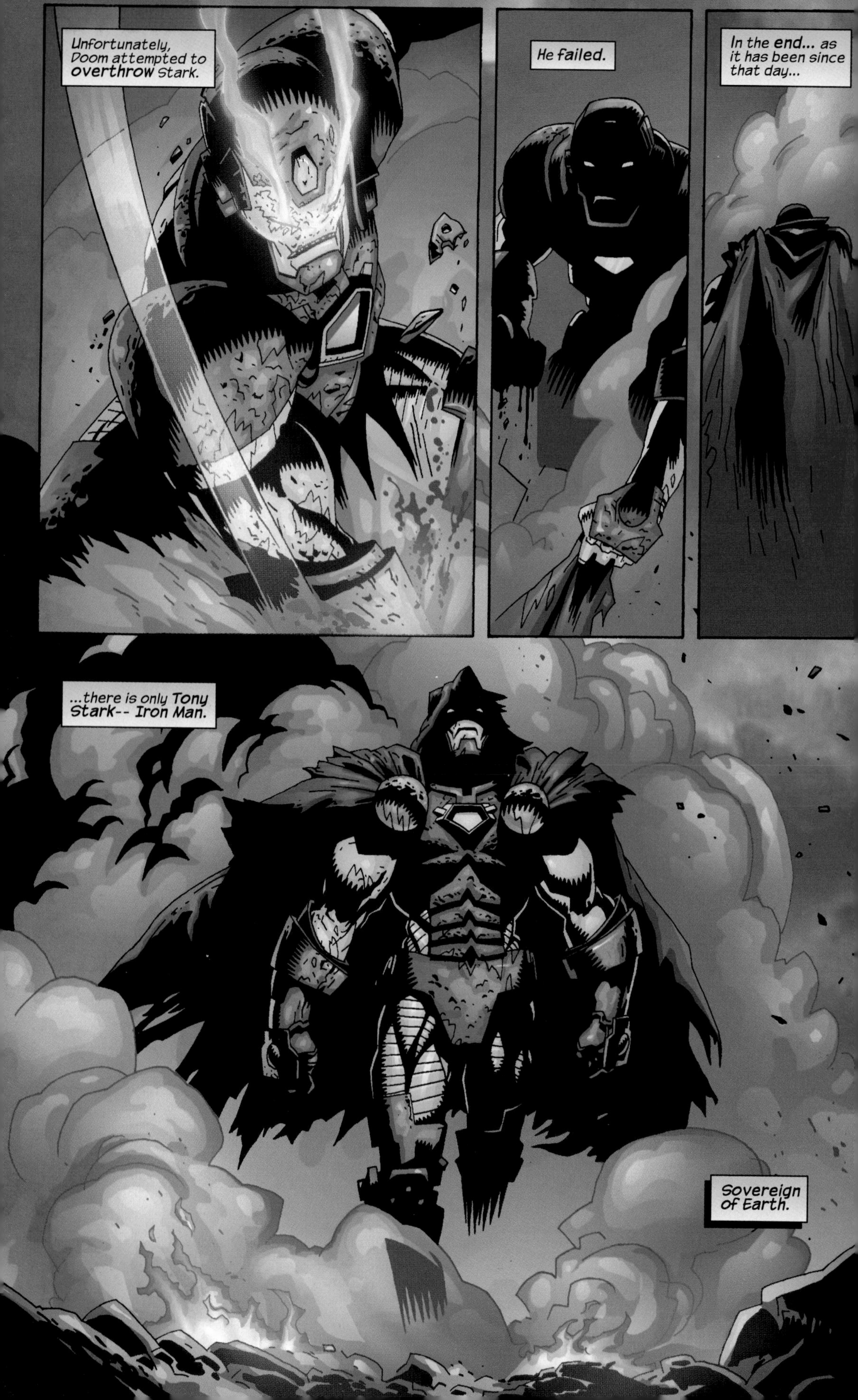
Unfortunately, Doom attempted to overthrow Stark.
He failed.
In the end... as it has been since that day...
...there is only Tony Stark-- Iron Man.
Sovereign of Earth.

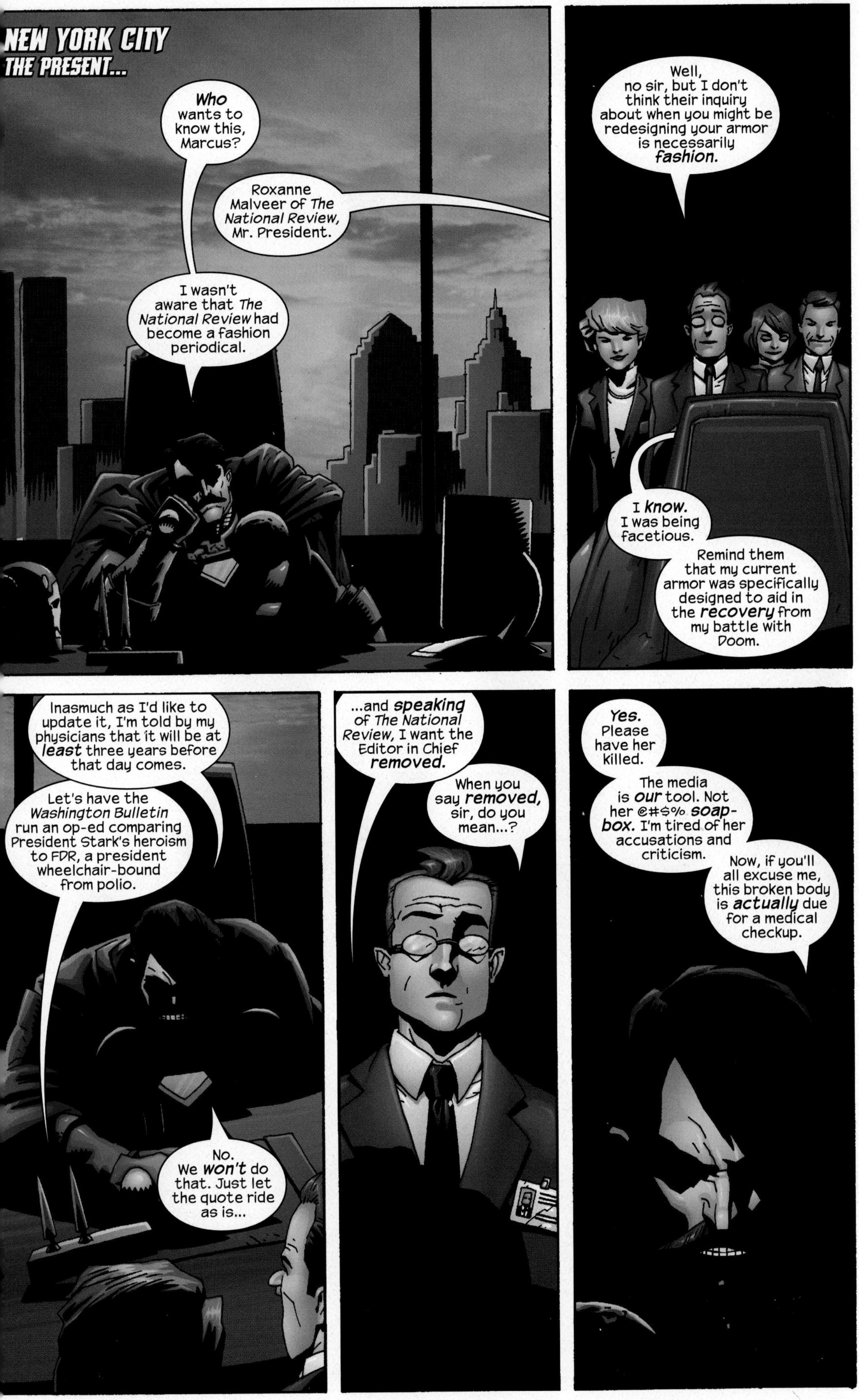
NEW YORK CITY
THE PRESENT...
Who wants to know this, Marcus?
Roxanne Malveer of The National Review, Mr. President.
I wasn't aware that The National Review had become a fashion periodical.
Well, no sir, but I don't think their inquiry about when you might be redesigning your armor is necessarily fashion.
I know. I was being facetious.
Remind them that my current armor was specifically designed to aid in the recovery from my battle with Doom.
Inasmuch as I'd like to update it, I'm told by my physicians that it will be at least three years before that day comes.
Let's have the Washington Bulletin run an op-ed comparing President Stark's heroism to FDR, a president wheelchair-bound from polio.
No. We won't do that. Just let the quote ride as is...
...and speaking of The National Review, I want the Editor in Chief removed.
When you say removed, sir, do you mean...?
Yes. Please have her killed.
The media is our tool. Not her @#$% soapbox. I'm tired of her accusations and criticism.
Now, if you'll all excuse me, this broken body is actually due for a medical checkup.

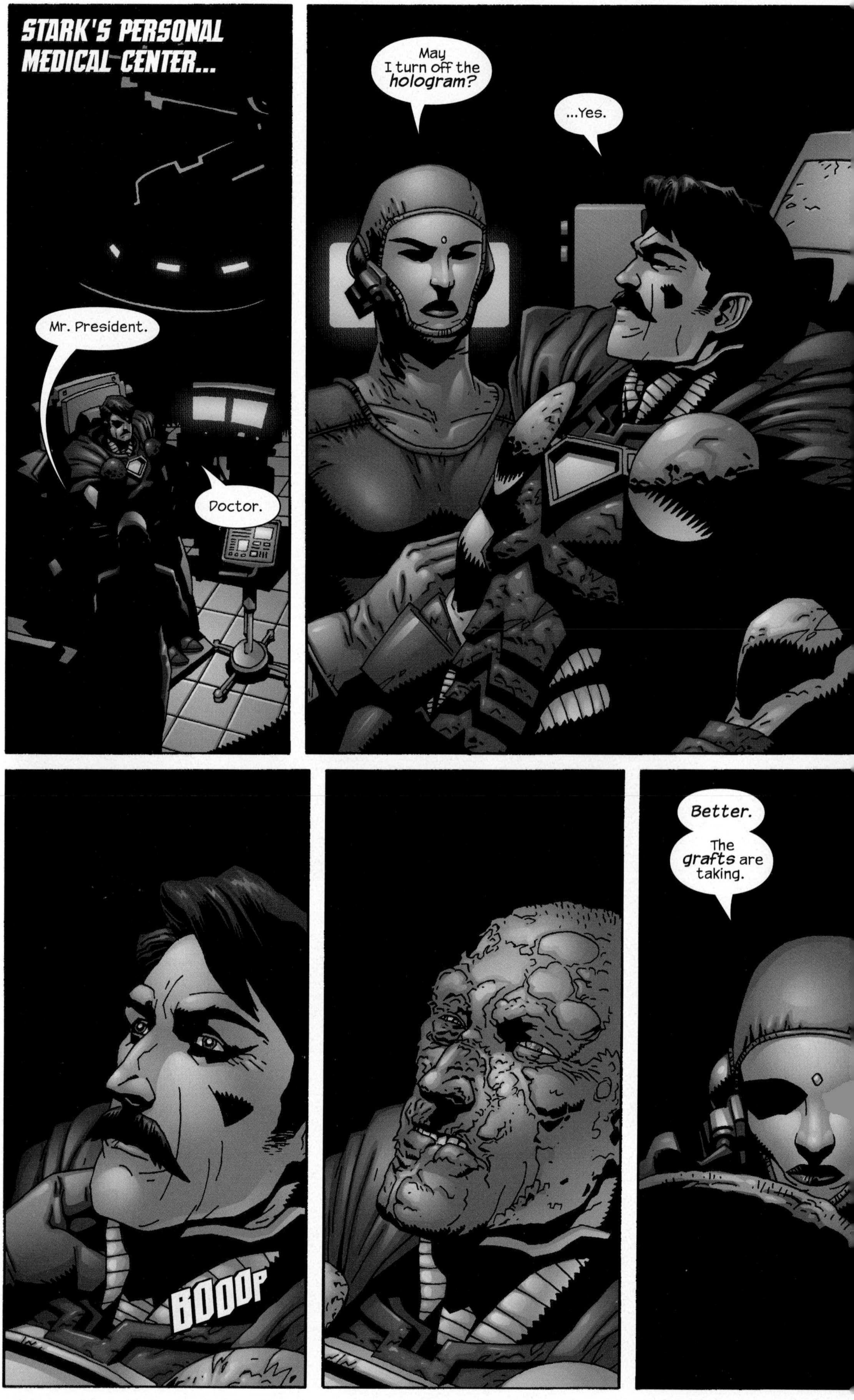
STARK'S PERSONAL MEDICAL CENTER...
Mr. President.
Doctor.
May I turn off the *hologram?*
...Yes.
BOOOP
Better.
The *grafts* are taking.

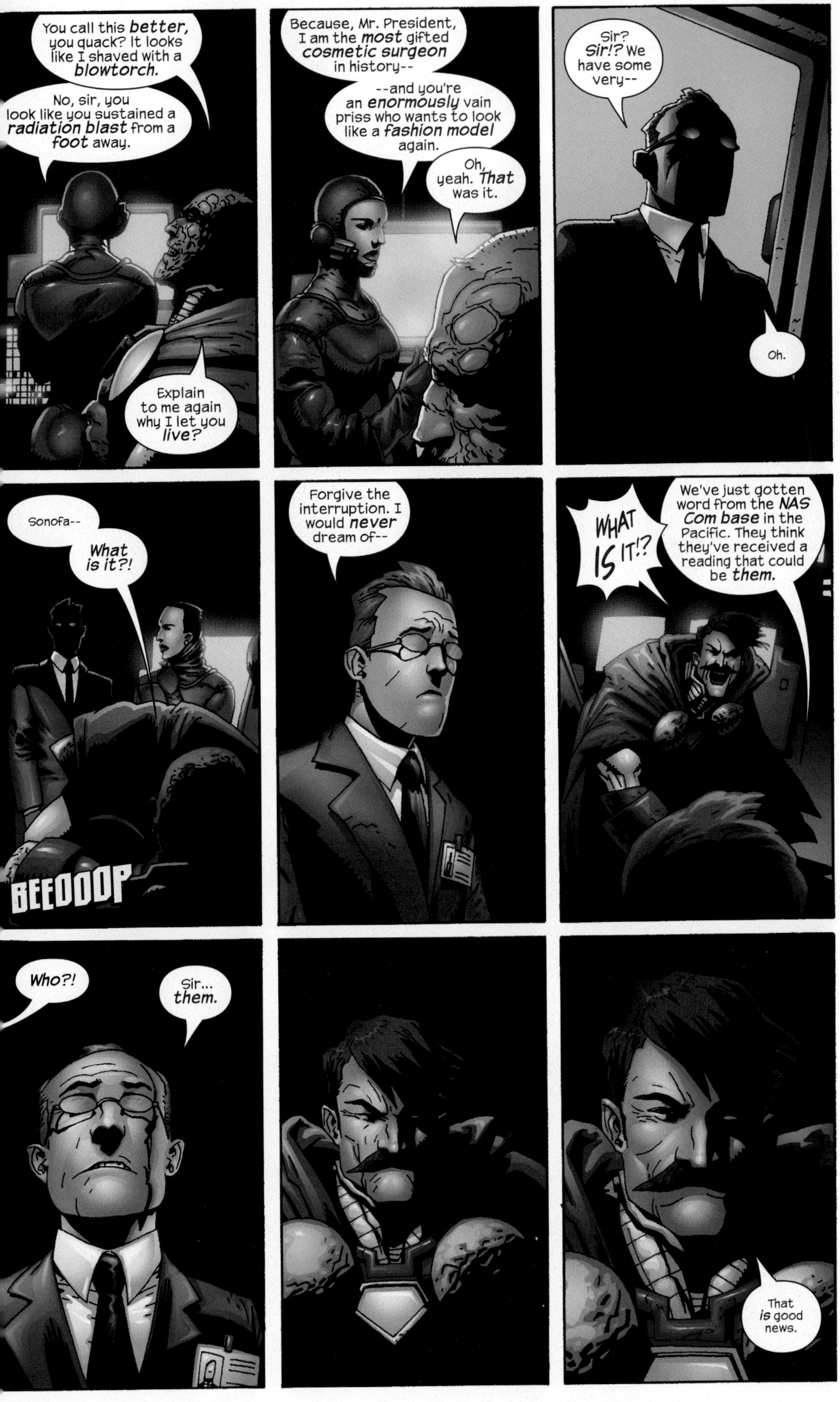
You call this better, you quack? It looks like I shaved with a blowtorch.
No, sir, you look like you sustained a radiation blast from a foot away.
Explain to me again why I let you live?
Because, Mr. President, I am the most gifted cosmetic surgeon in history--
--and you're an enormously vain priss who wants to look like a fashion model again.
Oh, yeah. That was it.
Sir? Sir!? We have some very--
Oh.
Sonofa--
What is it?!
BEEOOOP
Forgive the interruption. I would never dream of--
WHAT IS IT!?
We've just gotten word from the NAS Com base in the Pacific. They think they've received a reading that could be them.
Who?!
Sir... them.
That is good news.

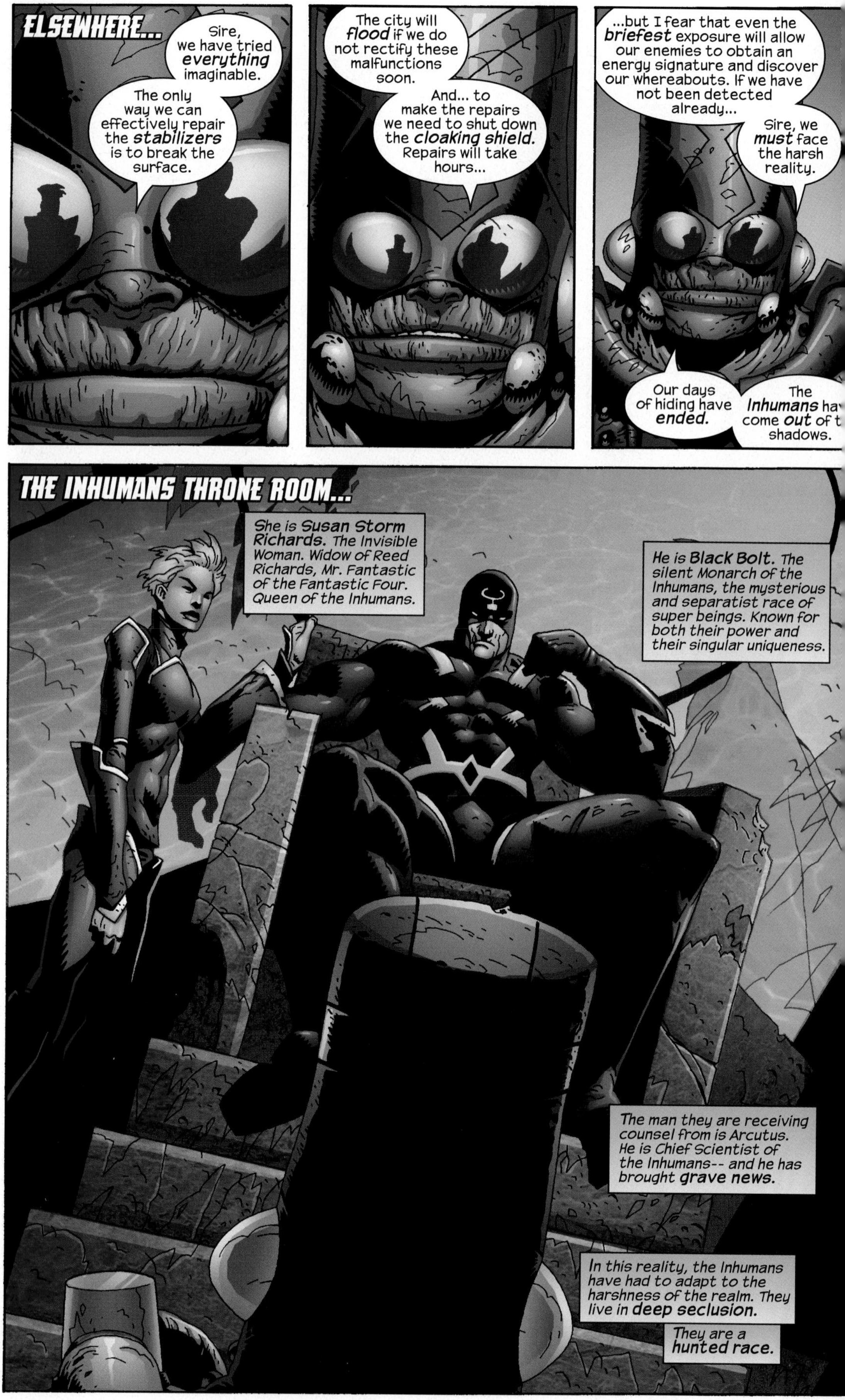
ELSEWHERE...
Sire, we have tried everything imaginable.
The only way we can effectively repair the stabilizers is to break the surface.
The city will flood if we do not rectify these malfunctions soon.
And... to make the repairs we need to shut down the cloaking shield. Repairs will take hours...
...but I fear that even the briefest exposure will allow our enemies to obtain an energy signature and discover our whereabouts. If we have not been detected already...
Sire, we must face the harsh reality.
Our days of hiding have ended.
The Inhumans ha come out of t shadows.
THE INHUMANS THRONE ROOM...
She is Susan Storm Richards. The Invisible Woman. Widow of Reed Richards, Mr. Fantastic of the Fantastic Four. Queen of the Inhumans.
He is Black Bolt. The silent Monarch of the Inhumans, the mysterious and separatist race of super beings. Known for both their power and their singular uniqueness.
The man they are receiving counsel from is Arcutus. He is Chief Scientist of the Inhumans-- and he has brought grave news.
In this reality, the Inhumans have had to adapt to the harshness of the realm. They live in deep seclusion.
They are a hunted race.

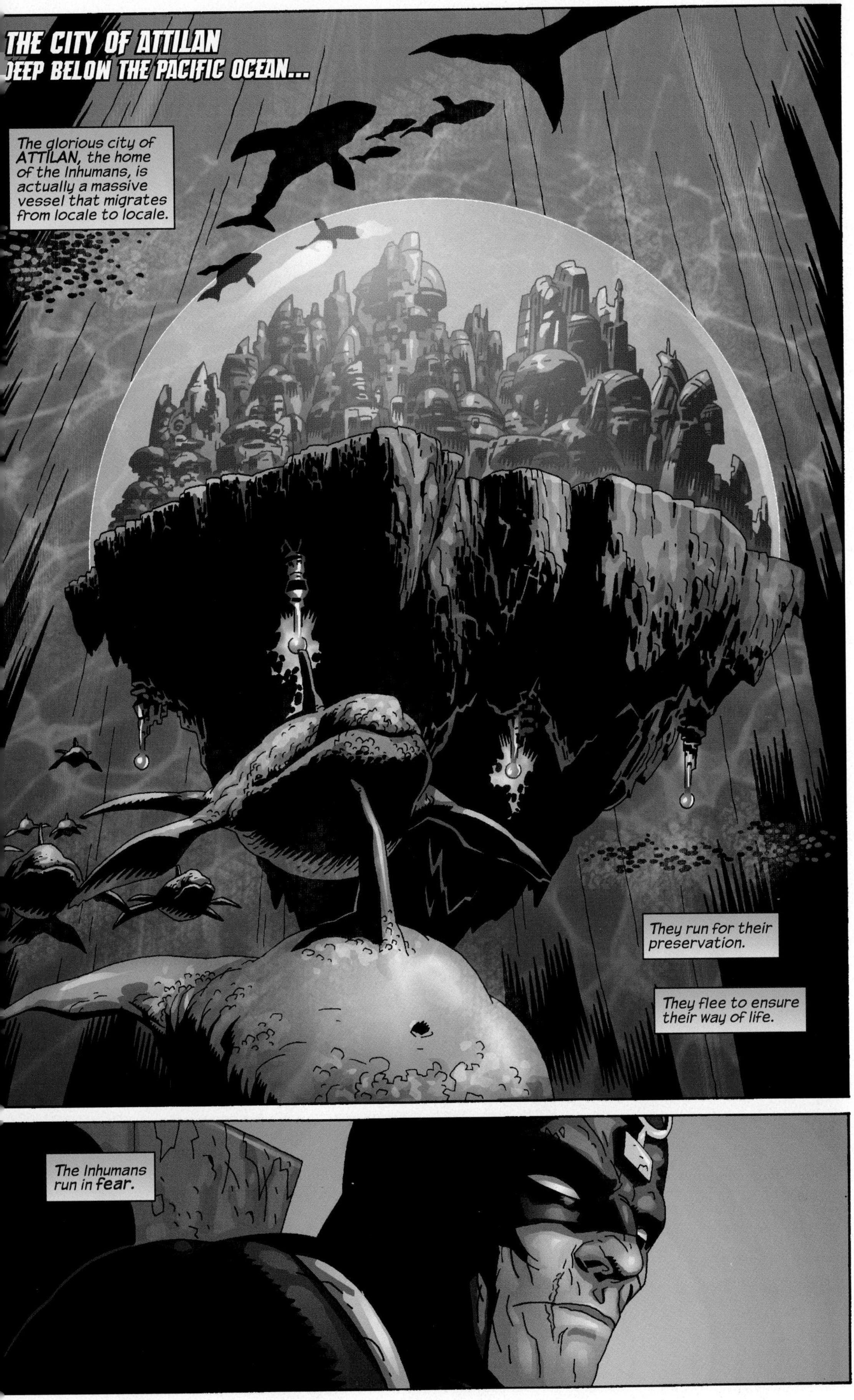
THE CITY OF ATTILAN
DEEP BELOW THE PACIFIC OCEAN...
The glorious city of ATTILAN, the home of the Inhumans, is actually a massive vessel that migrates from locale to locale.
They run for their preservation.
They flee to ensure their way of life.
The Inhumans run in fear.

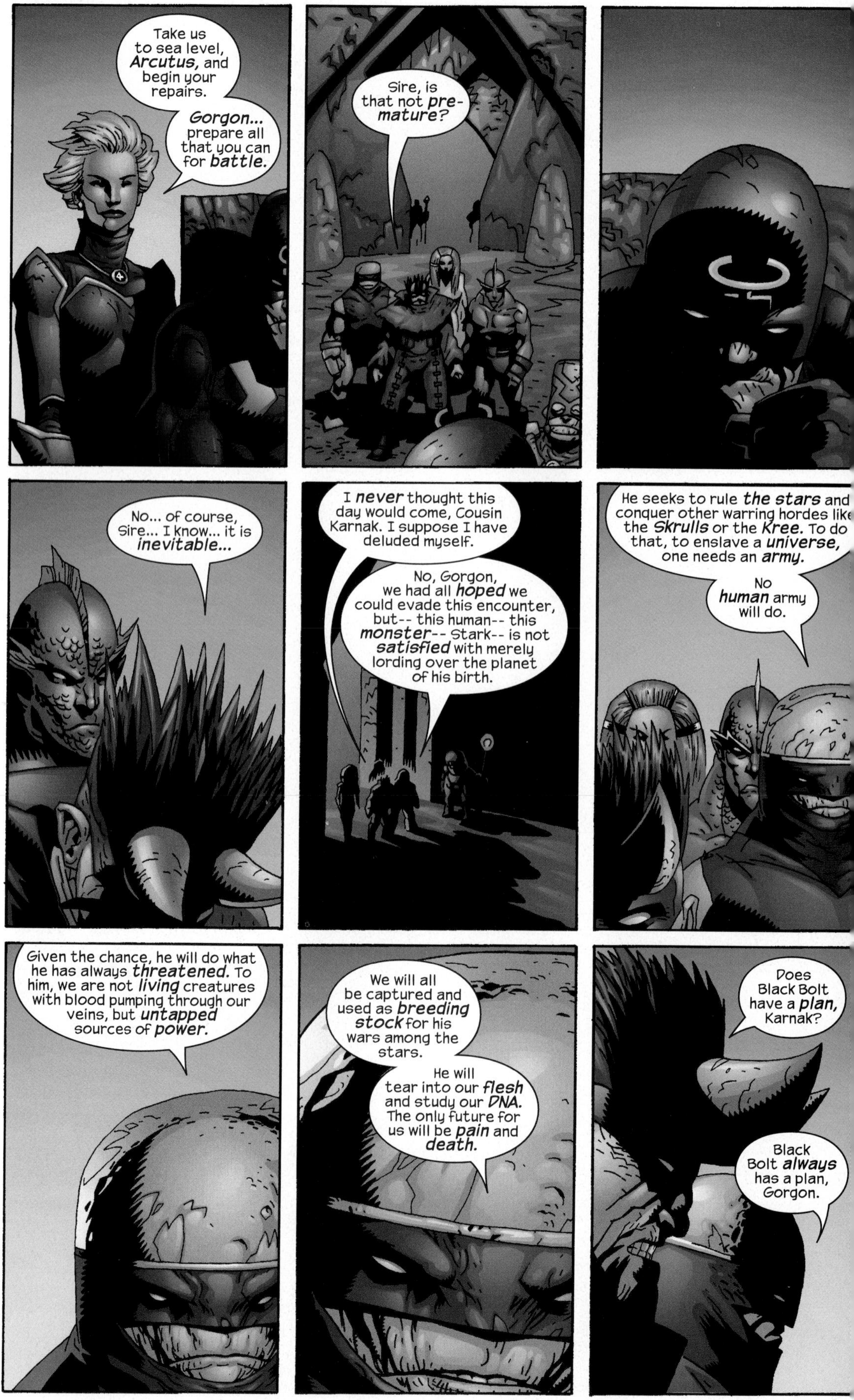

Take us to sea level, Arcutus, and begin your repairs.
Gorgon... prepare all that you can for battle.
Sire, is that not premature?
No... of course, Sire... I know... it is inevitable...
I never thought this day would come, Cousin Karnak. I suppose I have deluded myself.
No, Gorgon, we had all hoped we could evade this encounter, but-- this human-- this monster-- Stark-- is not satisfied with merely lording over the planet of his birth.
He seeks to rule the stars and conquer other warring hordes like the Skrulls or the Kree. To do that, to enslave a universe, one needs an army.
No human army will do.
Given the chance, he will do what he has always threatened. To him, we are not living creatures with blood pumping through our veins, but untapped sources of power.
We will all be captured and used as breeding stock for his wars among the stars.
He will tear into our flesh and study our DNA. The only future for us will be pain and death.
Does Black Bolt have a plan, Karnak?
Black Bolt always has a plan, Gorgon.

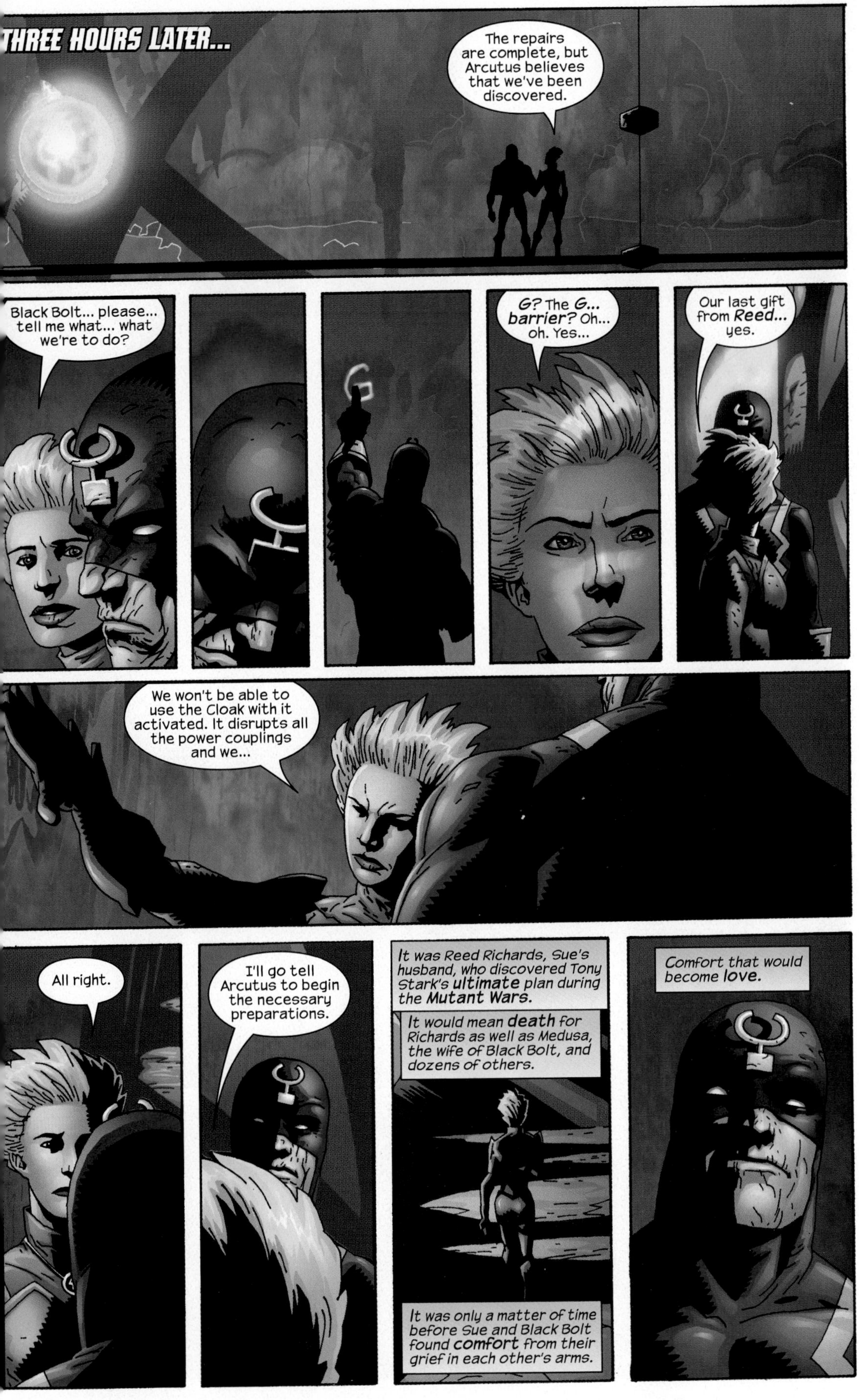
THREE HOURS LATER...
The repairs are complete, but Arcutus believes that we've been discovered.
Black Bolt... please... tell me what... what we're to do?
G? The G... barrier? Oh... oh. Yes...
Our last gift from Reed... yes.
We won't be able to use the Cloak with it activated. It disrupts all the power couplings and we...
All right.
I'll go tell Arcutus to begin the necessary preparations.
It was Reed Richards, Sue's husband, who discovered Tony Stark's ultimate plan during the Mutant Wars.
It would mean death for Richards as well as Medusa, the wife of Black Bolt, and dozens of others.
It was only a matter of time before Sue and Black Bolt found comfort from their grief in each other's arms.
Comfort that would become love.

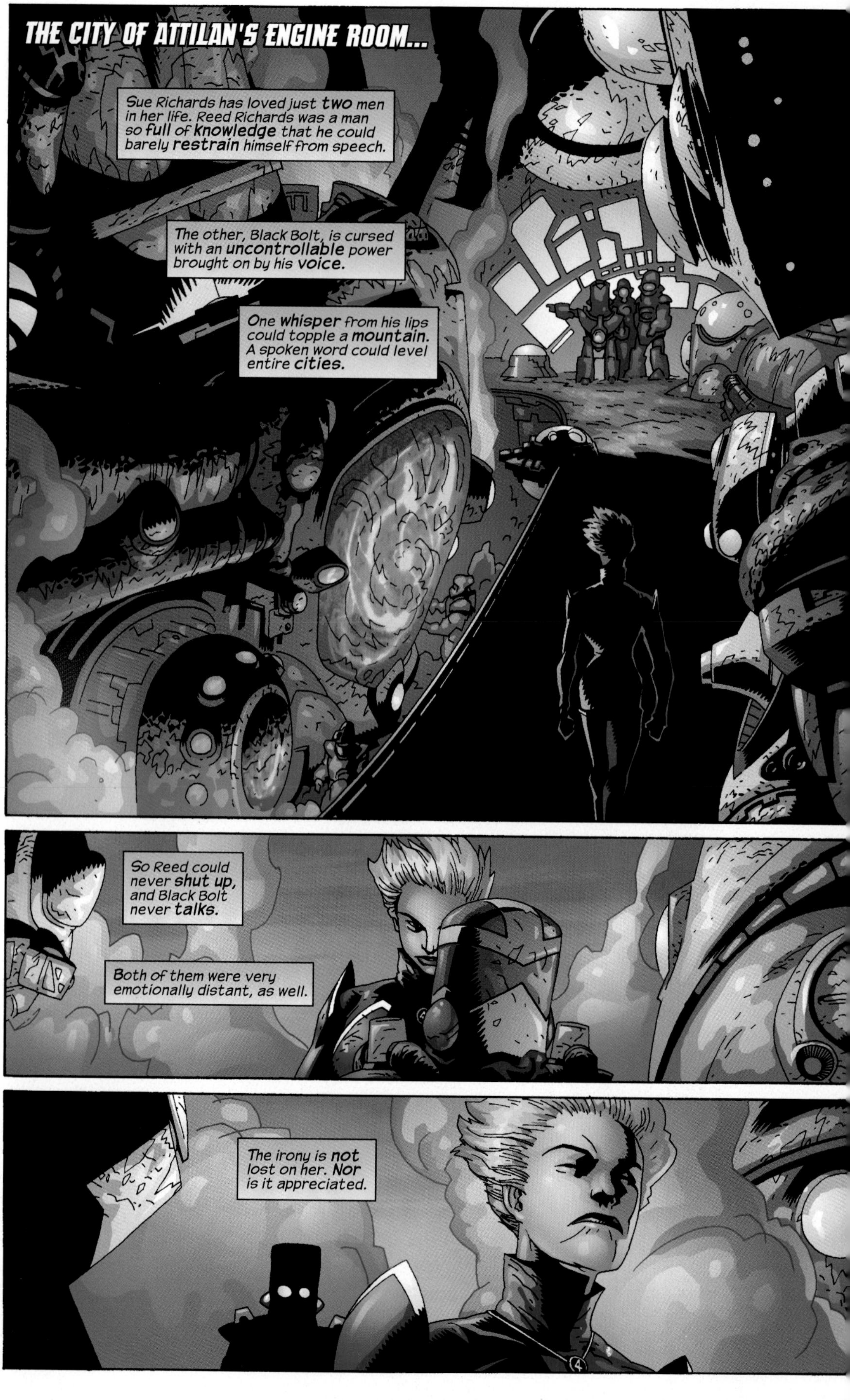
THE CITY OF ATTILAN'S ENGINE ROOM...
Sue Richards has loved just two men in her life. Reed Richards was a man so full of knowledge that he could barely restrain himself from speech.
The other, Black Bolt, is cursed with an uncontrollable power brought on by his voice.
One whisper from his lips could topple a mountain. A spoken word could level entire cities.
So Reed could never shut up, and Black Bolt never talks.
Both of them were very emotionally distant, as well.
The irony is not lost on her. Nor is it appreciated.

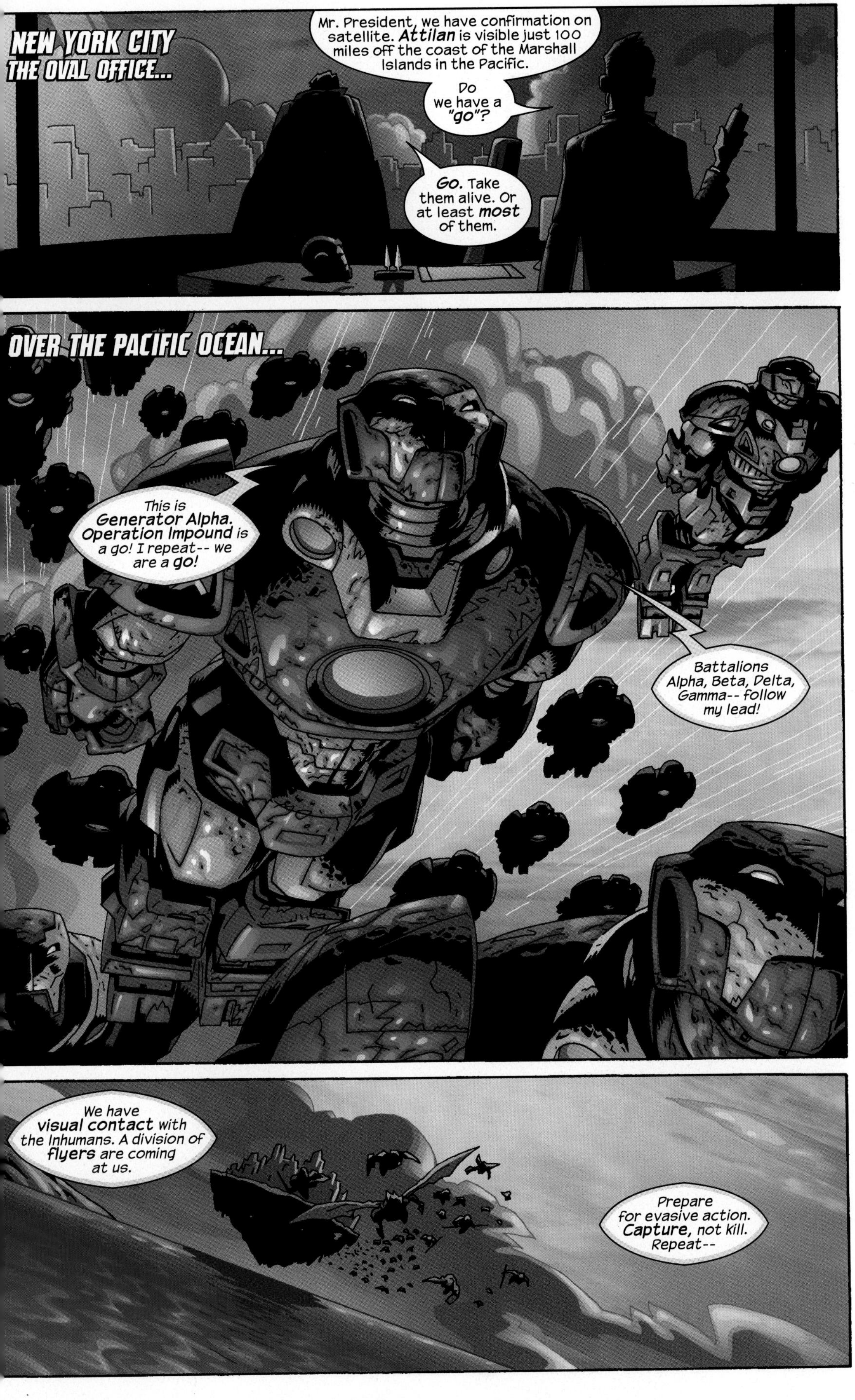
NEW YORK CITY
THE OVAL OFFICE...
Mr. President, we have confirmation on satellite. Attilan is visible just 100 miles off the coast of the Marshall Islands in the Pacific.
Do we have a "go"?
Go. Take them alive. Or at least most of them.
OVER THE PACIFIC OCEAN...
This is Generator Alpha. Operation Impound is a go! I repeat-- we are a go!
Battalions Alpha, Beta, Delta, Gamma-- follow my lead!
We have visual contact with the Inhumans. A division of flyers are coming at us.
Prepare for evasive action. Capture, not kill. Repeat--

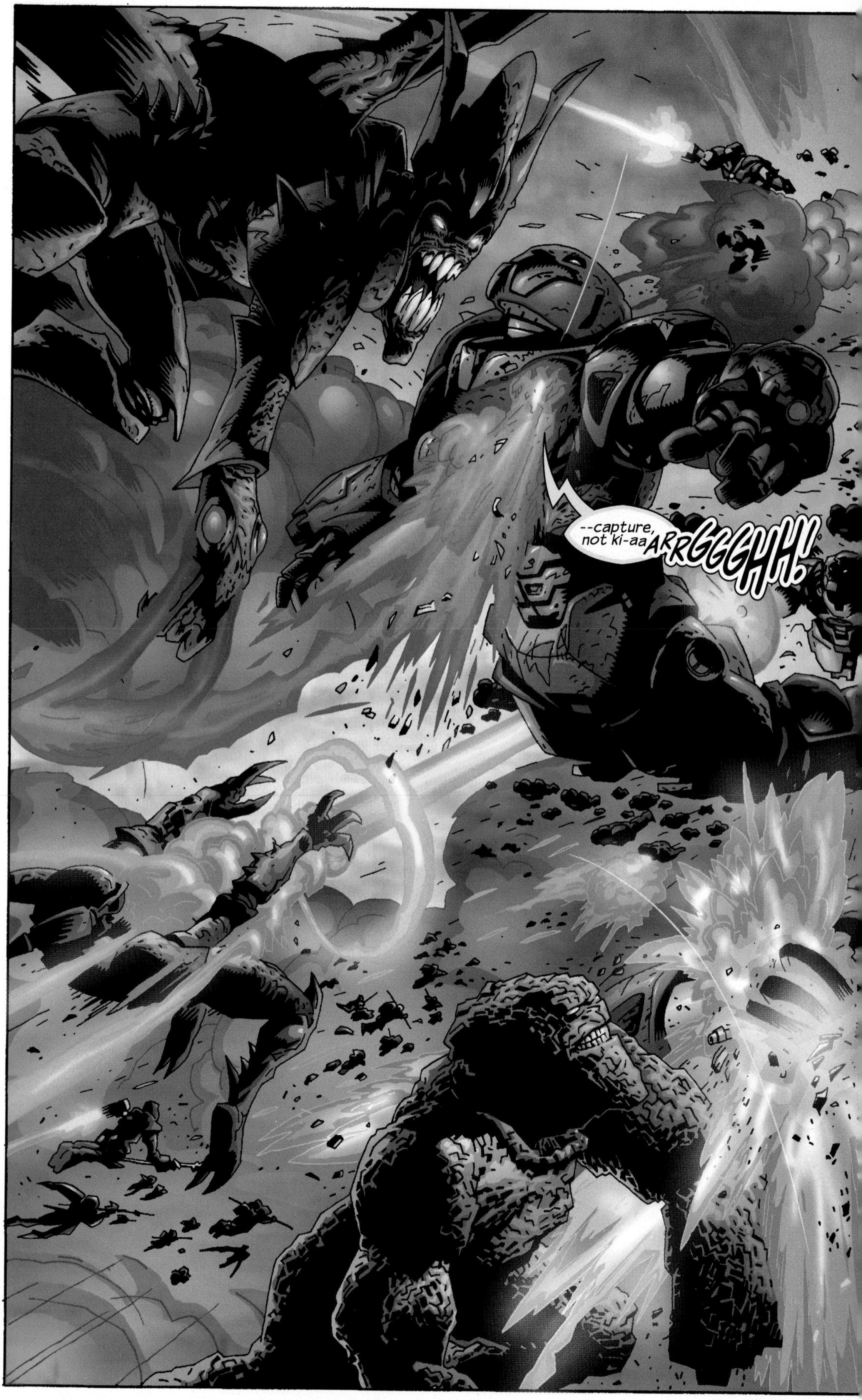
--capture, not ki-aaARRGGGHH!

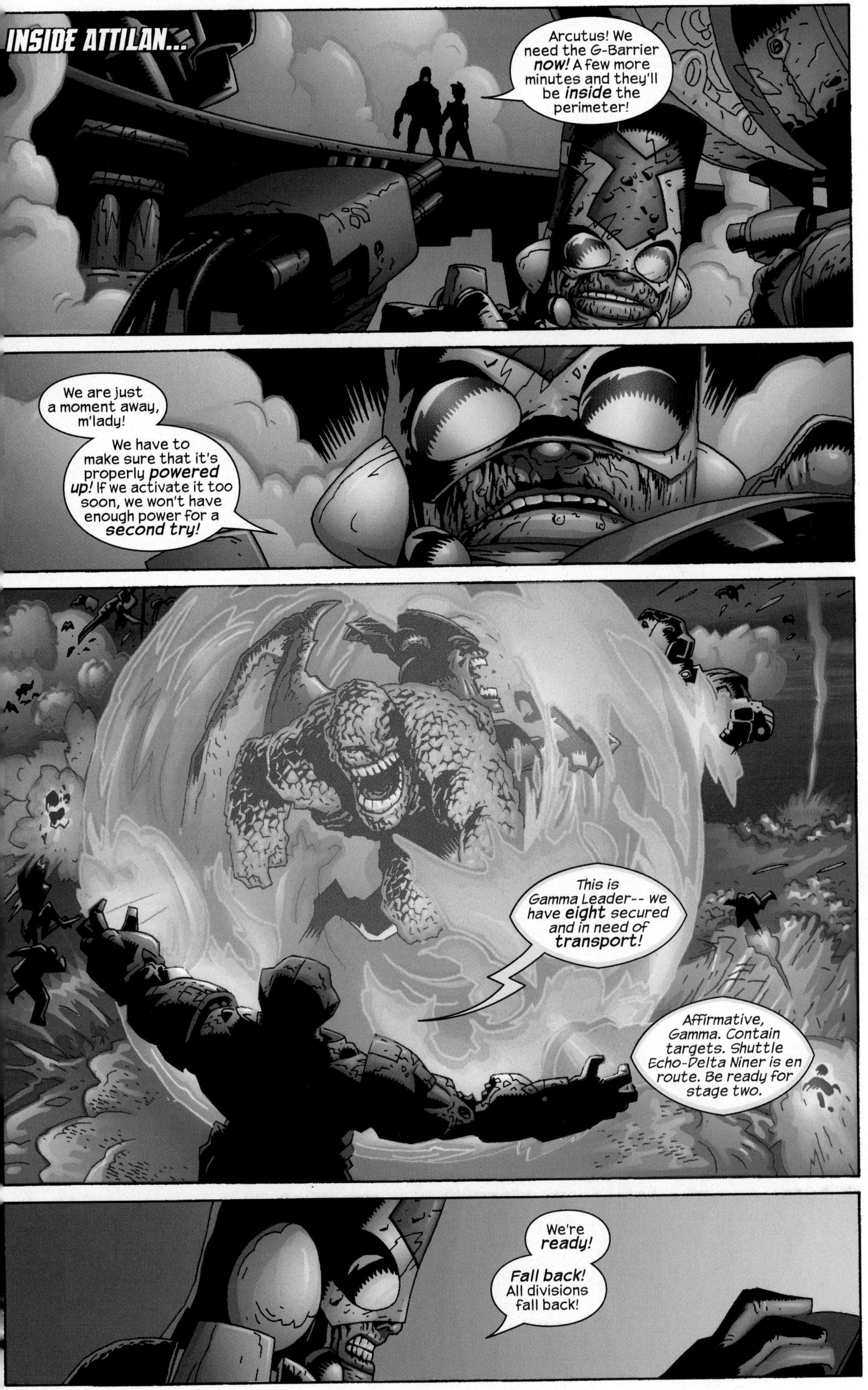
INSIDE ATTILAN...
Arcutus! We need the G-Barrier now! A few more minutes and they'll be inside the perimeter!
We are just a moment away, m'lady!
We have to make sure that it's properly powered up! If we activate it too soon, we won't have enough power for a second try!
This is Gamma Leader-- we have eight secured and in need of transport!
Affirmative, Gamma. Contain targets. Shuttle Echo-Delta Niner is en route. Be ready for stage two.
We're ready!
Fall back! All divisions fall back!

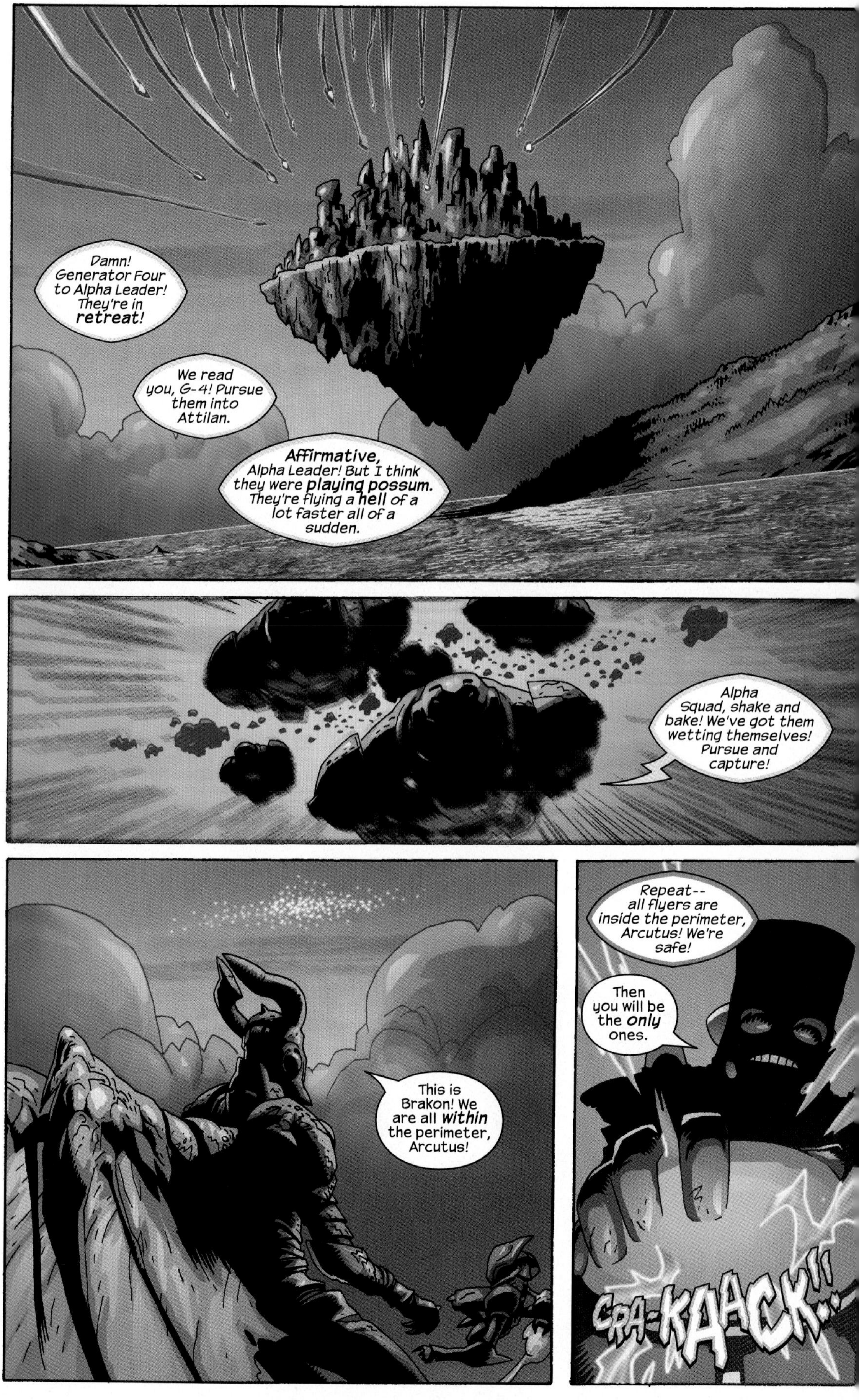
Damn! Generator Four to Alpha Leader! They're in **retreat**!
We read you, G-4! Pursue them into Attilan.
Affirmative, Alpha Leader! But I think they were **playing possum**. They're flying a **hell** of a lot faster all of a sudden.
Alpha Squad, shake and bake! We've got them wetting themselves! Pursue and capture!
This is Brakon! We are all ***within*** the perimeter, Arcutus!
Repeat-- all flyers are inside the perimeter, Arcutus! We're safe!
Then you will be the ***only*** ones.
CRA-KAACK!!..

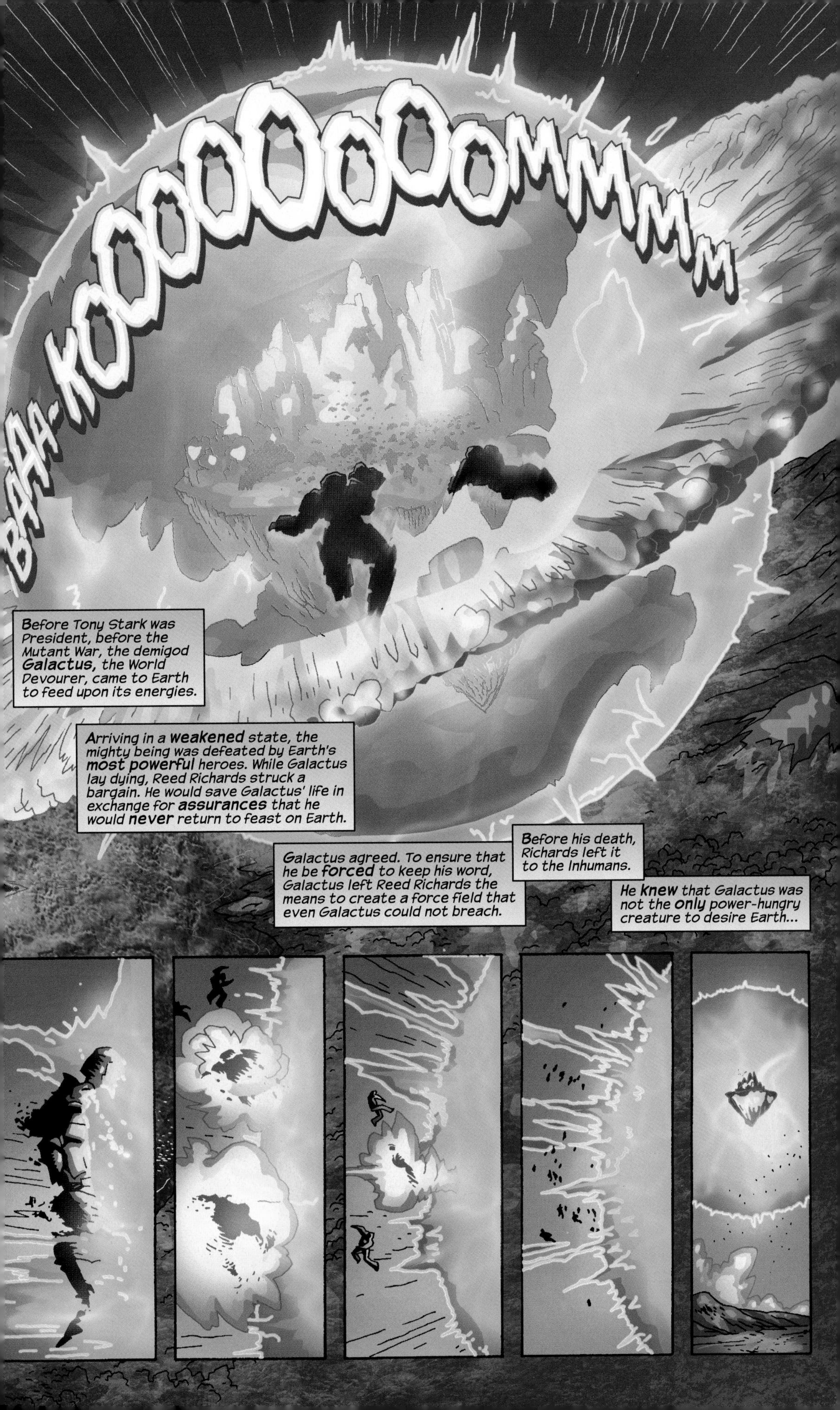

BRAA-KOOOOOOOOMMMMM
Before Tony Stark was President, before the Mutant War, the demigod Galactus, the World Devourer, came to Earth to feed upon its energies.
Arriving in a weakened state, the mighty being was defeated by Earth's most powerful heroes. While Galactus lay dying, Reed Richards struck a bargain. He would save Galactus' life in exchange for assurances that he would never return to feast on Earth.
Galactus agreed. To ensure that he be forced to keep his word, Galactus left Reed Richards the means to create a force field that even Galactus could not breach.
Before his death, Richards left it to the Inhumans.
He knew that Galactus was not the only power-hungry creature to desire Earth...

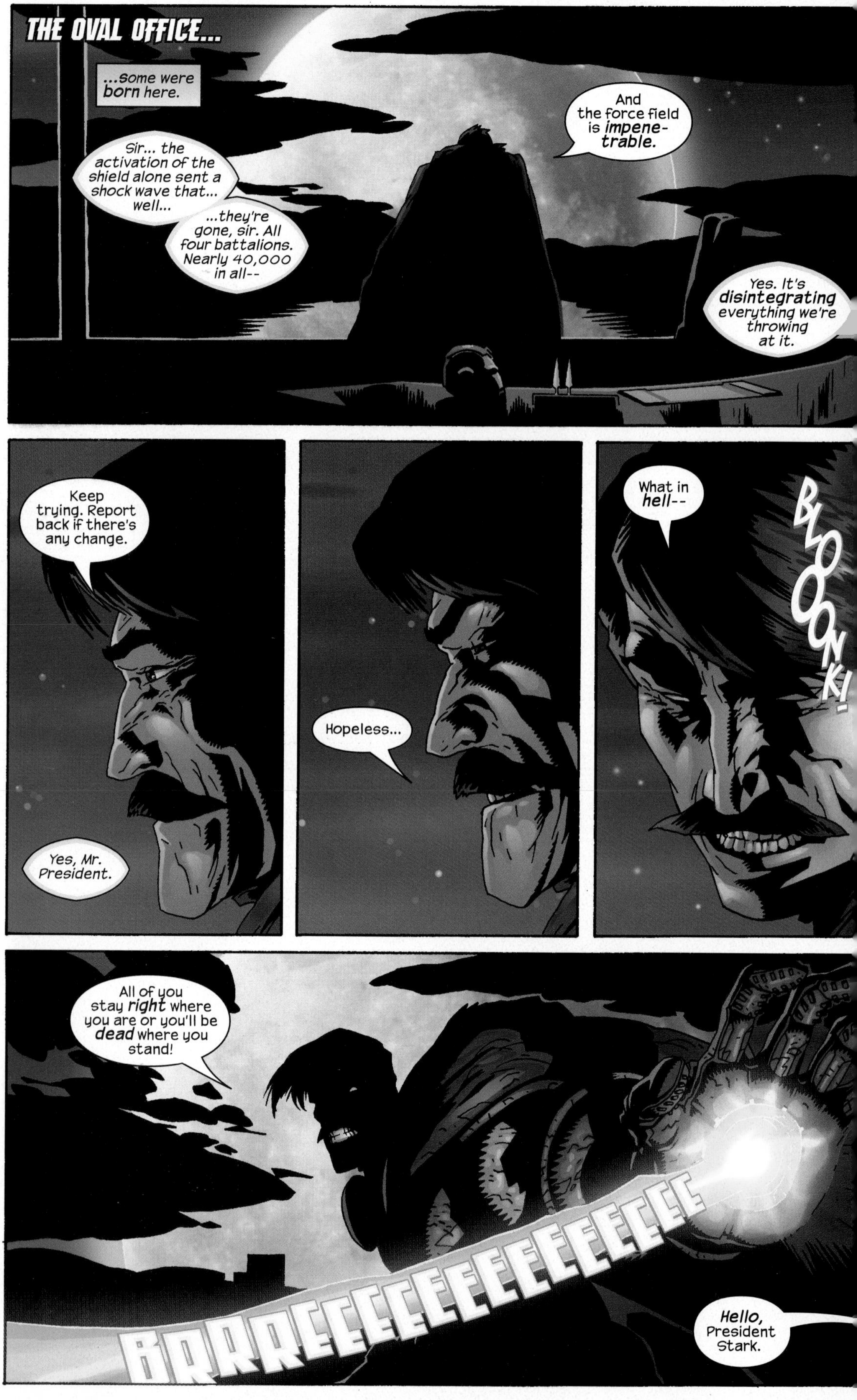
THE OVAL OFFICE...
...some were born here.
Sir... the activation of the shield alone sent a shock wave that... well...
...they're gone, sir. All four battalions. Nearly 40,000 in all--
And the force field is impenetrable.
Yes. It's disintegrating everything we're throwing at it.
Keep trying. Report back if there's any change.
Yes, Mr. President.
Hopeless...
What in hell--
BLOOONK!
All of you stay right where you are or you'll be dead where you stand!
BRRREEEEEEEEEEEEEEEE
Hello, President Stark.

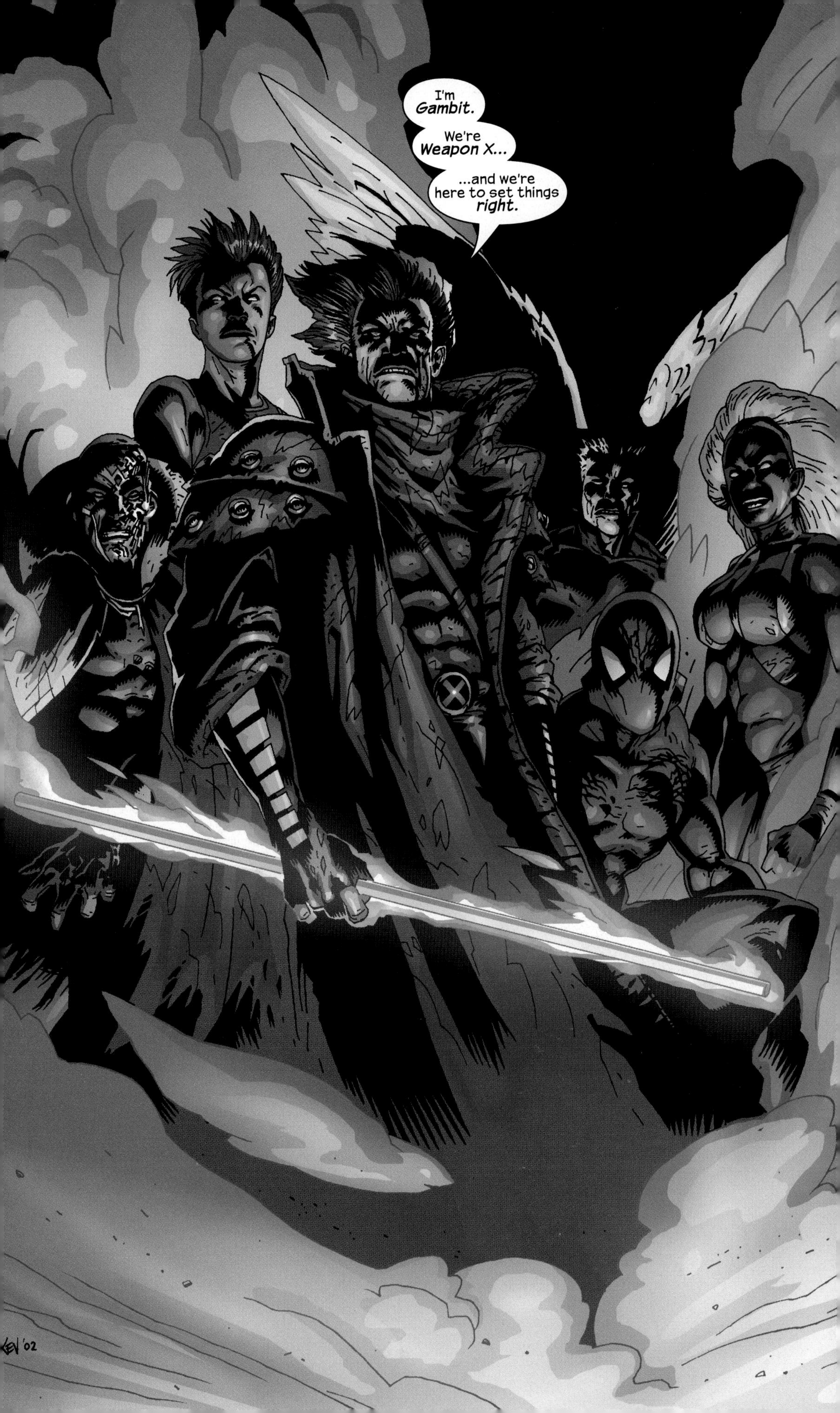
I'm Gambit.
We're Weapon X...
...and we're here to set things right.
KEV '02

24

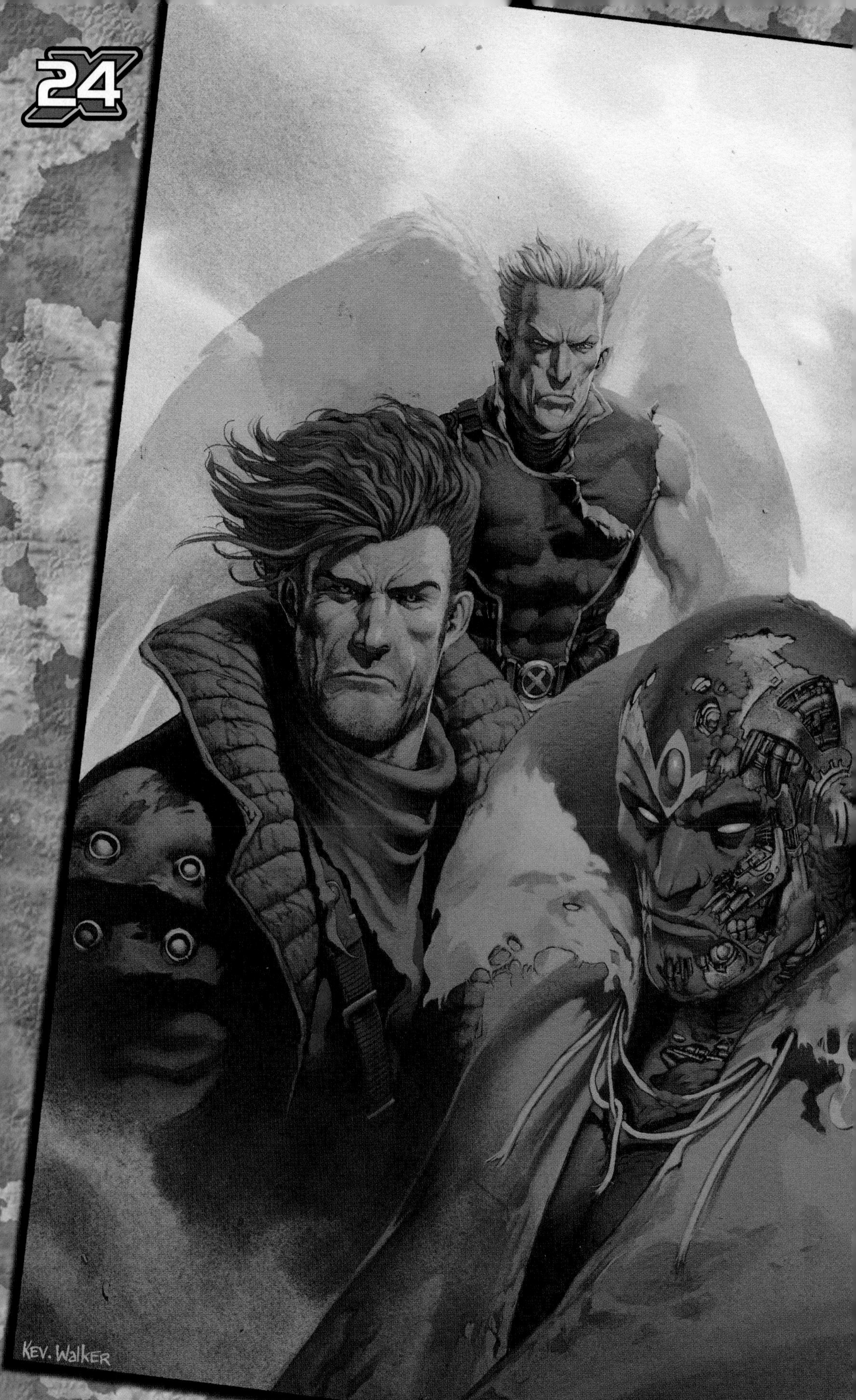
KEV. WALKER

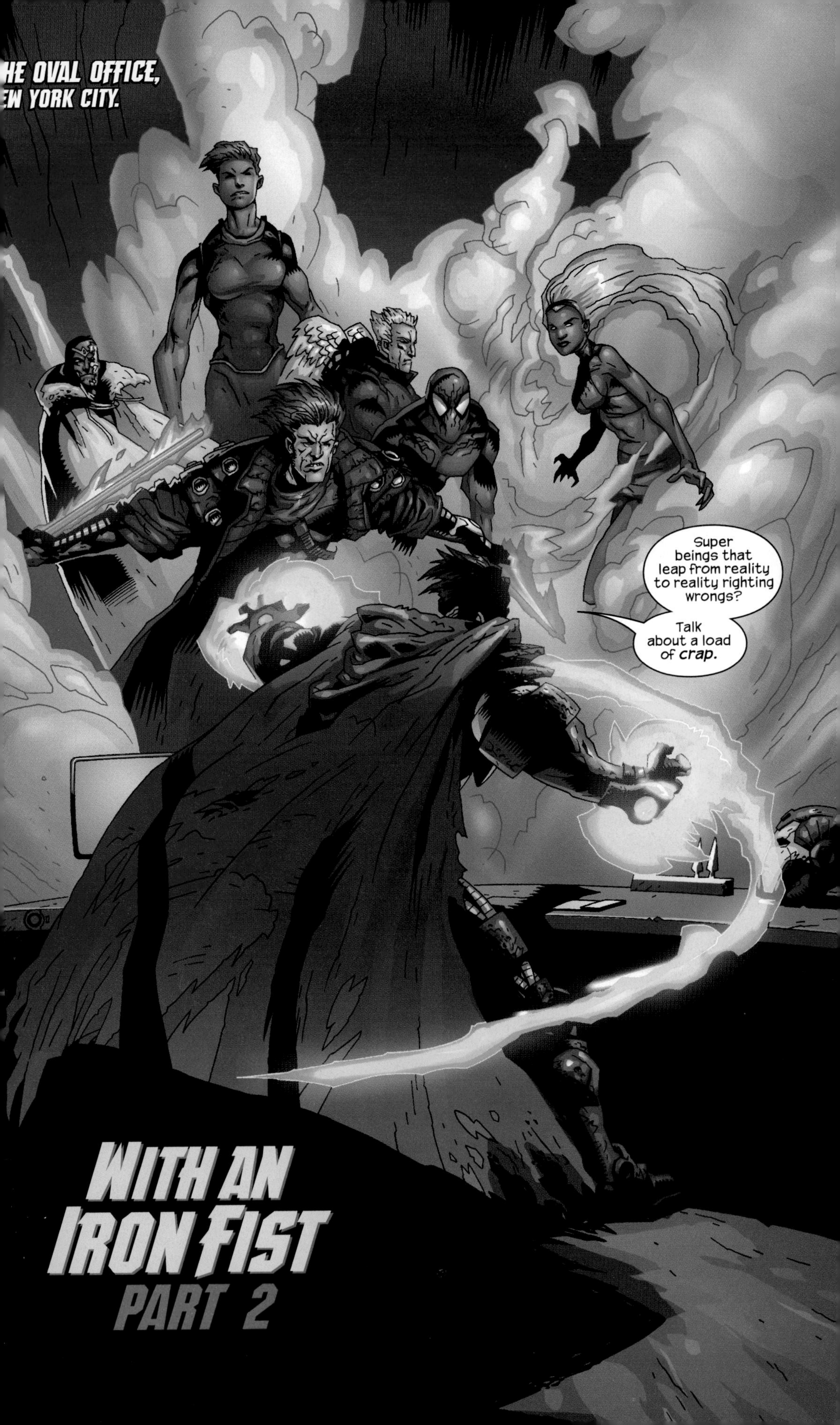
HE OVAL OFFICE,
EW YORK CITY.
Super beings that leap from reality to reality righting wrongs?
Talk about a load of *crap.*
WITH AN IRON FIST
PART 2

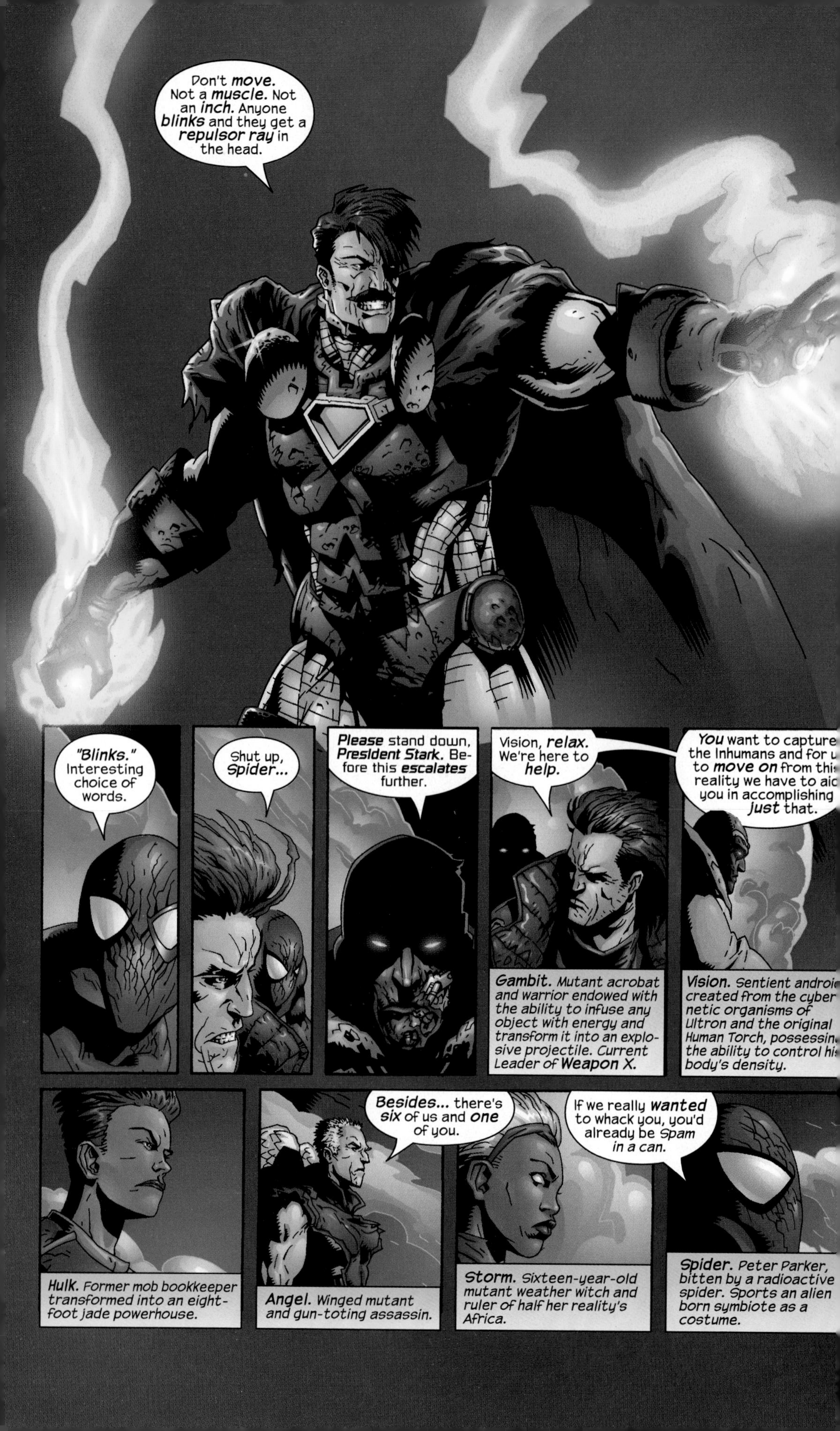
Don't move. Not a muscle. Not an inch. Anyone blinks and they get a repulsor ray in the head.
"Blinks." Interesting choice of words.
Shut up, Spider...
Please stand down, President Stark. Before this escalates further.
Vision, relax. We're here to help.
You want to capture the Inhumans and for u to move on from thi reality we have to aic you in accomplishing just that.
Gambit. Mutant acrobat and warrior endowed with the ability to infuse any object with energy and transform it into an explosive projectile. Current Leader of Weapon X.
Vision. Sentient androi created from the cyber netic organisms of Ultron and the original Human Torch, possessin the ability to control hi body's density.
Hulk. Former mob bookkeeper transformed into an eight-foot jade powerhouse.
Besides... there's six of us and one of you.
Angel. Winged mutant and gun-toting assassin.
If we really wanted to whack you, you'd already be Spam in a can.
Storm. Sixteen-year-old mutant weather witch and ruler of half her reality's Africa.
Spider. Peter Parker, bitten by a radioactive spider. Sports an alien born symbiote as a costume.

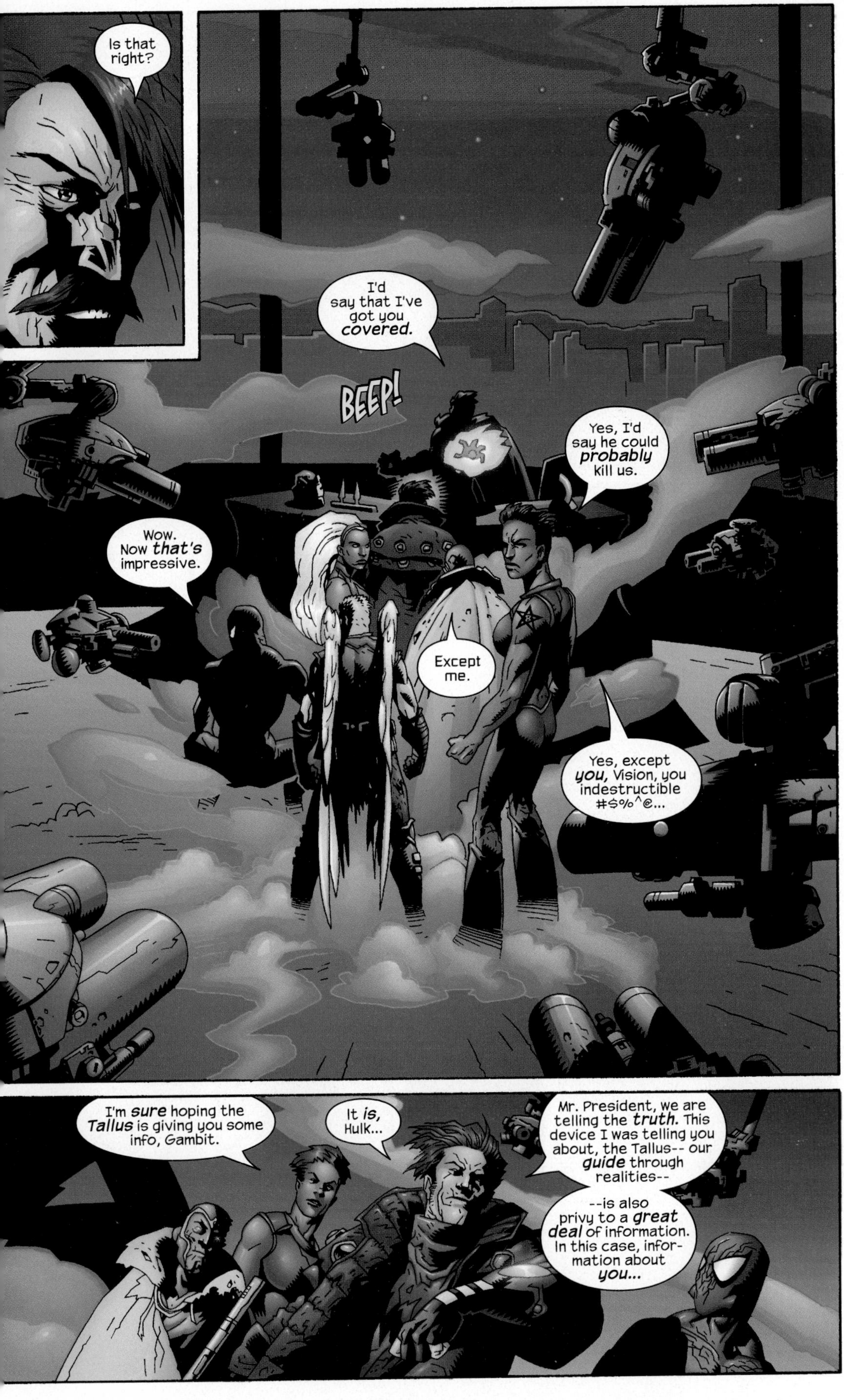

Is that right?
I'd say that I've got you *covered.*
BEEP!
Yes, I'd say he could *probably* kill us.
Wow. Now *that's* impressive.
Except me.
Yes, except *you,* Vision, you indestructible #$%^@...
I'm *sure* hoping the *Tallus* is giving you some info, Gambit.
It *is,* Hulk...
Mr. President, we are telling the *truth.* This device I was telling you about, the Tallus-- our *guide* through realities--
--is also privy to a *great deal* of information. In this case, information about *you...*

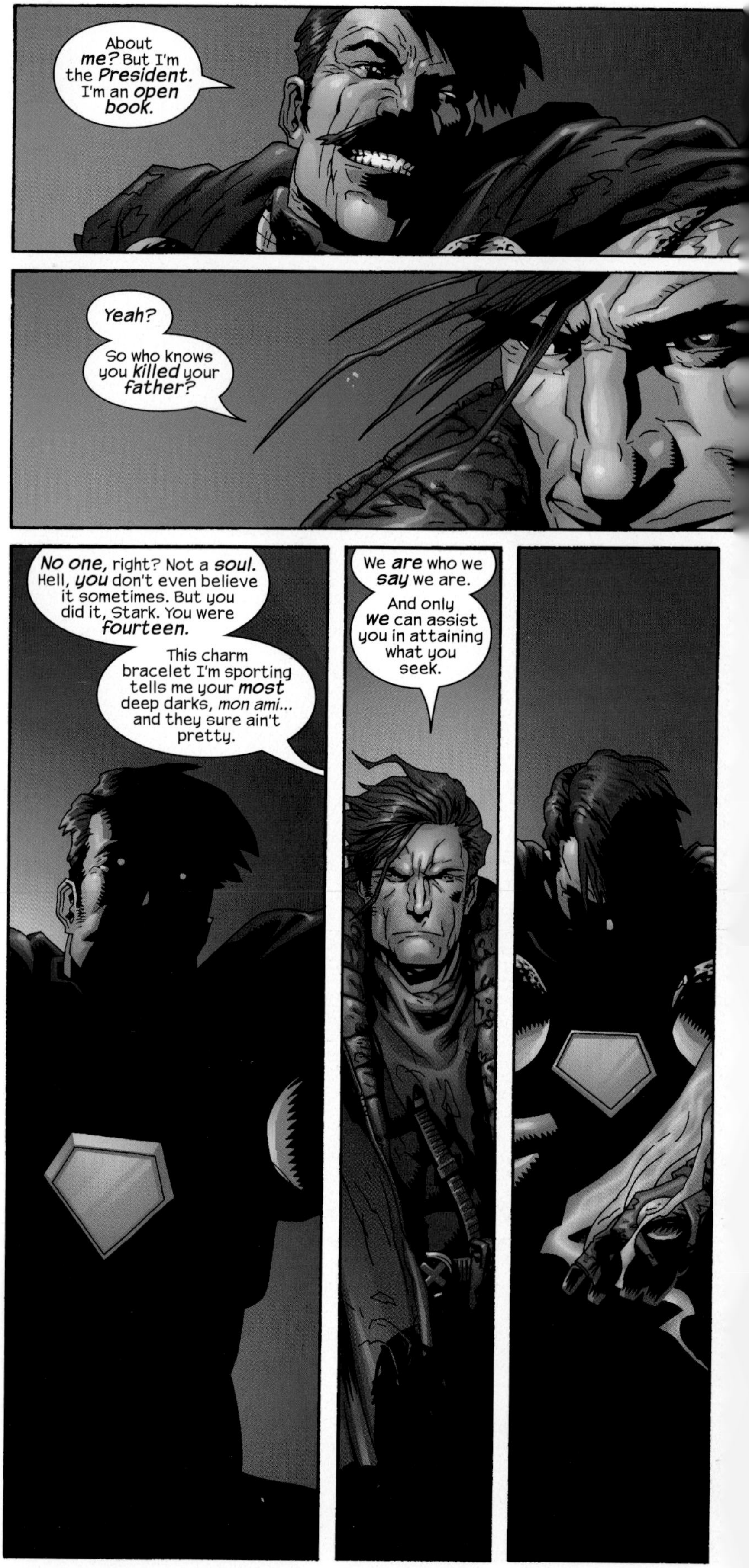
About me? But I'm the President. I'm an open book.
Yeah?
So who knows you killed your father?
No one, right? Not a soul. Hell, you don't even believe it sometimes. But you did it, Stark. You were fourteen.
This charm bracelet I'm sporting tells me your most deep darks, mon ami... and they sure ain't pretty.
We are who we say we are.
And only we can assist you in attaining what you seek.

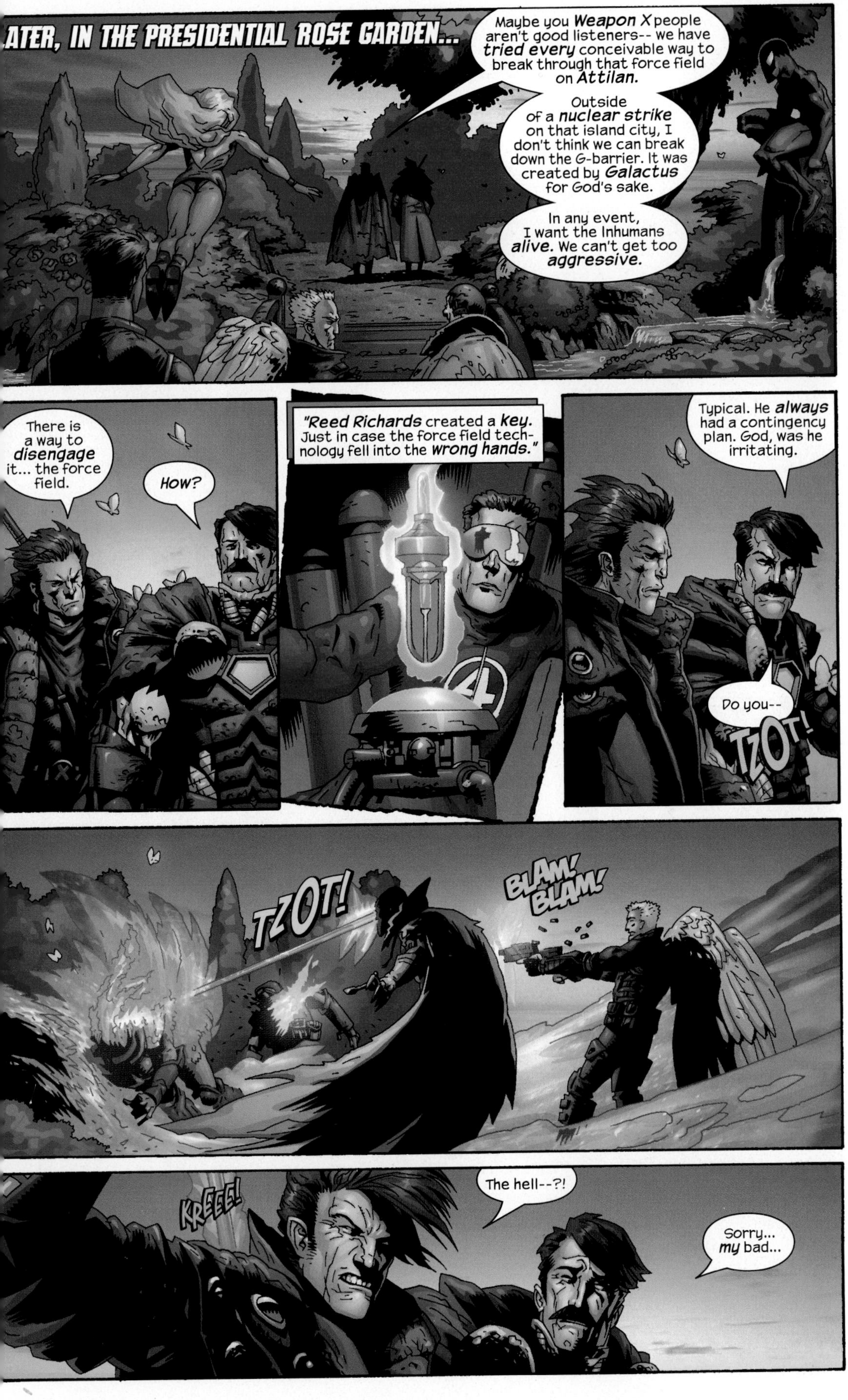
LATER, IN THE PRESIDENTIAL ROSE GARDEN...
Maybe you Weapon X people aren't good listeners-- we have tried every conceivable way to break through that force field on Attilan.
Outside of a nuclear strike on that island city, I don't think we can break down the G-barrier. It was created by Galactus for God's sake.
In any event, I want the Inhumans alive. We can't get too aggressive.
There is a way to disengage it... the force field.
How?
"Reed Richards created a key. Just in case the force field technology fell into the wrong hands."
Typical. He always had a contingency plan. God, was he irritating.
Do you--
TZOT!
TZOT!
BLAM! BLAM!
KREEE!
The hell--?!
Sorry... my bad...

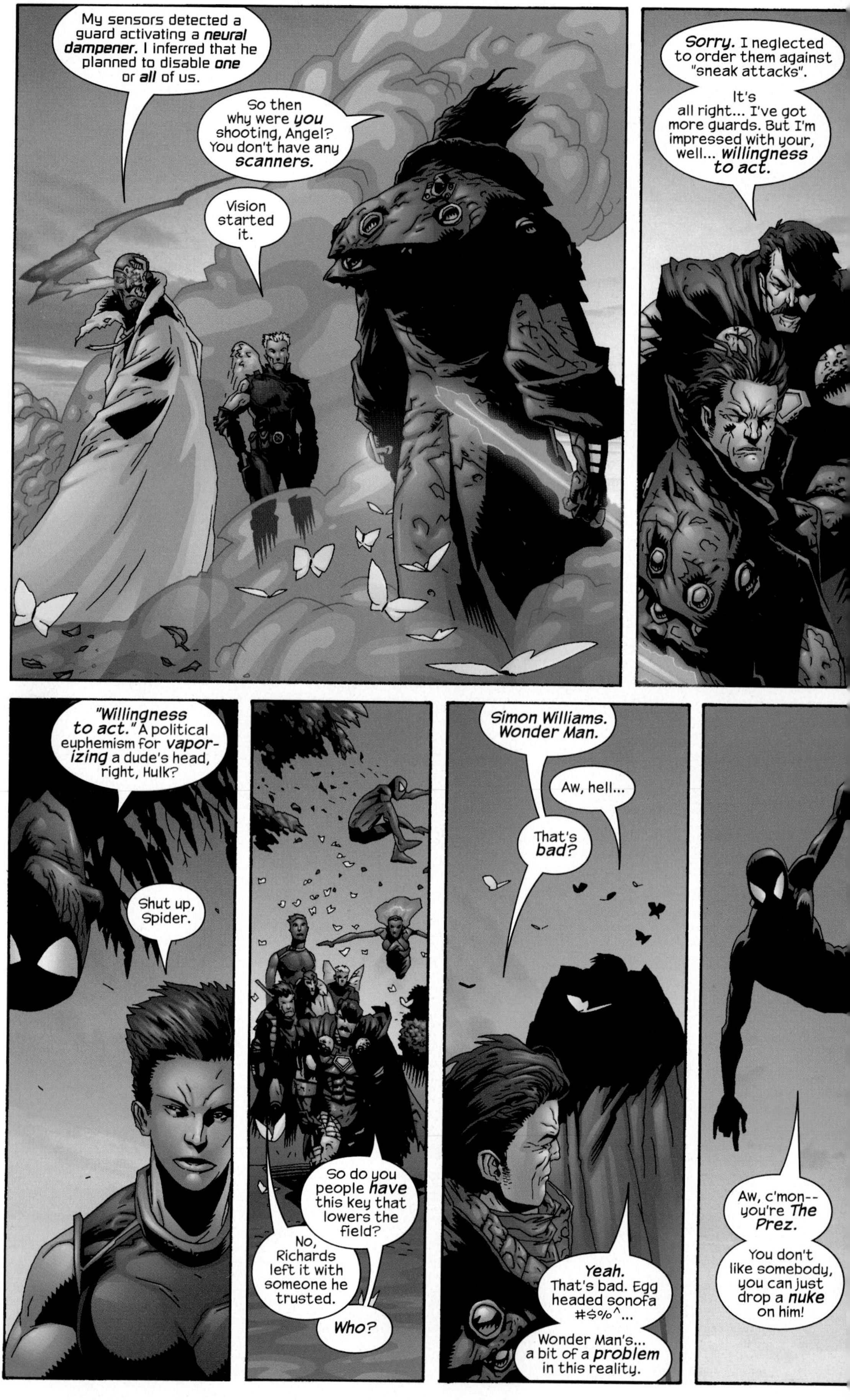

My sensors detected a guard activating a *neural dampener.* I inferred that he planned to disable *one* or *all* of us.
So then why were *you* shooting, Angel? You don't have any *scanners.*
Vision started it.
Sorry. I neglected to order them against "sneak attacks".
It's all right... I've got more guards. But I'm impressed with your, well... *willingness to act.*
"Willingness to act." A political euphemism for *vaporizing* a dude's head, right, Hulk?
Shut up, Spider.
So do you people *have* this key that lowers the field?
No, Richards left it with someone he trusted.
Who?
Simon Williams. Wonder Man.
Aw, hell...
That's *bad?*
Yeah. That's bad. Egg headed sonofa #$%^...
Wonder Man's... a bit of a *problem* in this reality.
Aw, c'mon-- you're *The Prez.*
You don't like somebody, you can just drop a *nuke* on him!

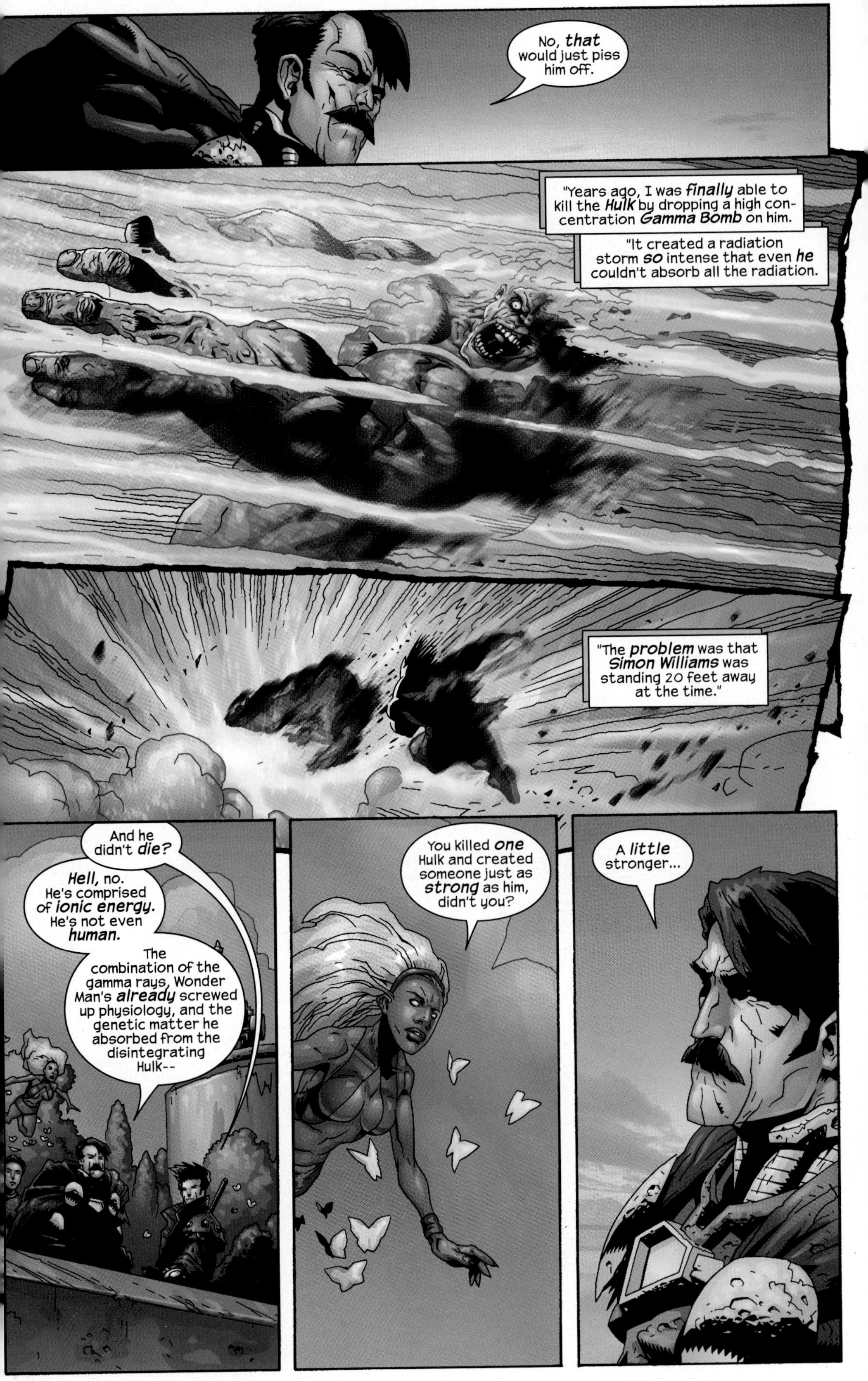

No, *that* would just piss him off.
"Years ago, I was *finally* able to kill the *Hulk* by dropping a high concentration *Gamma Bomb* on him.
"It created a radiation storm *so* intense that even *he* couldn't absorb all the radiation.
"The *problem* was that *Simon Williams* was standing 20 feet away at the time."
And he didn't *die?*
Hell, no. He's comprised of *ionic energy*. He's not even *human.*
The combination of the gamma rays, Wonder Man's *already* screwed up physiology, and the genetic matter he absorbed from the disintegrating Hulk--
You killed *one* Hulk and created someone just as *strong* as him, didn't you?
A *little* stronger...

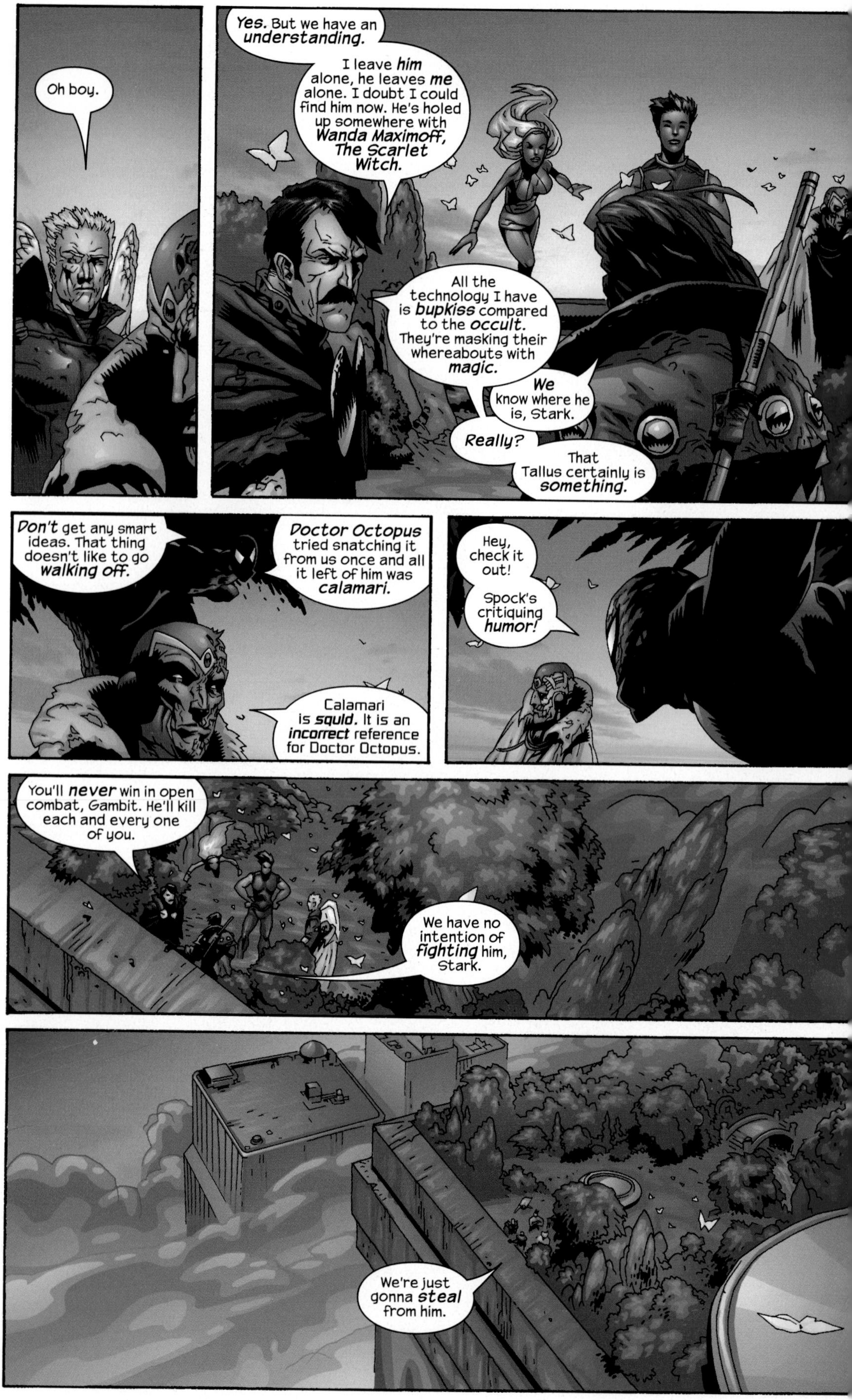
Oh boy.
Yes. But we have an understanding.
I leave him alone, he leaves me alone. I doubt I could find him now. He's holed up somewhere with Wanda Maximoff, The Scarlet Witch.
All the technology I have is bupkiss compared to the occult. They're masking their whereabouts with magic.
We know where he is, Stark.
Really?
That Tallus certainly is something.
Don't get any smart ideas. That thing doesn't like to go walking off.
Doctor Octopus tried snatching it from us once and all it left of him was calamari.
Calamari is squid. It is an incorrect reference for Doctor Octopus.
Hey, check it out!
Spock's critiquing humor!
You'll never win in open combat, Gambit. He'll kill each and every one of you.
We have no intention of fighting him, Stark.
We're just gonna steal from him.

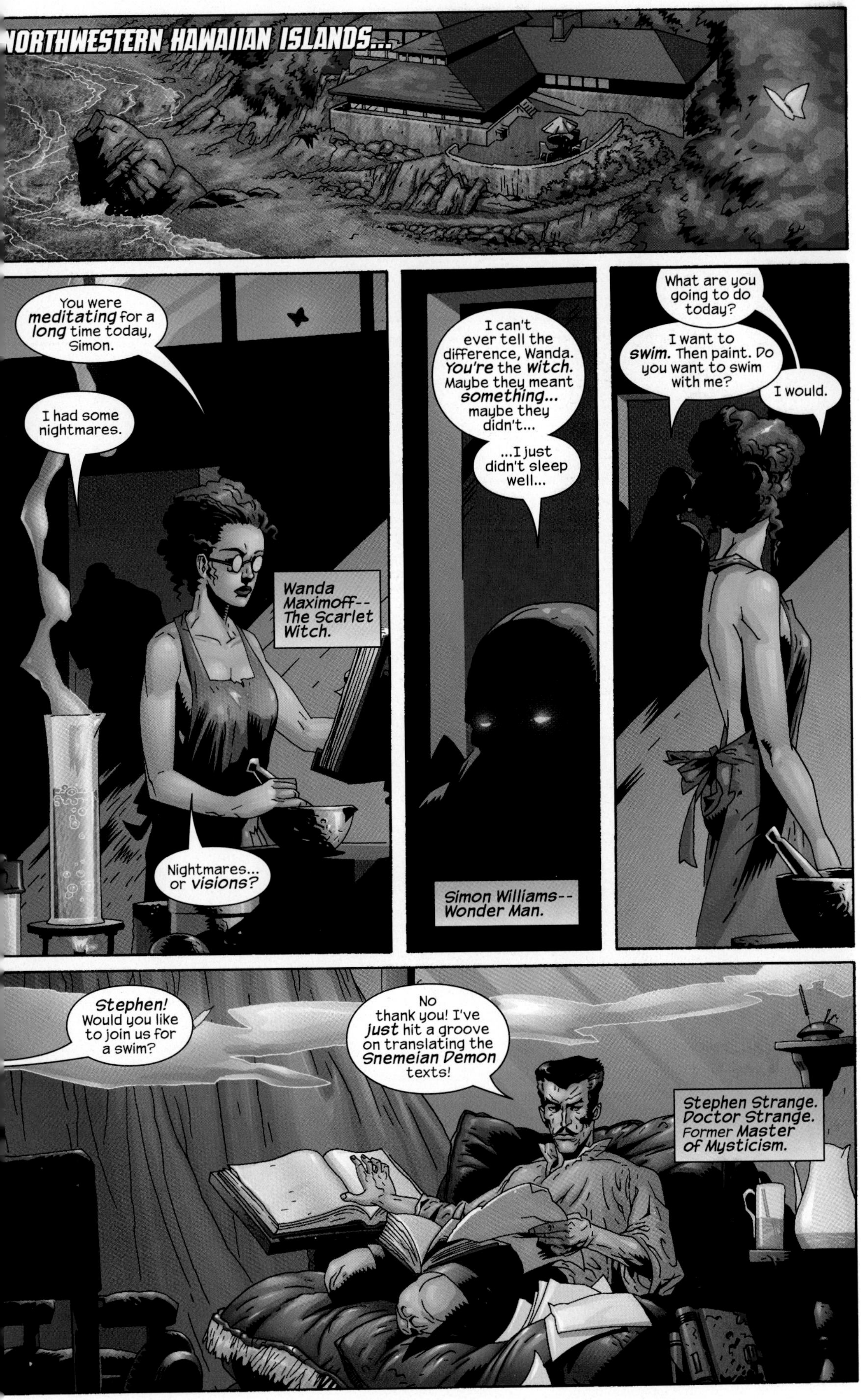

NORTHWESTERN HAWAIIAN ISLANDS...
You were meditating for a long time today, Simon.
I had some nightmares.
Wanda Maximoff-- The Scarlet Witch.
Nightmares... or visions?
I can't ever tell the difference, Wanda. You're the witch. Maybe they meant something... maybe they didn't...
...I just didn't sleep well...
Simon Williams-- Wonder Man.
What are you going to do today?
I want to swim. Then paint. Do you want to swim with me?
I would.
Stephen! Would you like to join us for a swim?
No thank you! I've just hit a groove on translating the Snemeian Demon texts!
Stephen Strange. Doctor Strange. Former Master of Mysticism.

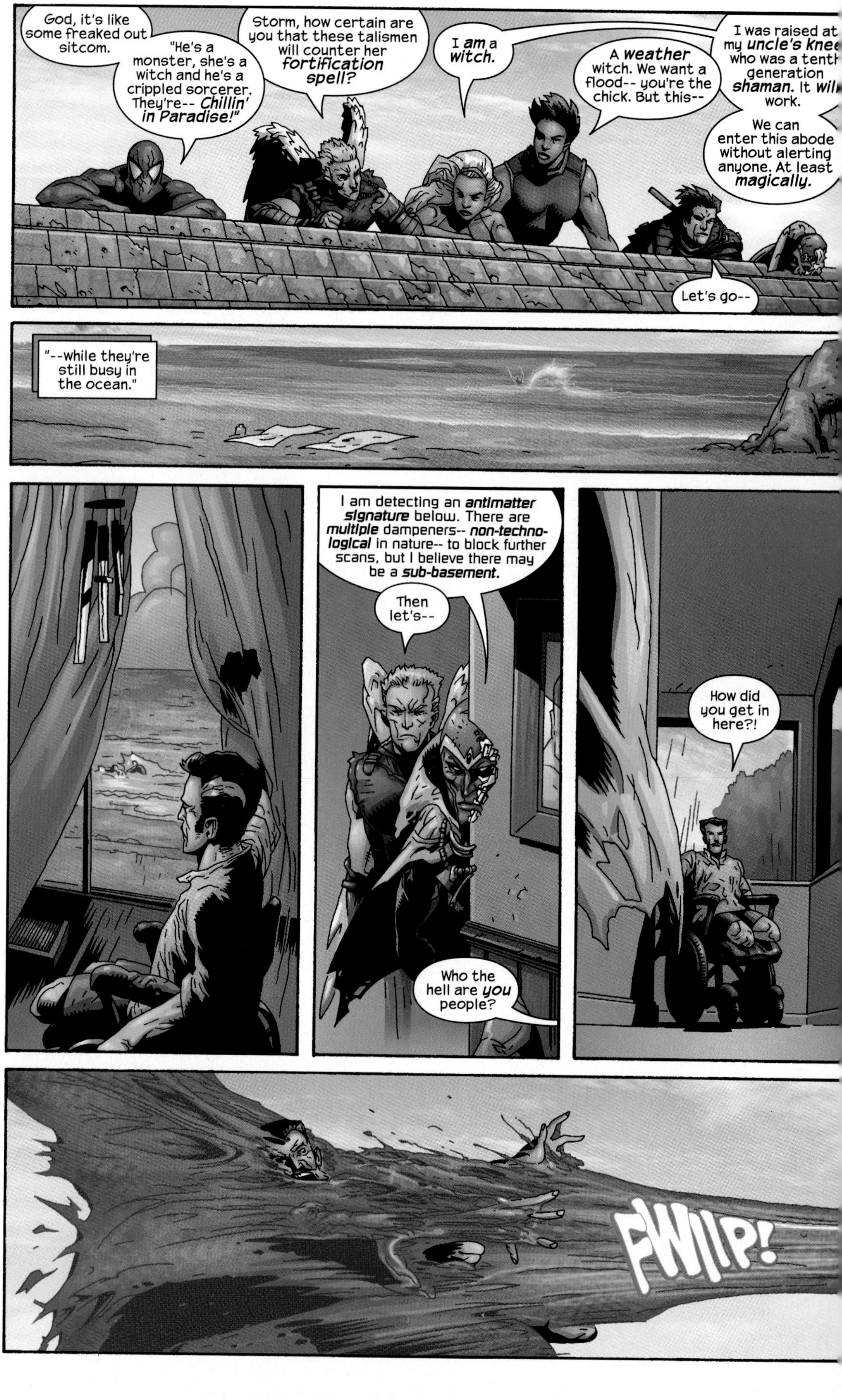

God, it's like some freaked out sitcom.
"He's a monster, she's a witch and he's a crippled sorcerer. They're-- Chillin' in Paradise!"
Storm, how certain are you that these talismen will counter her fortification spell?
I am a witch.
A weather witch. We want a flood-- you're the chick. But this--
I was raised at my uncle's kne who was a tent generation shaman. It wil work.
We can enter this abode without alerting anyone. At least magically.
Let's go--
"--while they're still busy in the ocean."
I am detecting an antimatter signature below. There are multiple dampeners-- non-technological in nature-- to block further scans, but I believe there may be a sub-basement.
Then let's--
Who the hell are you people?
How did you get in here?!
FWIIP!

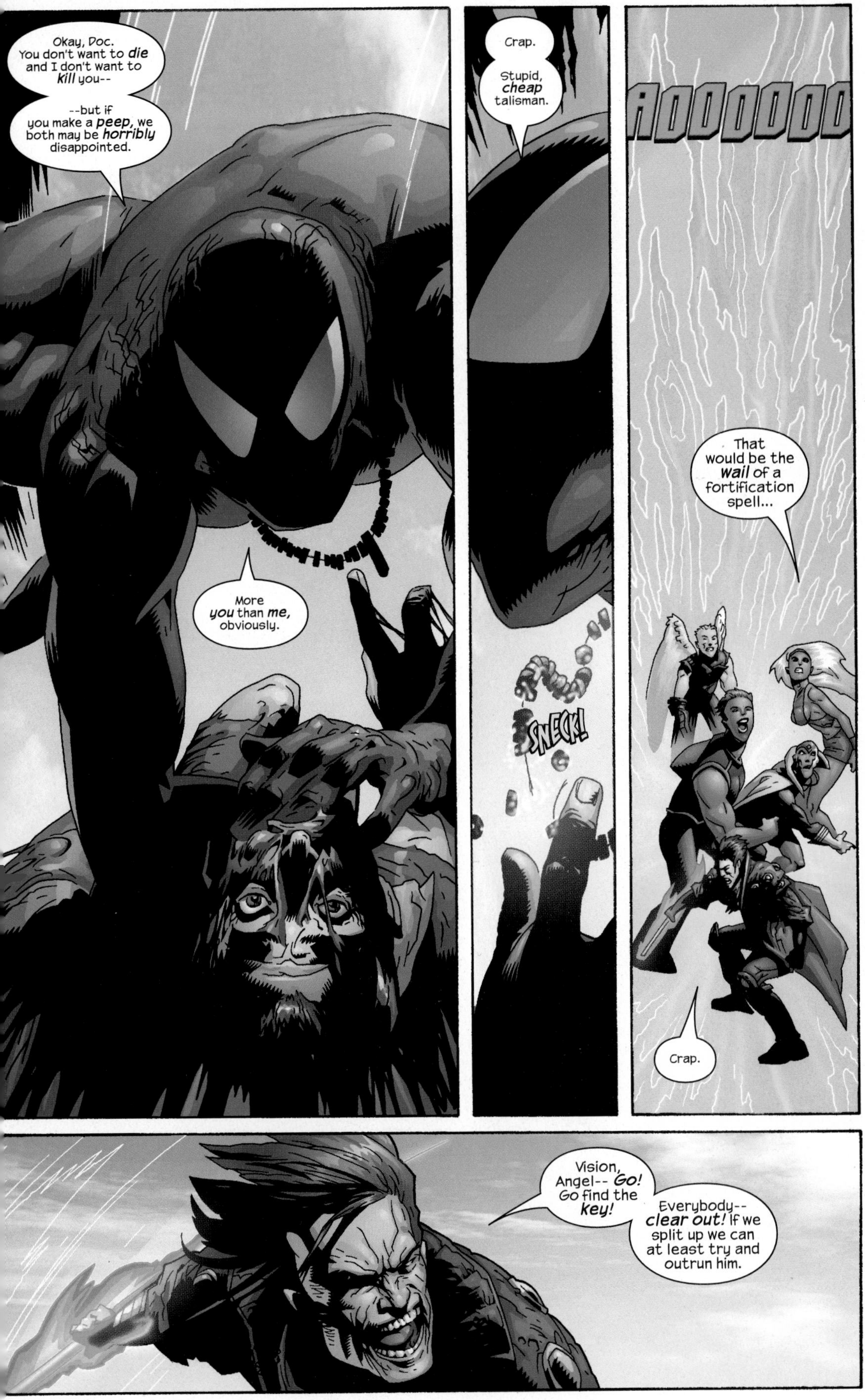
Okay, Doc. You don't want to *die* and I don't want to *kill* you--
--but if you make a *peep*, we both may be *horribly* disappointed.
More *you* than *me*, obviously.
Crap.
Stupid, *cheap* talisman.
SNECK!
AOOOOOO
That would be the *wail* of a fortification spell...
Crap.
Vision, Angel-- *Go!* Go find the *key!*
Everybody-- *clear out!* If we split up we can at least try and outrun him.

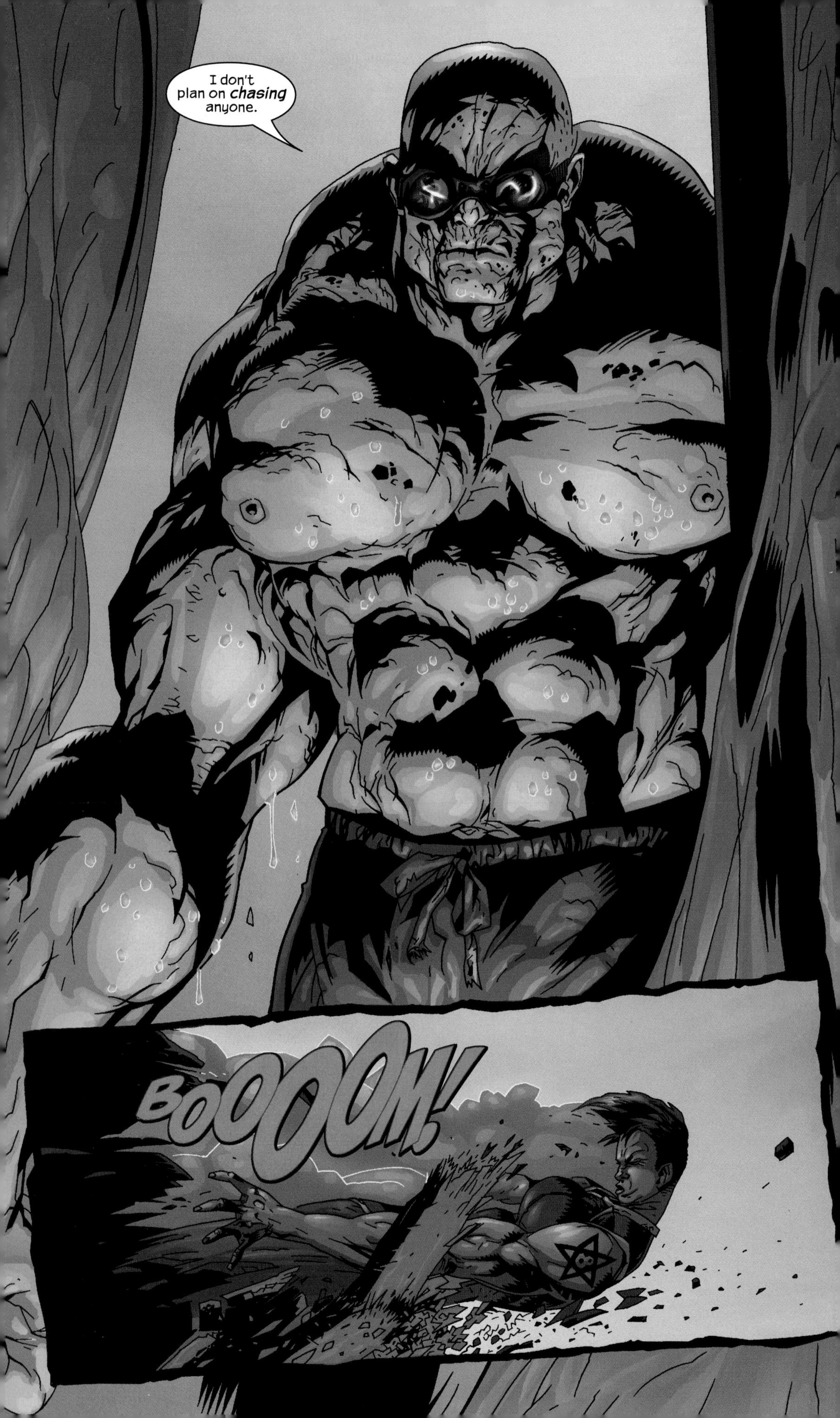
I don't plan on *chasing* anyone.
BOOOOOM!

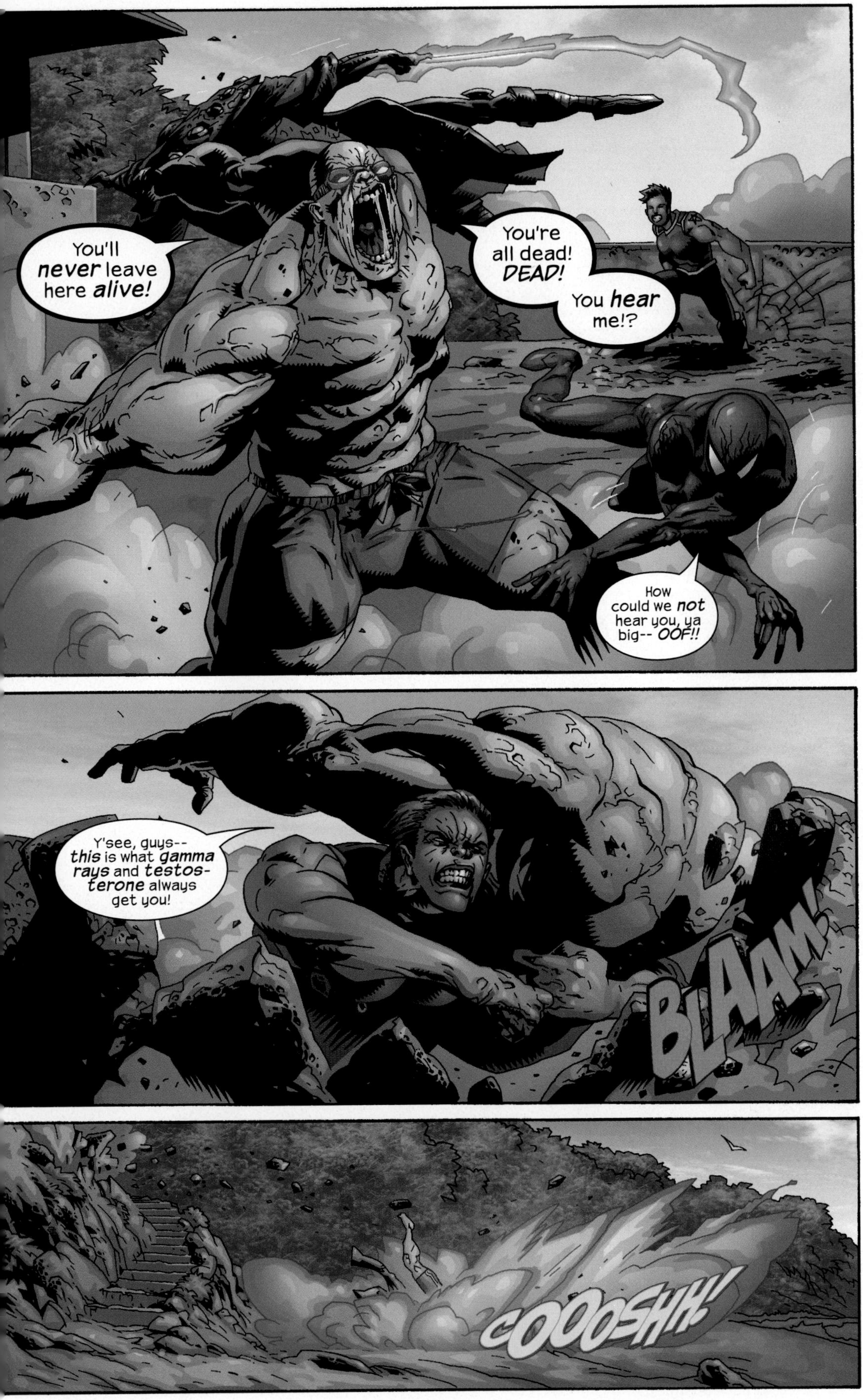
You'll never leave here alive!
You're all dead! DEAD!
You hear me!?
How could we not hear you, ya big-- OOF!!
Y'see, guys-- this is what gamma rays and testosterone always get you!
BLAAM!
COOOSHH!

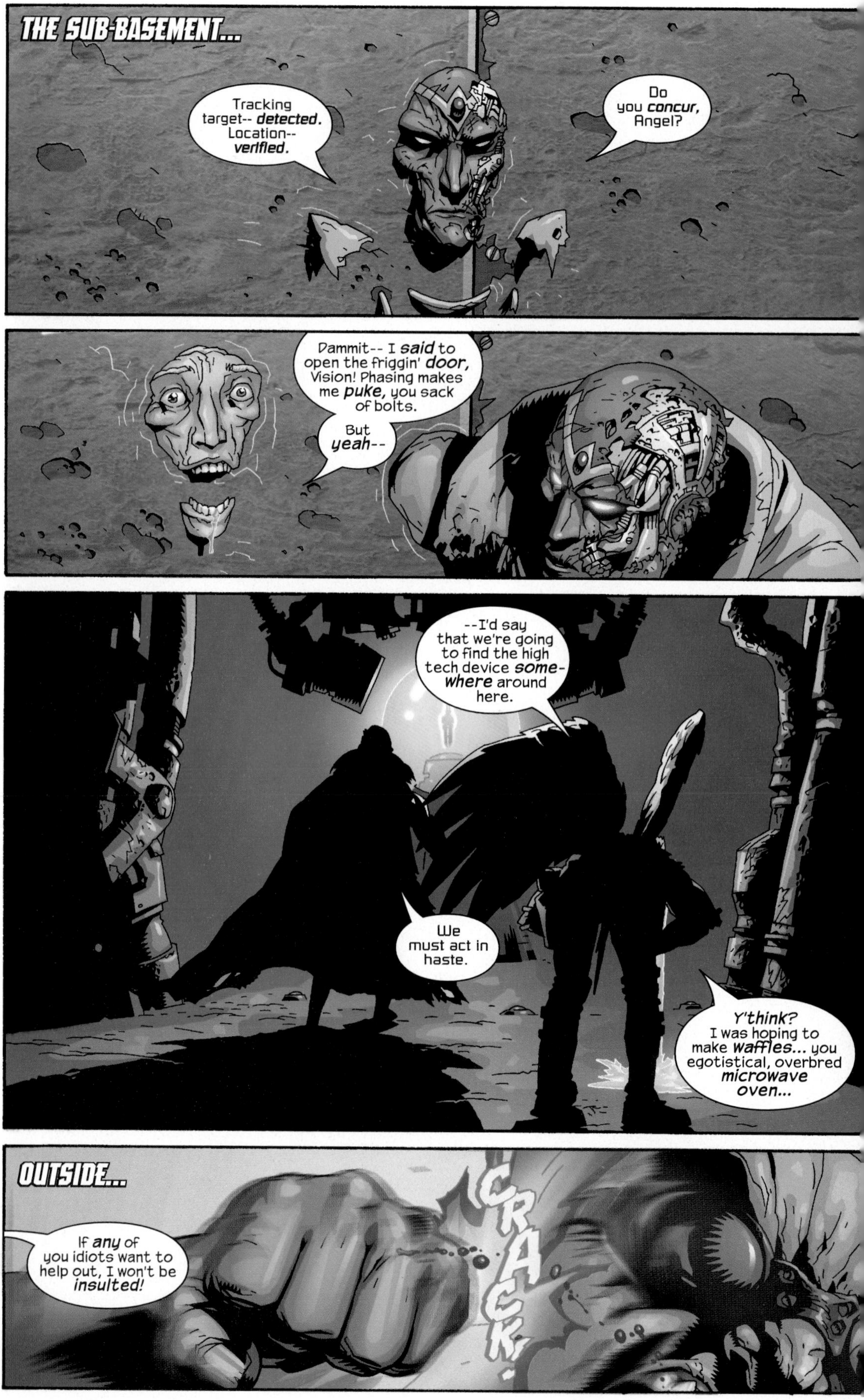
THE SUB-BASEMENT...
Tracking target-- detected. Location-- verified.
Do you concur, Angel?
Dammit-- I said to open the friggin' door, Vision! Phasing makes me puke, you sack of bolts.
But yeah--
--I'd say that we're going to find the high tech device some-where around here.
We must act in haste.
Y'think? I was hoping to make waffles... you egotistical, overbred microwave oven...
OUTSIDE...
If any of you idiots want to help out, I won't be insulted!
CRACK!

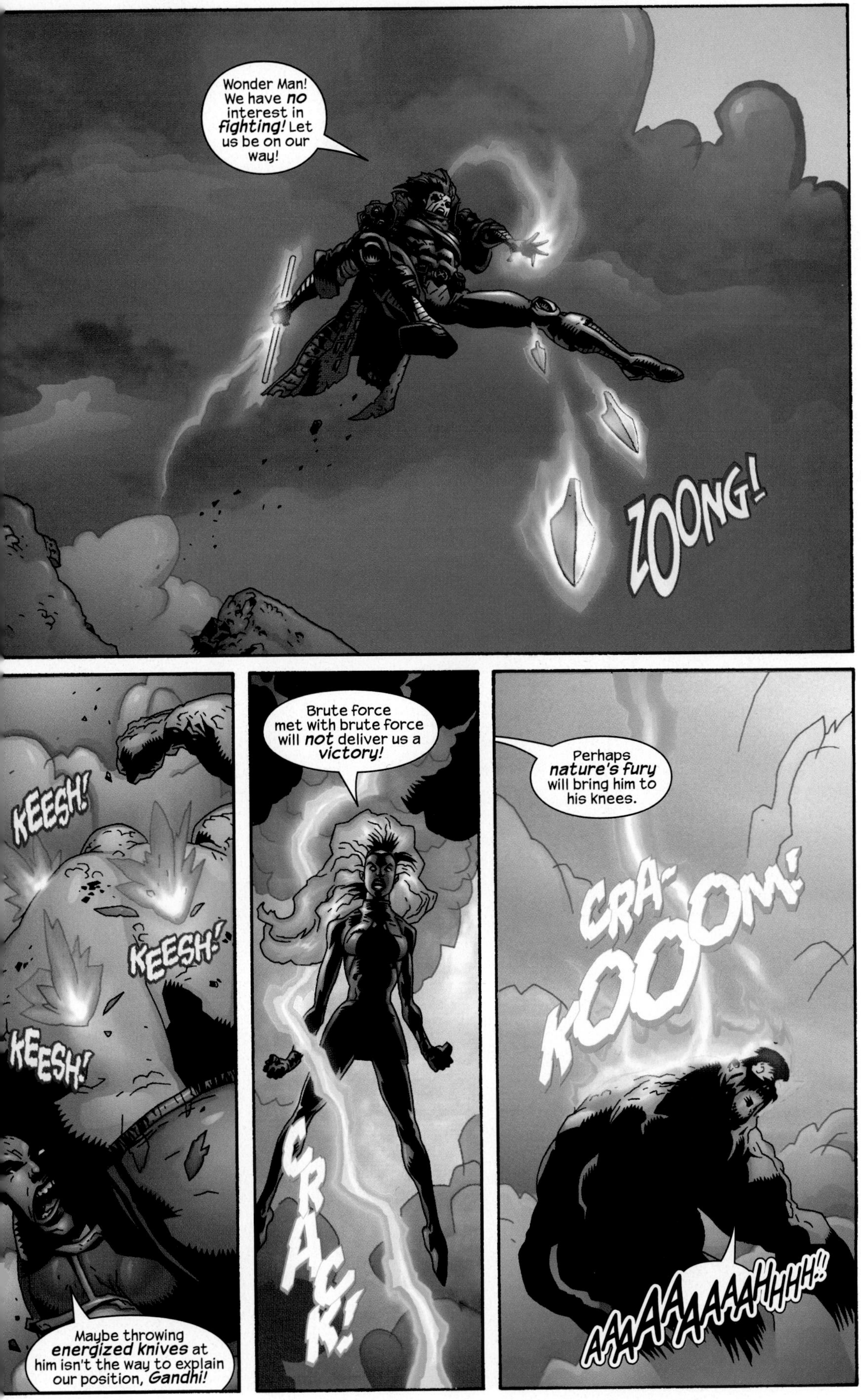

Wonder Man! We have *no* interest in *fighting!* Let us be on our way!
ZOONG!
KEESH!
KEESH!
KEESH!
Maybe throwing *energized knives* at him isn't the way to explain our position, *Gandhi!*
Brute force met with brute force will *not* deliver us a *victory!*
CRACK!
Perhaps *nature's fury* will bring him to his knees.
CRA-KOOOOM!
AAAAAAAAHHHH!!

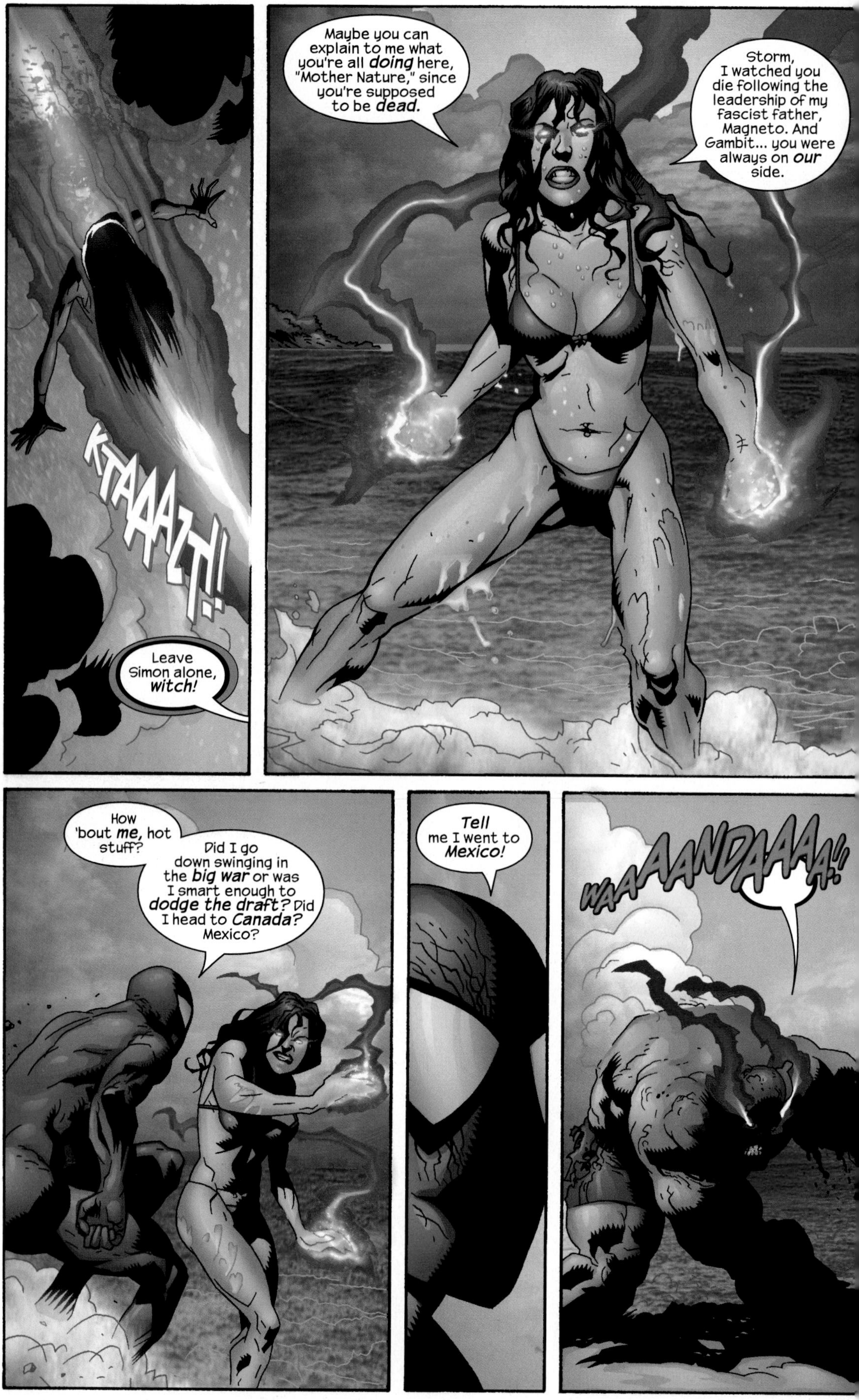
KTAAAZT!!
Leave Simon alone, *witch!*
Maybe you can explain to me what you're all *doing* here, "Mother Nature," since you're supposed to be *dead*.
Storm, I watched you die following the leadership of my fascist father, Magneto. And Gambit... you were always on *our* side.
How 'bout *me,* hot stuff?
Did I go down swinging in the *big war* or was I smart enough to *dodge the draft?* Did I head to *Canada?* Mexico?
Tell me I went to *Mexico!*
WAAAANDAAAA!!

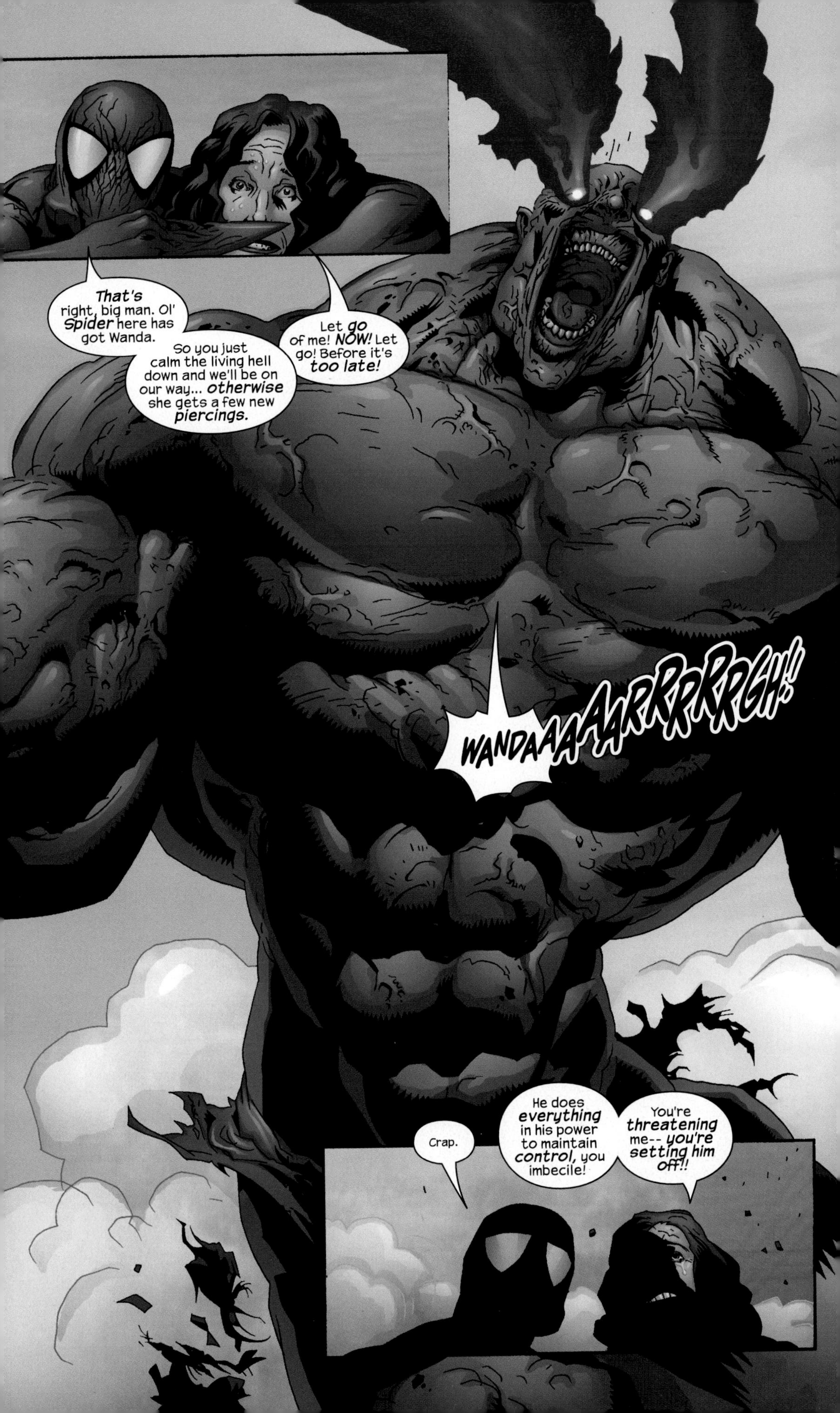
That's right, big man. Ol' Spider here has got Wanda.
So you just calm the living hell down and we'll be on our way... otherwise she gets a few new piercings.
Let go of me! NOW! Let go! Before it's too late!
WANDAAAAARRRRRGH!!
Crap.
He does everything in his power to maintain control, you imbecile!
You're threatening me-- you're setting him off!!

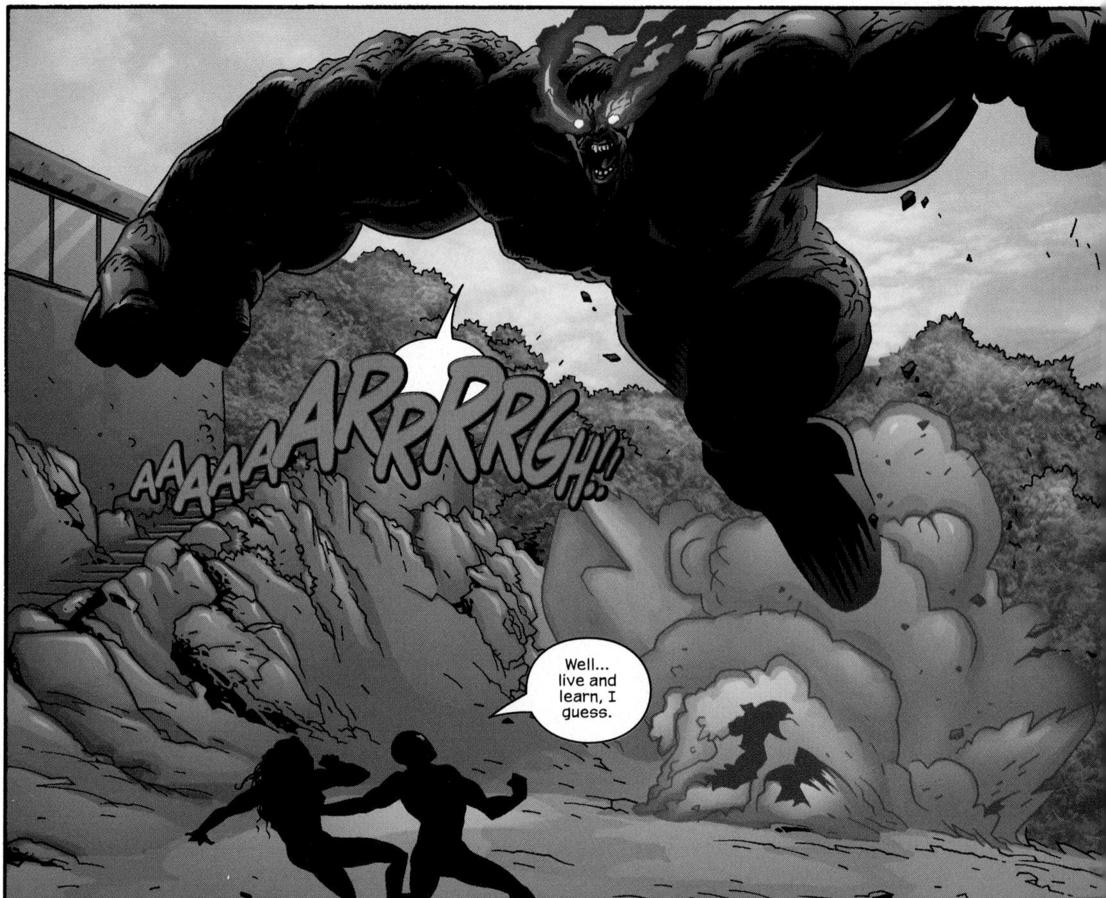
AAAAARRRRRGH!!
Well... live and learn, I guess.

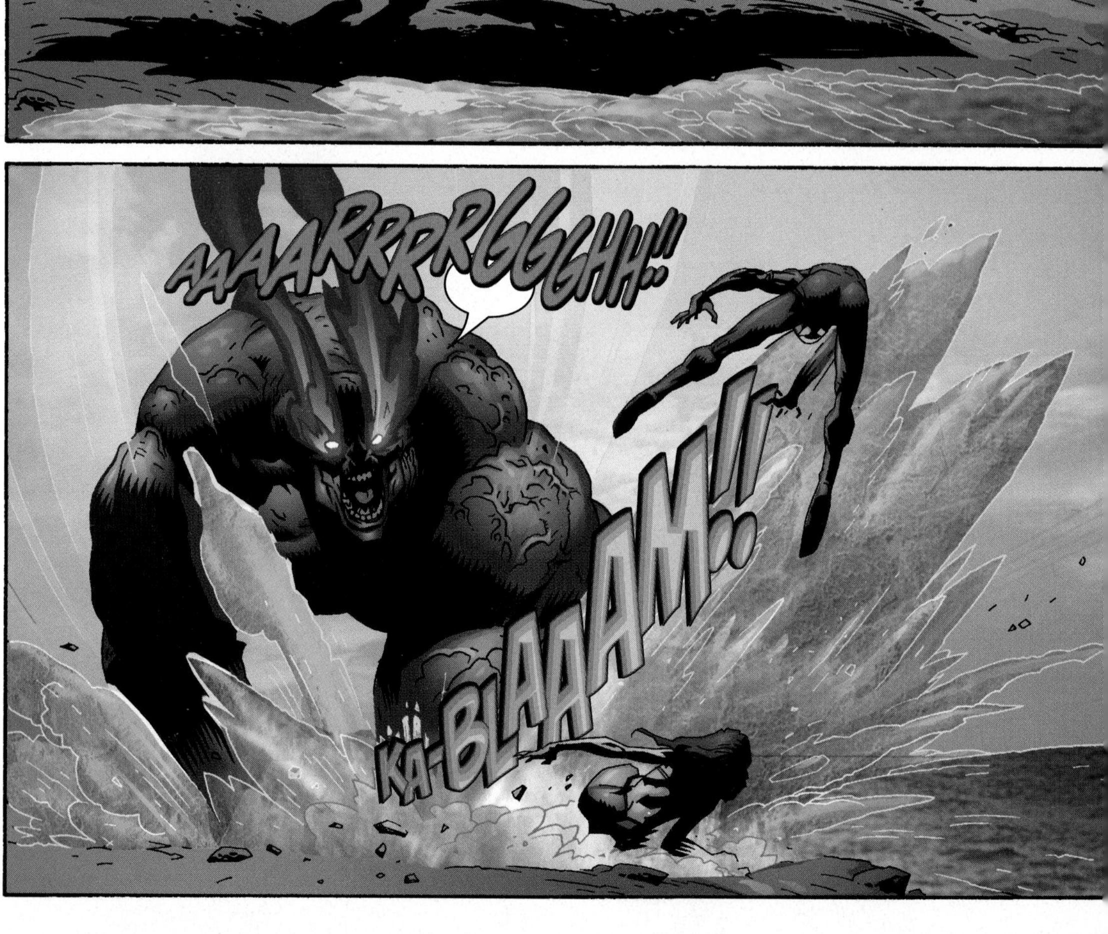
AAAARRRRGGGHH!!
KA-BLAAAM!!

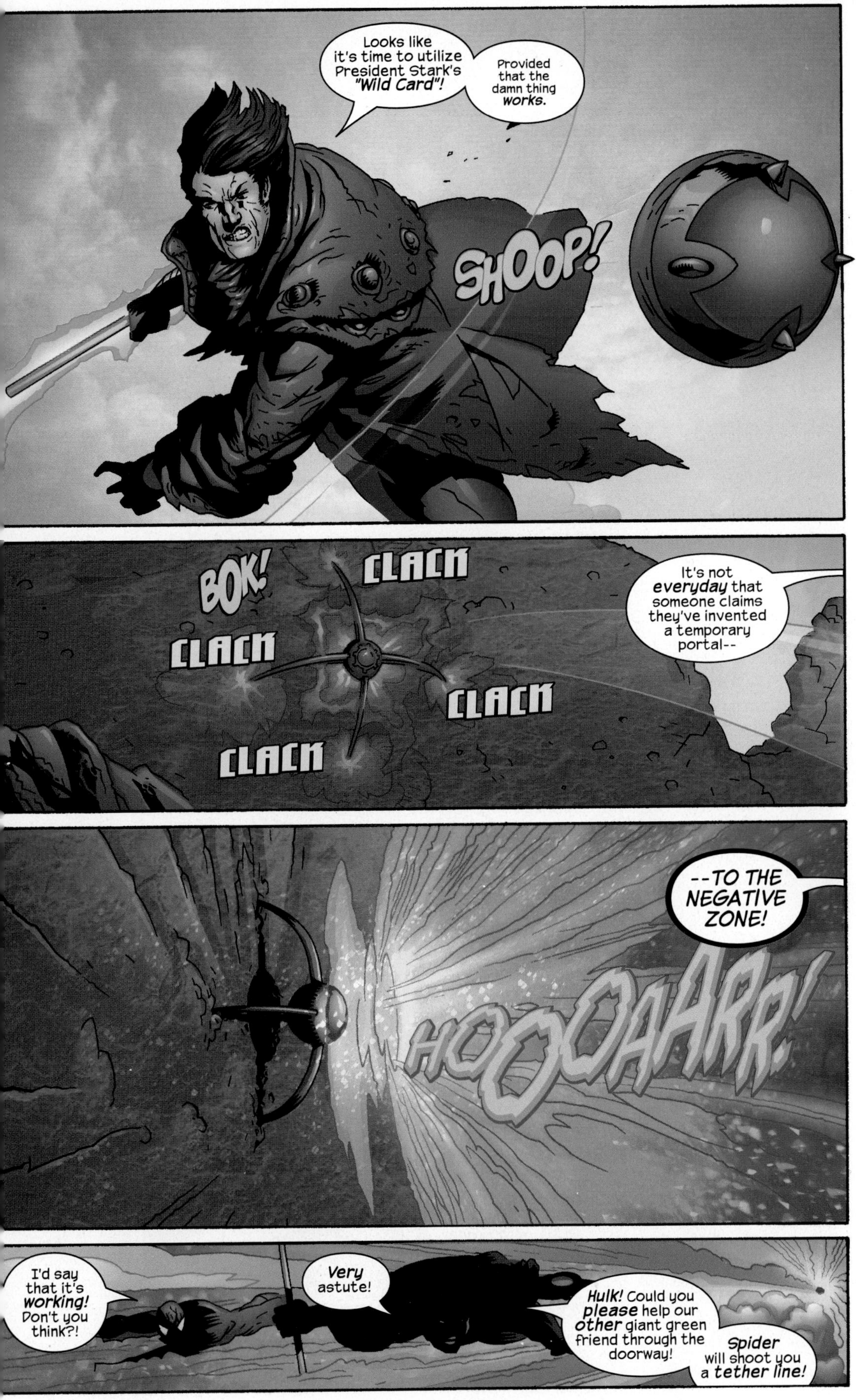

Looks like it's time to utilize President Stark's "Wild Card"!
Provided that the damn thing works.
SHOOP!
BOK!
CLACK
CLACK
CLACK
CLACK
It's not everyday that someone claims they've invented a temporary portal--
--TO THE NEGATIVE ZONE!
HOOOOAARR!
I'd say that it's working! Don't you think?!
Very astute!
Hulk! Could you please help our other giant green friend through the doorway!
Spider will shoot you a tether line!

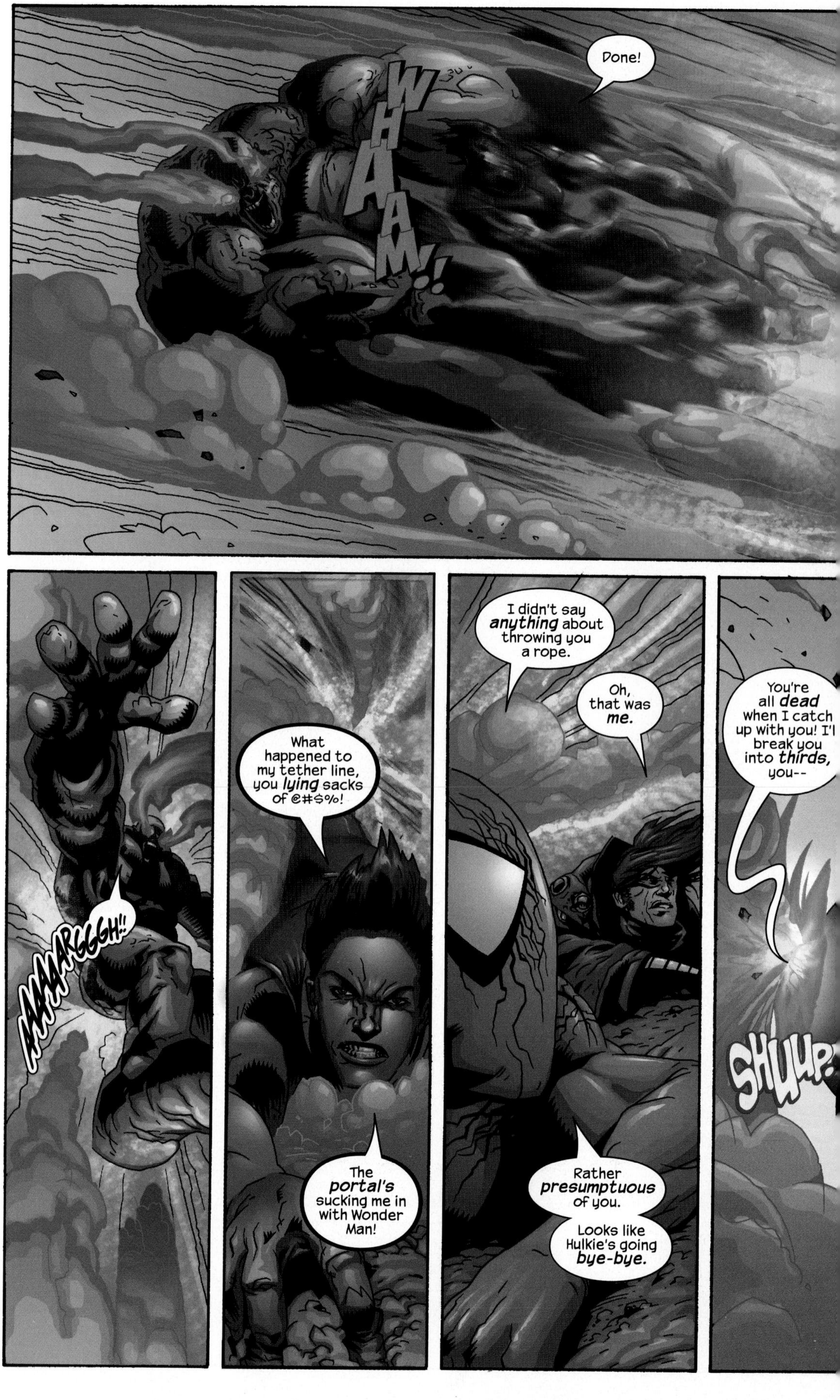
WHAAM!!
Done!
AAAAARGGGH!!
What happened to my tether line, you *lying* sacks of @#$%!
The *portal's* sucking me in with Wonder Man!
I didn't say *anything* about throwing you a rope.
Oh, that was *me.*
Rather *presumptuous* of you.
Looks like Hulkie's going *bye-bye.*
You're all *dead* when I catch up with you! I'l break you into *thirds,* you--
SHUUP

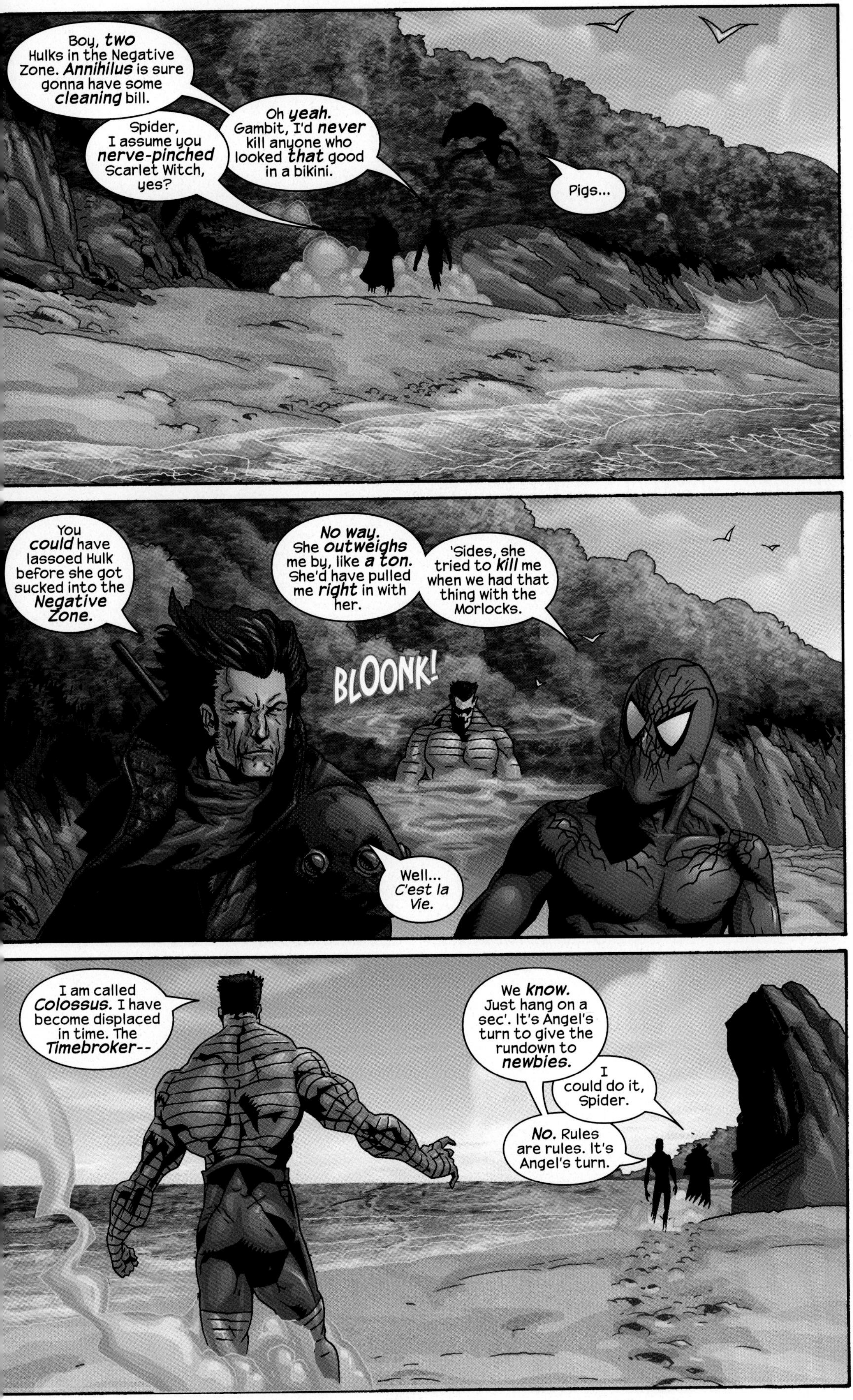

Boy, two Hulks in the Negative Zone. Annihilus is sure gonna have some cleaning bill.
Spider, I assume you nerve-pinched Scarlet Witch, yes?
Oh yeah. Gambit, I'd never kill anyone who looked that good in a bikini.
Pigs...
You could have lassoed Hulk before she got sucked into the Negative Zone.
No way. She outweighs me by, like a ton. She'd have pulled me right in with her.
'Sides, she tried to kill me when we had that thing with the Morlocks.
BLOONK!
Well... C'est la Vie.
I am called Colossus. I have become displaced in time. The Timebroker--
We know. Just hang on a sec'. It's Angel's turn to give the rundown to newbies.
I could do it, Spider.
No. Rules are rules. It's Angel's turn.

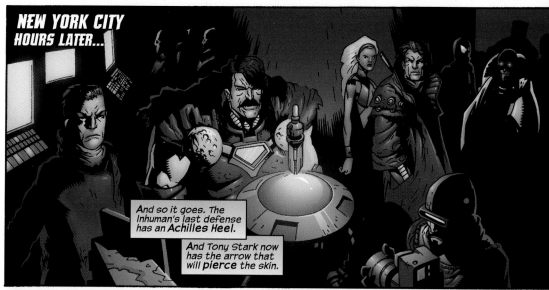

NEW YORK CITY
HOURS LATER...

And so it goes. The Inhuman's last defense has an *Achilles Heel.*

And Tony Stark now has the arrow that will *pierce* the skin.

THE INHUMANS THRONE ROOM...

Black Bolt knew this was unavoidable. He knew that his people's long journey was *ending.*

They are *tired,* he thinks. His people-- his fellow Inhumans-- have run for so long, gone without so much...

...known so little joy in past decades.

The Inhuman children do not remember a time other than *this.* They never knew the *majesty* that was their kingdom.

The *pride* their people once possessed. They know only what it is to be *hunted.*

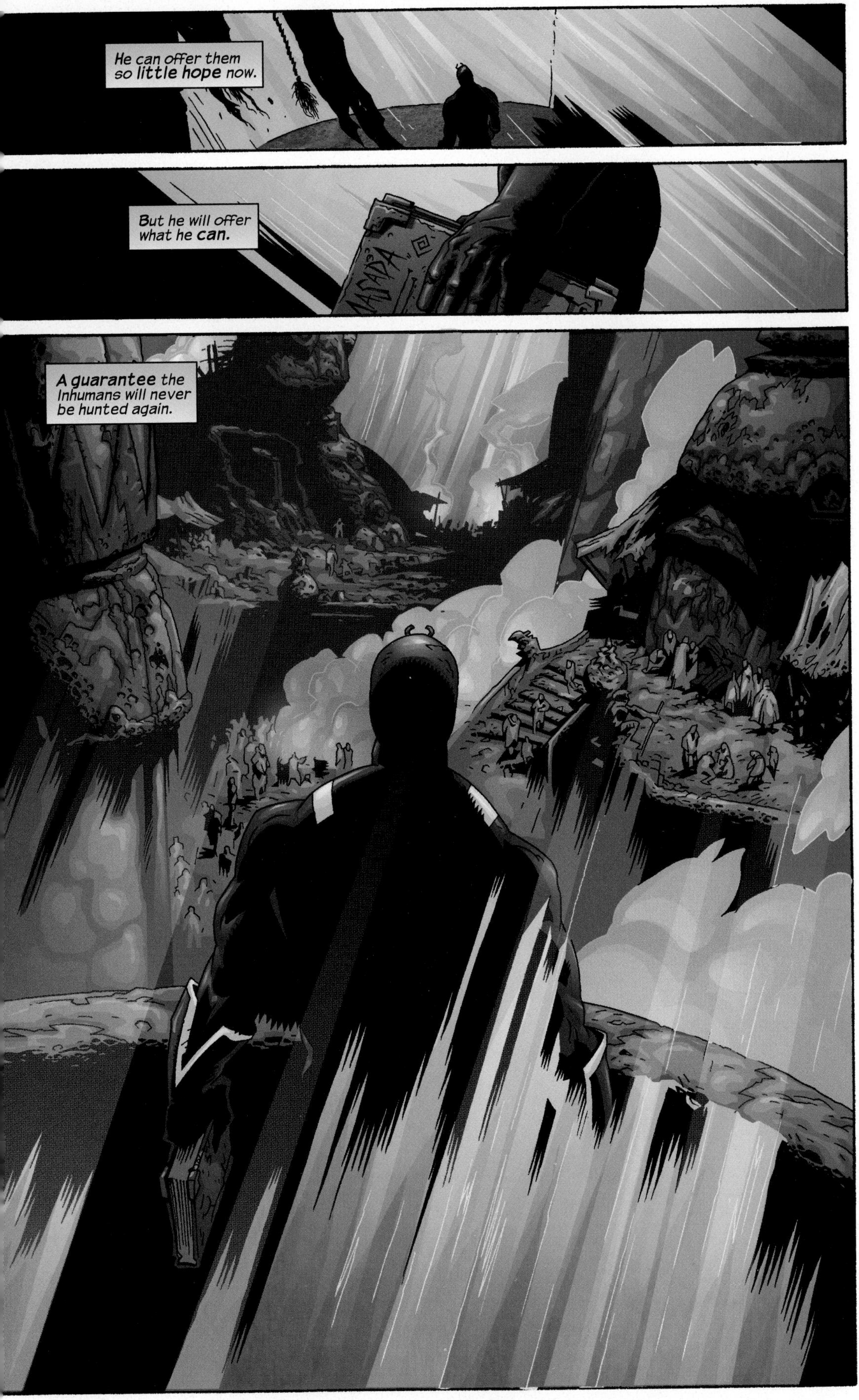
He can offer them so little hope now.
But he will offer what he can.
MASADA
A guarantee the Inhumans will never be hunted again.

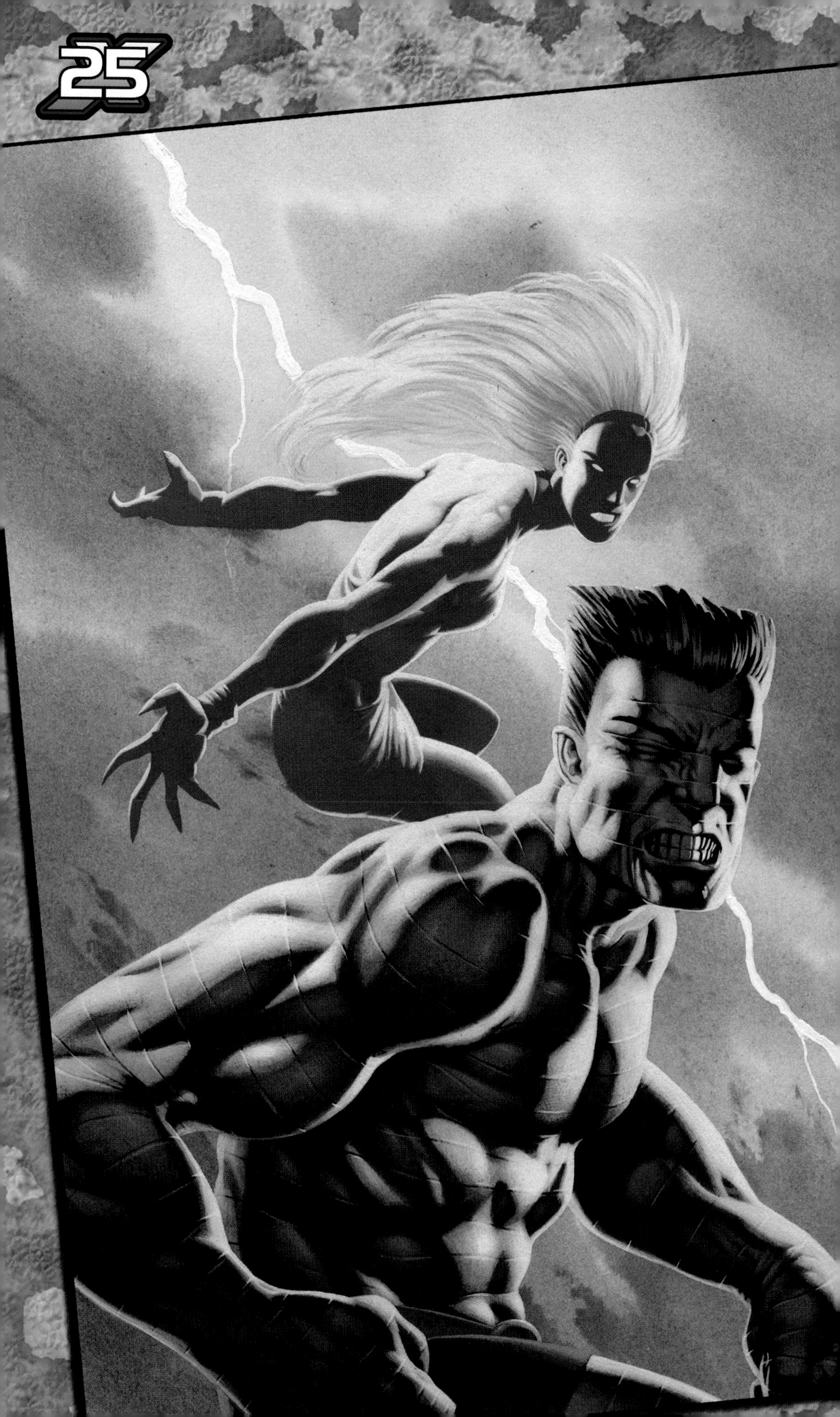
25

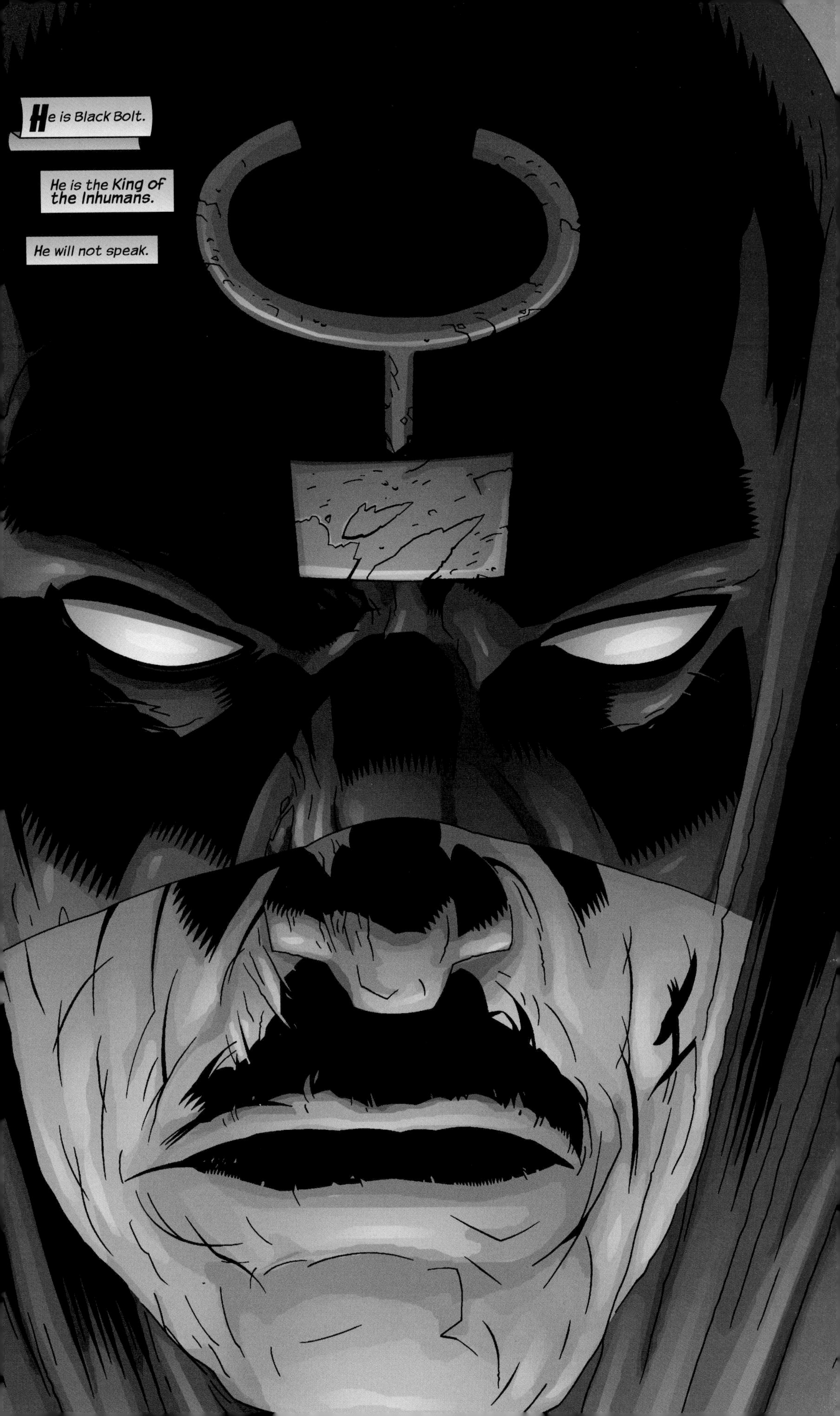
He is Black Bolt.
He is the King of the Inhumans.
He will not speak.

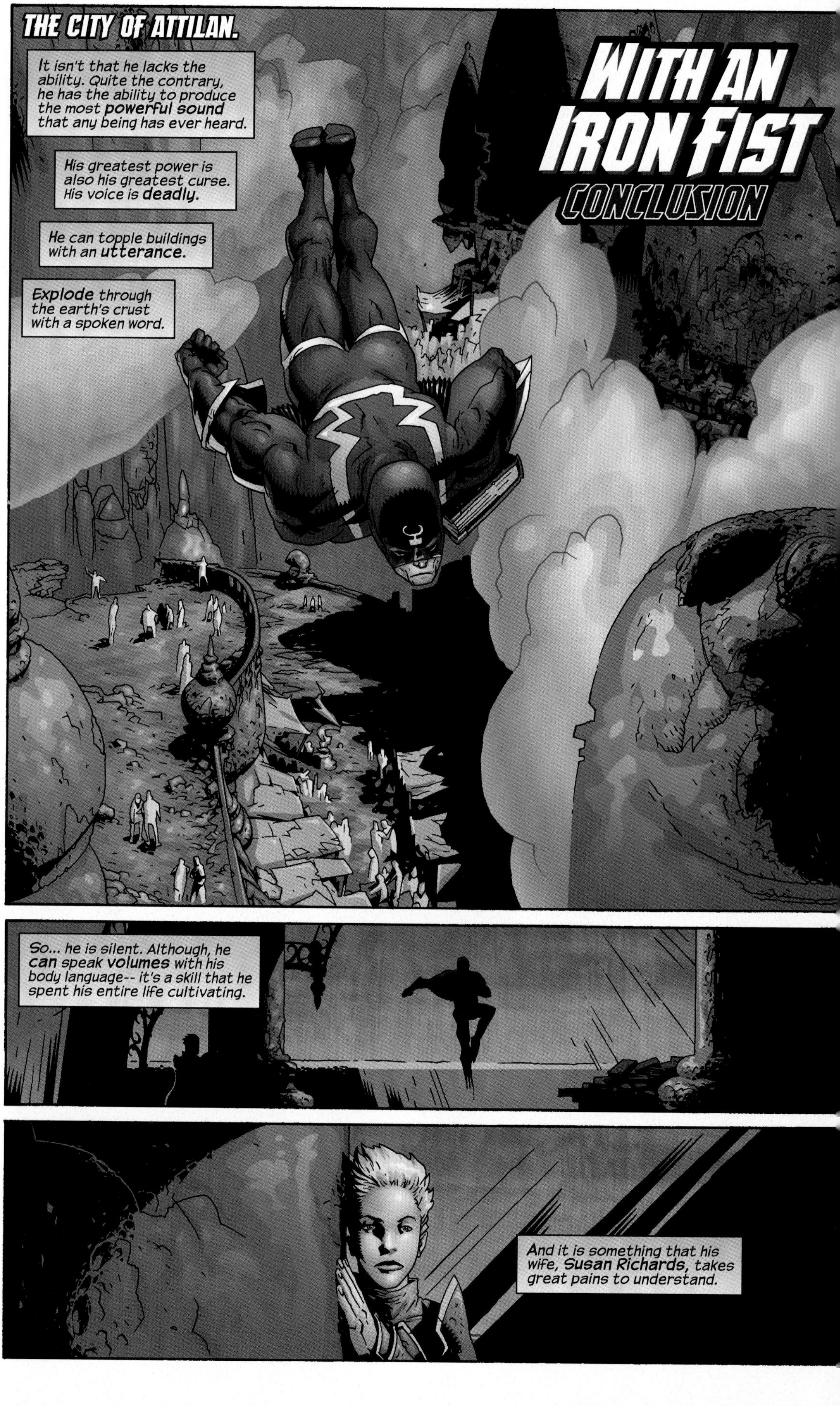
THE CITY OF ATTILAN.
WITH AN IRON FIST
CONCLUSION
It isn't that he lacks the ability. Quite the contrary, he has the ability to produce the most powerful sound that any being has ever heard.
His greatest power is also his greatest curse. His voice is deadly.
He can topple buildings with an utterance.
Explode through the earth's crust with a spoken word.
So... he is silent. Although, he can speak volumes with his body language-- it's a skill that he spent his entire life cultivating.
And it is something that his wife, Susan Richards, takes great pains to understand.

As a wife who shares her life with a husband who is without speech, she must interpret, search, and fight to comprehend his every gesture.

It is difficult... *especially of late.*

He has kept completely to himself. Even for a man of **no words** like Black Bolt, it is out of character.

Why have you been reading all these?

These are *books*...

...books on races that have been *slaughtered.*

The American Indians, the African slave trade to the New World, the Mongol Emperor of China, The Teiping Rebellion--

--The French Revolution, The Aztecs, Jews from all eras... modern texts... ancient books...

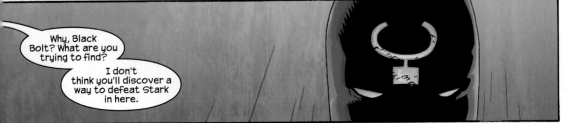

Why, Black Bolt? What are you trying to find?

I don't think you'll discover a way to defeat Stark in here.

Yes... I know the story of *Masada...*

Why would...?

No...

No!
No! No!
No!

You don't
mean to...
please...
please!

There *must* be
another way! You
can't just-- we
shouldn't--

Your
Majesty... my
Queen. Forgive my
intrusion.

We have just
received a communica-
tion from the *Scarlet
Witch* and *Doctor
Strange.*

Stark has
stolen the *Disruptor.*
He has the means to
bring the *G-Barrier*
down.

We assume
another attack
on Attilan is...
is *certain.*

We can't...

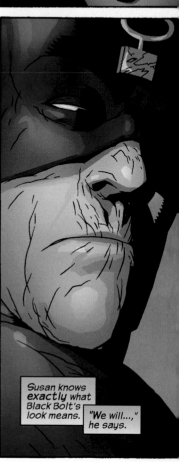

Susan knows
exactly what
Black Bolt's
look means.
"We will...,"
he says.

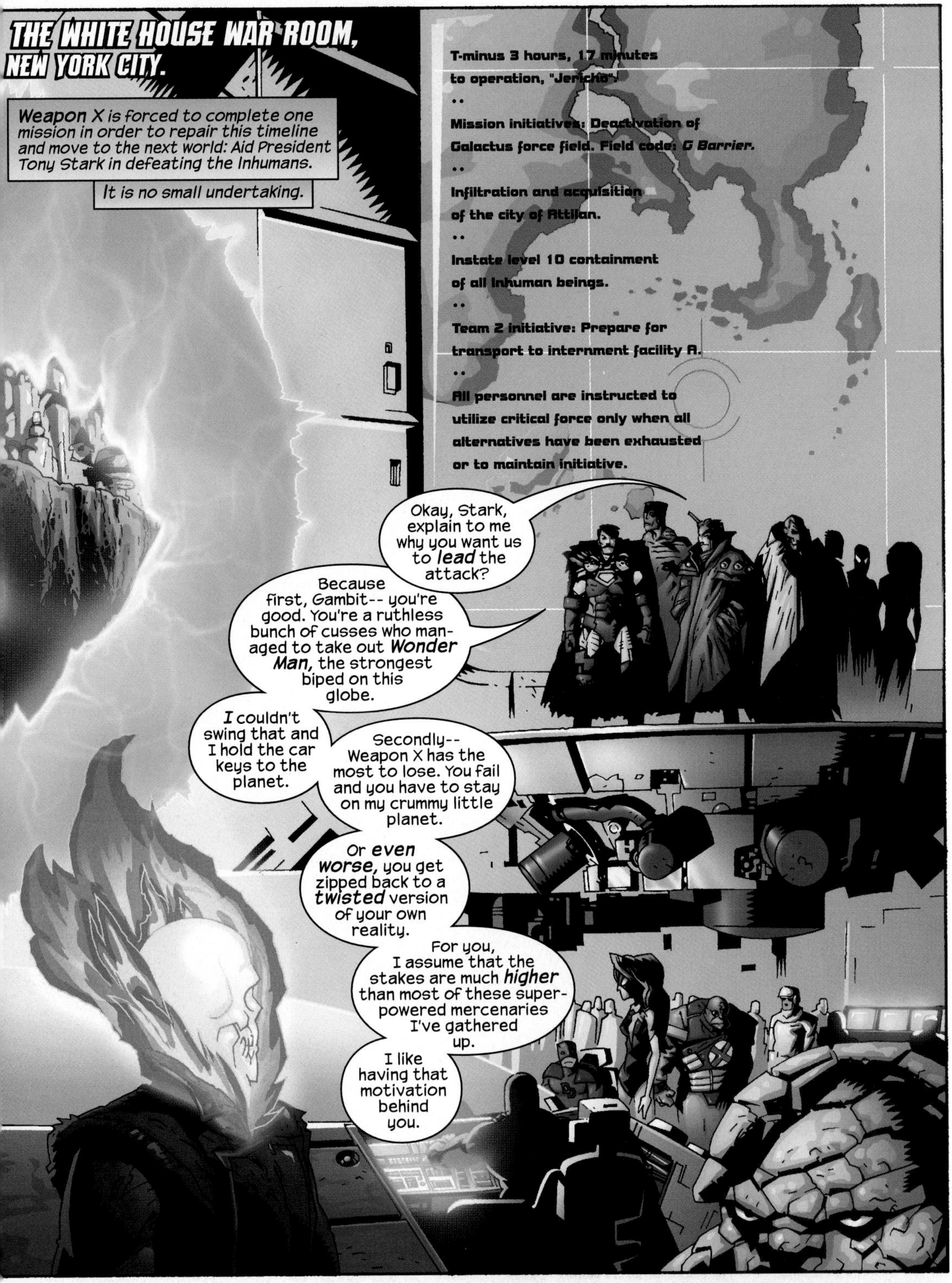
THE WHITE HOUSE WAR ROOM, NEW YORK CITY.
Weapon X is forced to complete one mission in order to repair this timeline and move to the next world: Aid President Tony Stark in defeating the Inhumans.
It is no small undertaking.
T-minus 3 hours, 17 minutes to operation, "Jericho".
Mission initiatives: Deactivation of Galactus force field. Field code: G Barrier.
Infiltration and acquisition of the city of Attilan.
Instate level 10 containment of all Inhuman beings.
Team 2 initiative: Prepare for transport to internment facility A.
All personnel are instructed to utilize critical force only when all alternatives have been exhausted or to maintain initiative.
Okay, Stark, explain to me why you want us to lead the attack?
Because first, Gambit-- you're good. You're a ruthless bunch of cusses who managed to take out Wonder Man, the strongest biped on this globe.
I couldn't swing that and I hold the car keys to the planet.
Secondly-- Weapon X has the most to lose. You fail and you have to stay on my crummy little planet.
Or even worse, you get zipped back to a twisted version of your own reality.
For you, I assume that the stakes are much higher than most of these super-powered mercenaries I've gathered up.
I like having that motivation behind you.

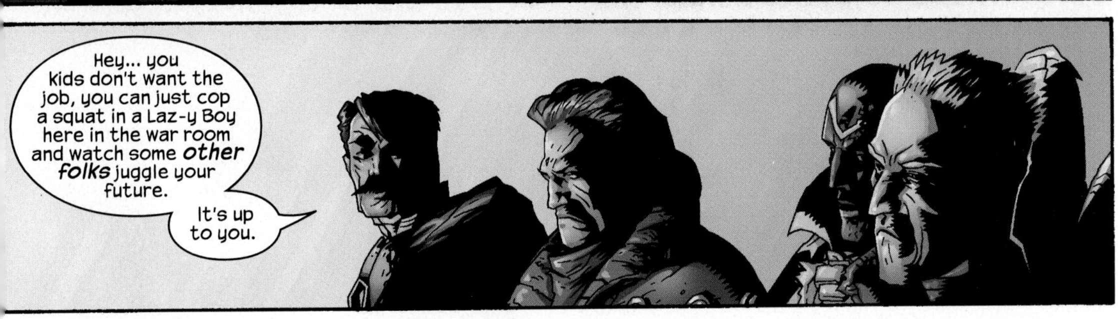
Hey... you kids don't want the job, you can just cop a squat in a Laz-y Boy here in the war room and watch some other folks juggle your future.
It's up to you.

NO.

We'll lead the charge.

Mr. President! We have movement! *Attilan* is moving *due east* over the Pacific at two hundred knots.

What are you up to, Black Bolt?

If they maintain this course, is there anything ahead of them?

Not much, Sir. No land masses-- but there is a four mile stretch of coral.

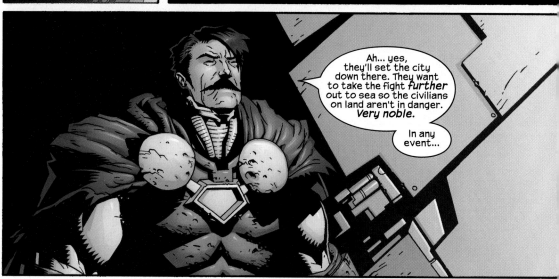

Ah... yes, they'll set the city down there. They want to take the fight *further* out to sea so the civilians on land aren't in danger. *Very noble.*

In any event...

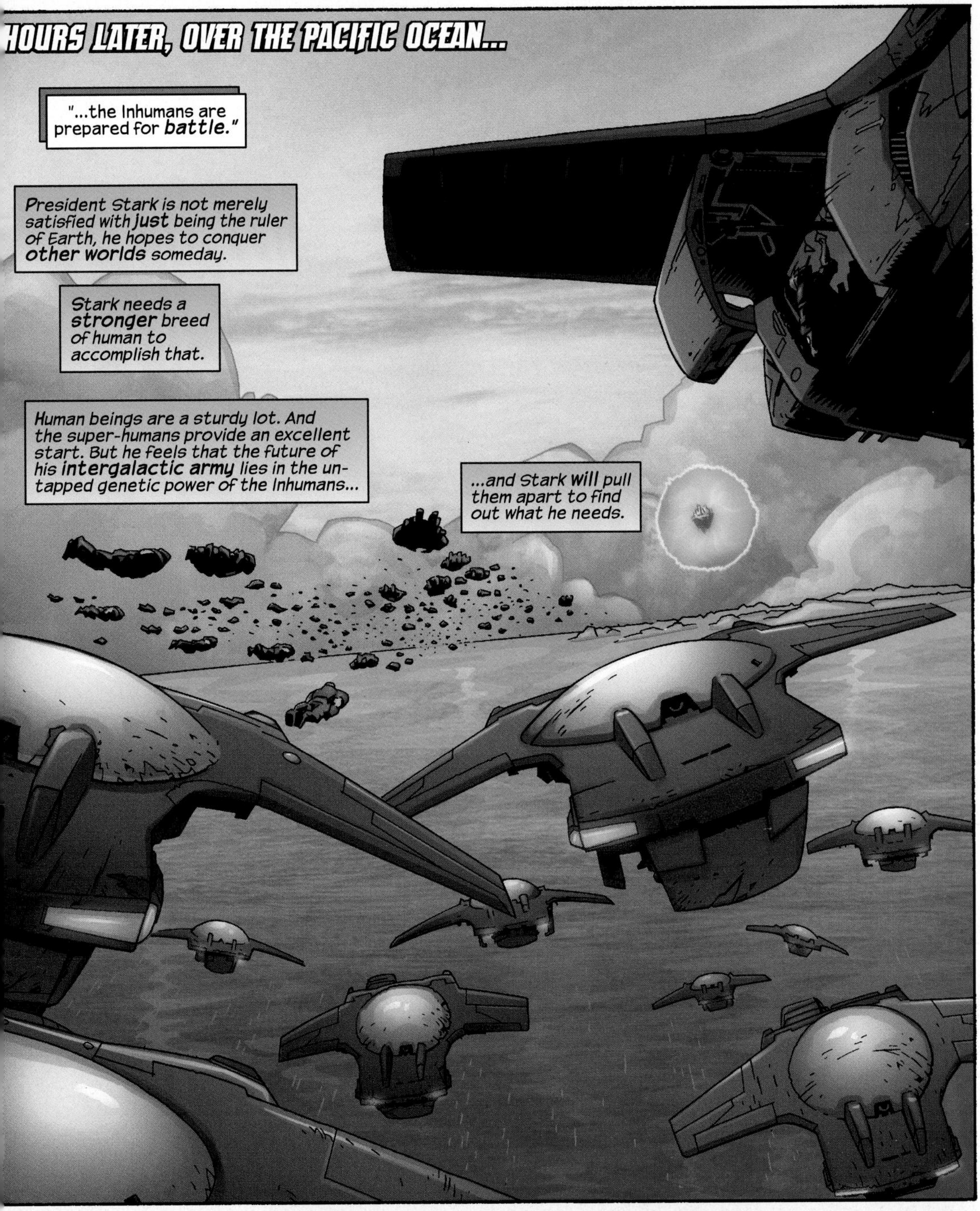
HOURS LATER, OVER THE PACIFIC OCEAN...
"...the Inhumans are prepared for battle."
President Stark is not merely satisfied with just being the ruler of Earth, he hopes to conquer other worlds someday.
Stark needs a stronger breed of human to accomplish that.
Human beings are a sturdy lot. And the super-humans provide an excellent start. But he feels that the future of his intergalactic army lies in the untapped genetic power of the Inhumans...
...and Stark will pull them apart to find out what he needs.

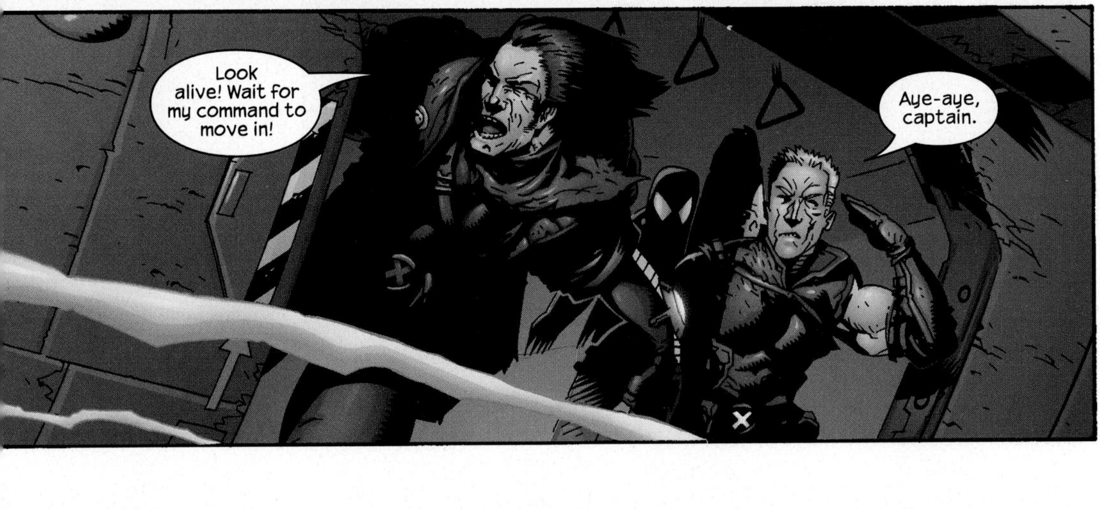
Look alive! Wait for my command to move in!
Aye-aye, captain.

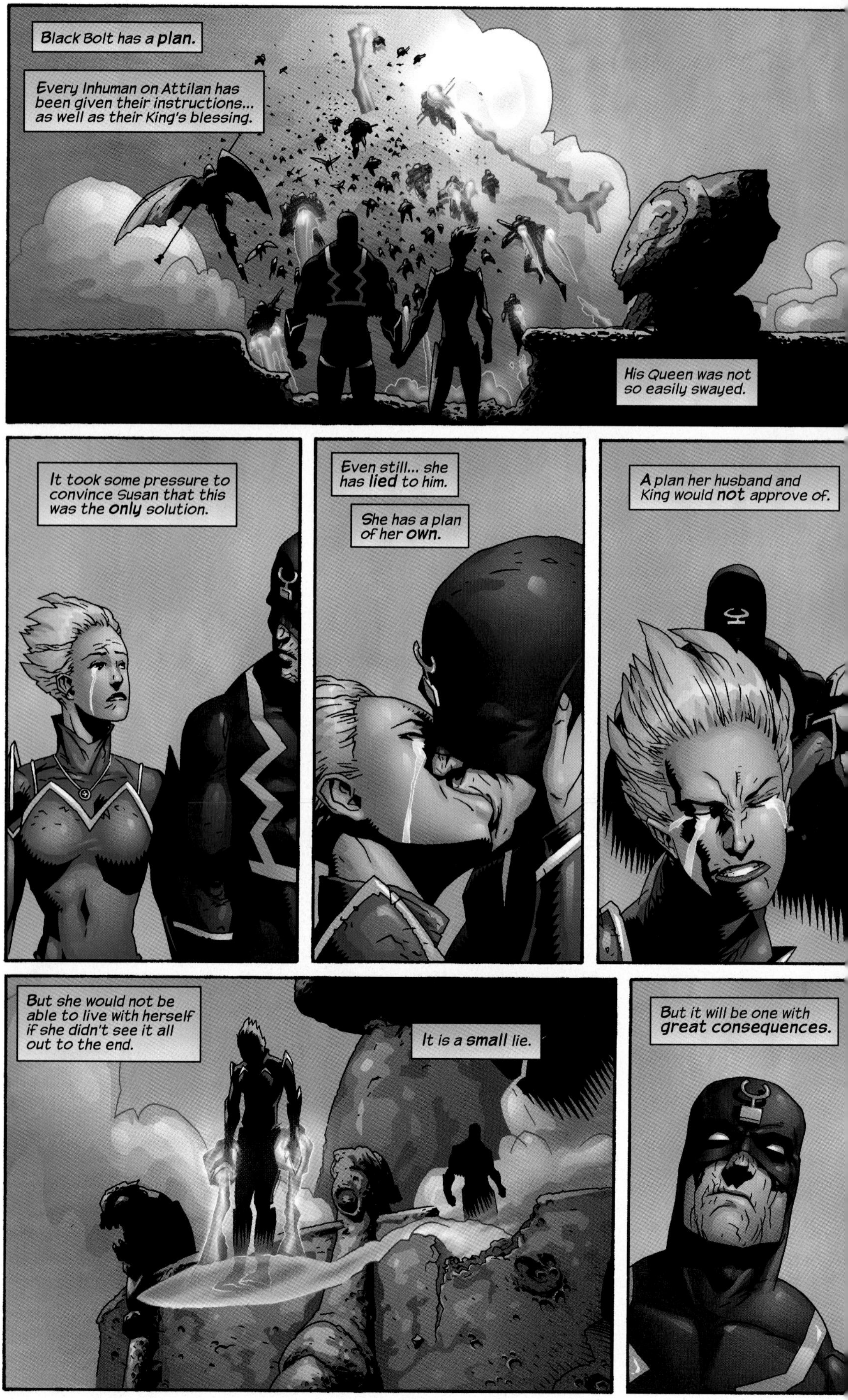
Black Bolt has a plan.
Every Inhuman on Attilan has been given their instructions... as well as their King's blessing.
His Queen was not so easily swayed.
It took some pressure to convince Susan that this was the only solution.
Even still... she has lied to him.
She has a plan of her own.
A plan her husband and King would not approve of.
But she would not be able to live with herself if she didn't see it all out to the end.
It is a small lie.
But it will be one with great consequences.

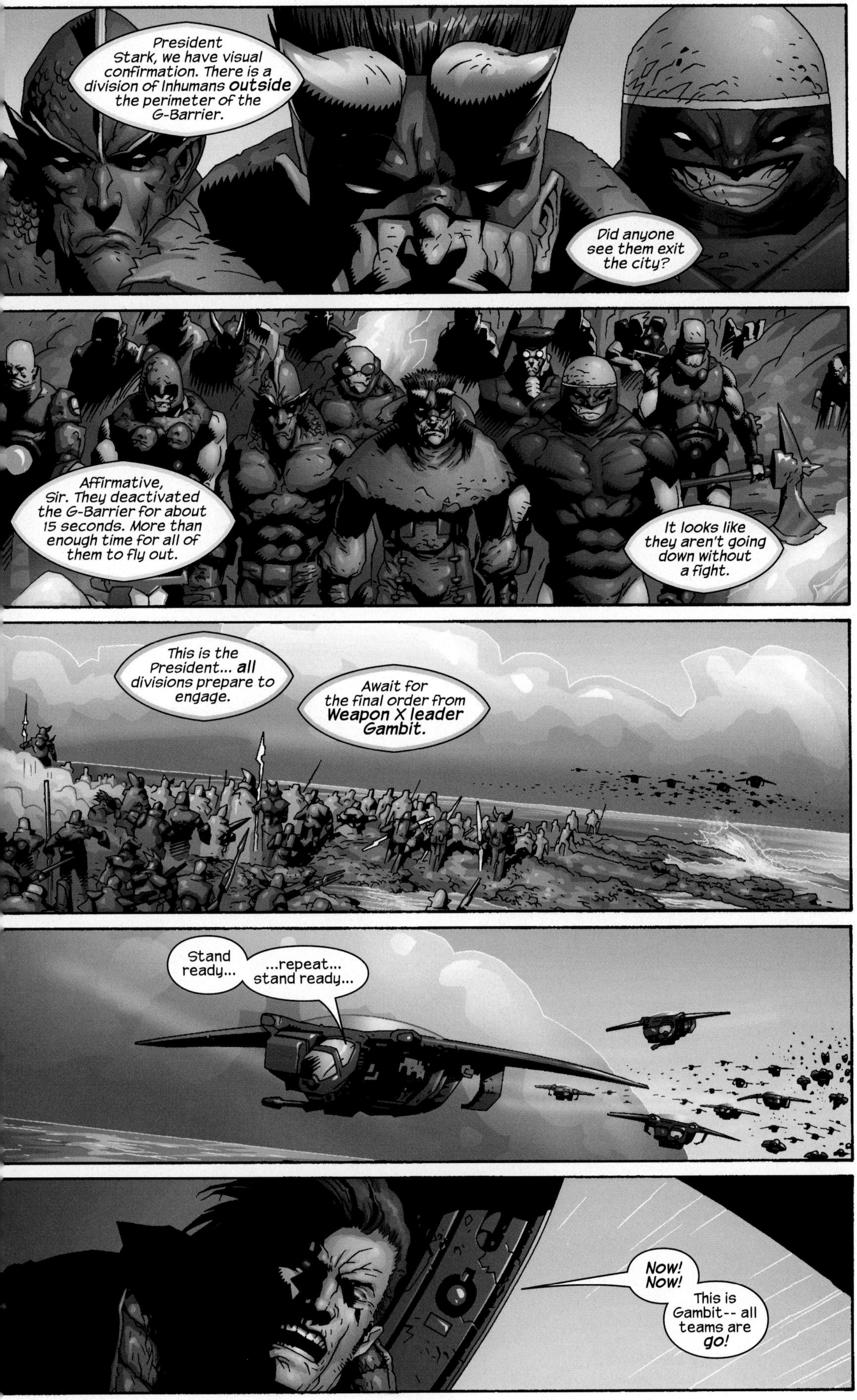
President Stark, we have visual confirmation. There is a division of Inhumans outside the perimeter of the G-Barrier.
Did anyone see them exit the city?
Affirmative, Sir. They deactivated the G-Barrier for about 15 seconds. More than enough time for all of them to fly out.
It looks like they aren't going down without a fight.
This is the President... all divisions prepare to engage.
Await for the final order from Weapon X leader Gambit.
Stand ready...
...repeat... stand ready...
Now! Now!
This is Gambit-- all teams are go!

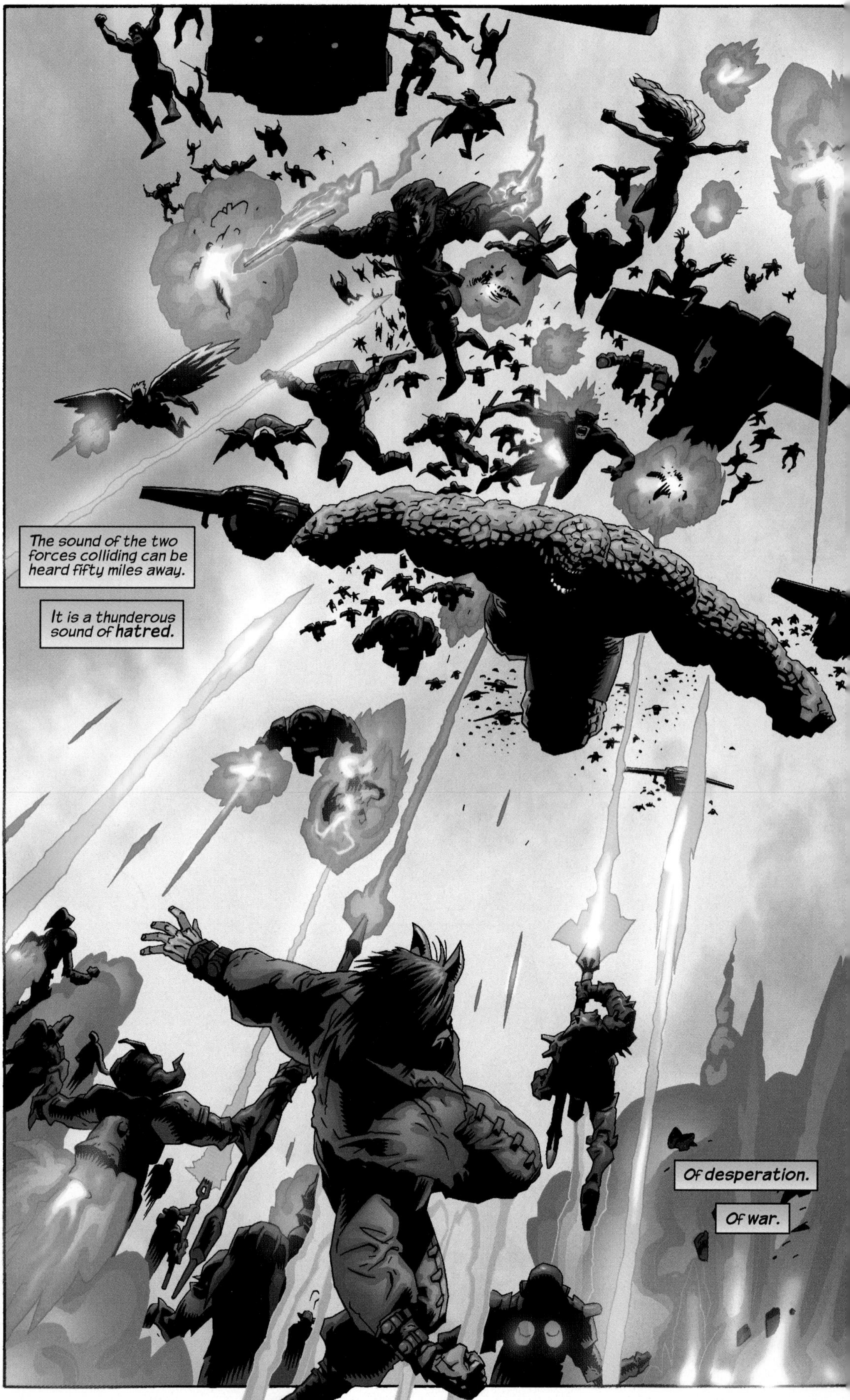
The sound of the two forces colliding can be heard fifty miles away.
It is a thunderous sound of **hatred**.
Of desperation.
Of war.

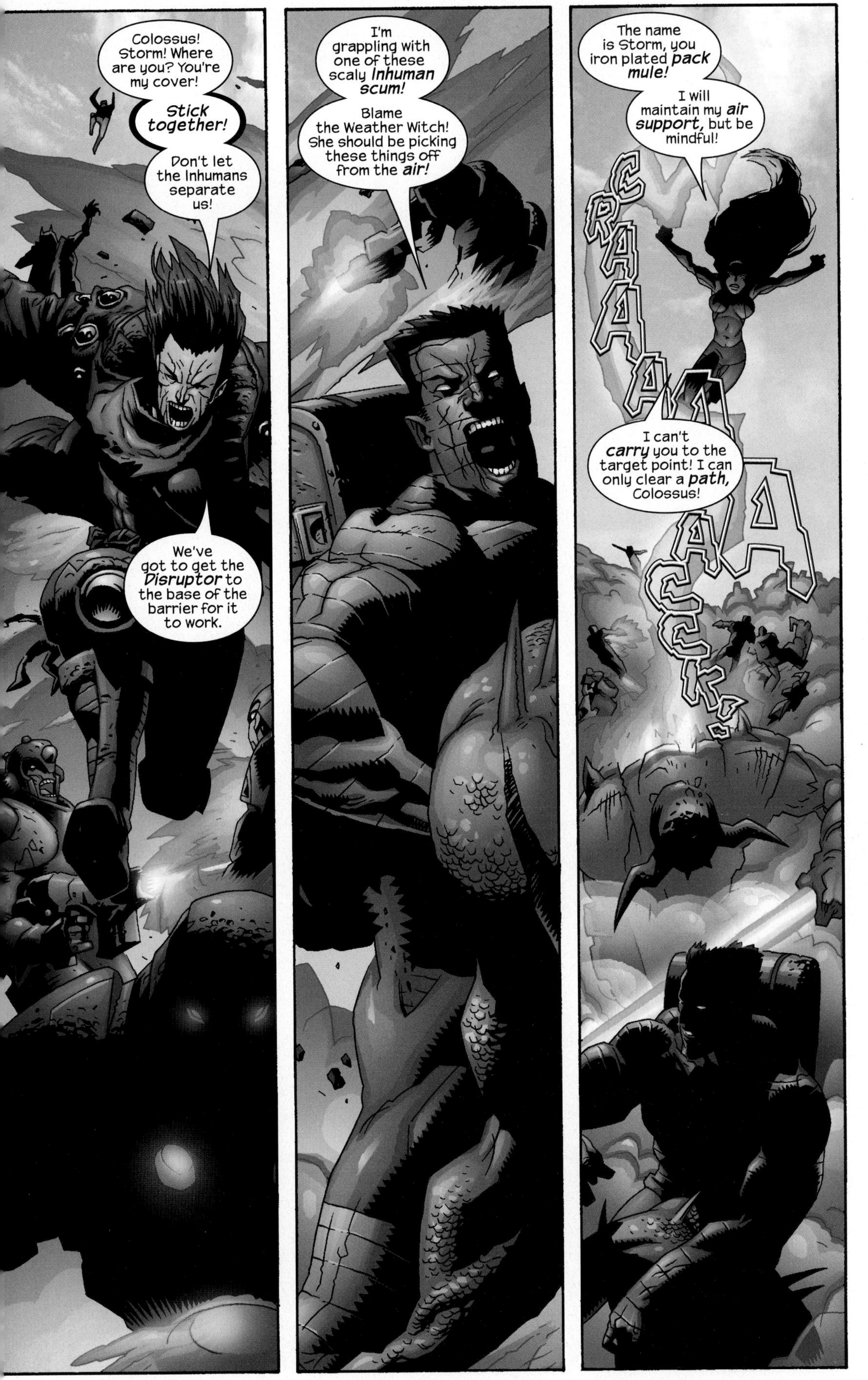
Colossus! Storm! Where are you? You're my cover!
Stick together!
Don't let the Inhumans separate us!
We've got to get the Disruptor to the base of the barrier for it to work.
I'm grappling with one of these scaly Inhuman scum!
Blame the Weather Witch! She should be picking these things off from the air!
The name is Storm, you iron plated pack mule!
I will maintain my air support, but be mindful!
CRAAAAACK!
I can't carry you to the target point! I can only clear a path, Colossus!

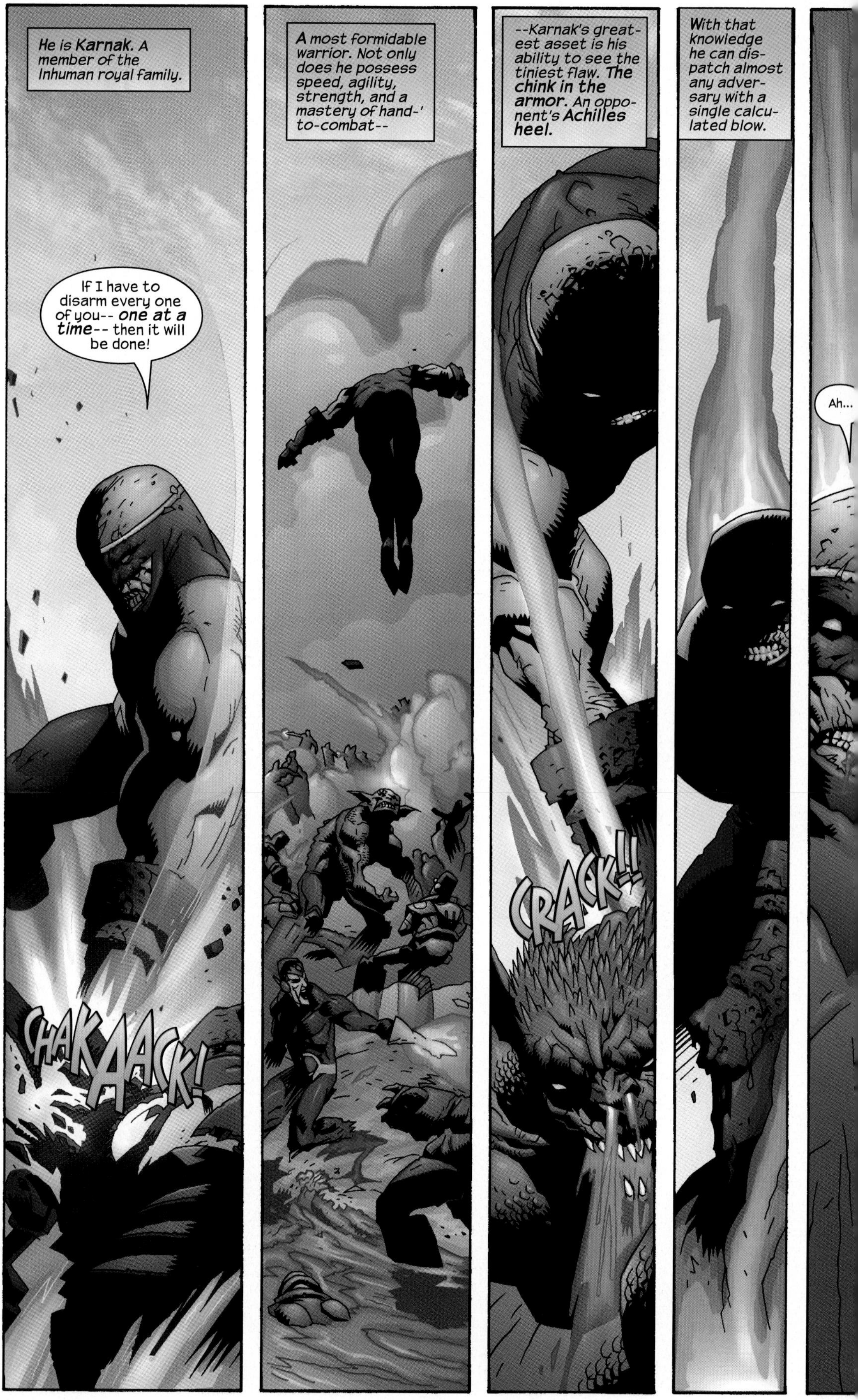
He is Karnak. A member of the Inhuman royal family.
If I have to disarm every one of you-- one at a time-- then it will be done!
CHAKAACK!
A most formidable warrior. Not only does he possess speed, agility, strength, and a mastery of hand-' to-combat--
--Karnak's greatest asset is his ability to see the tiniest flaw. The chink in the armor. An opponent's Achilles heel.
CRACK!!
With that knowledge he can dispatch almost any adversary with a single calculated blow.
Ah...

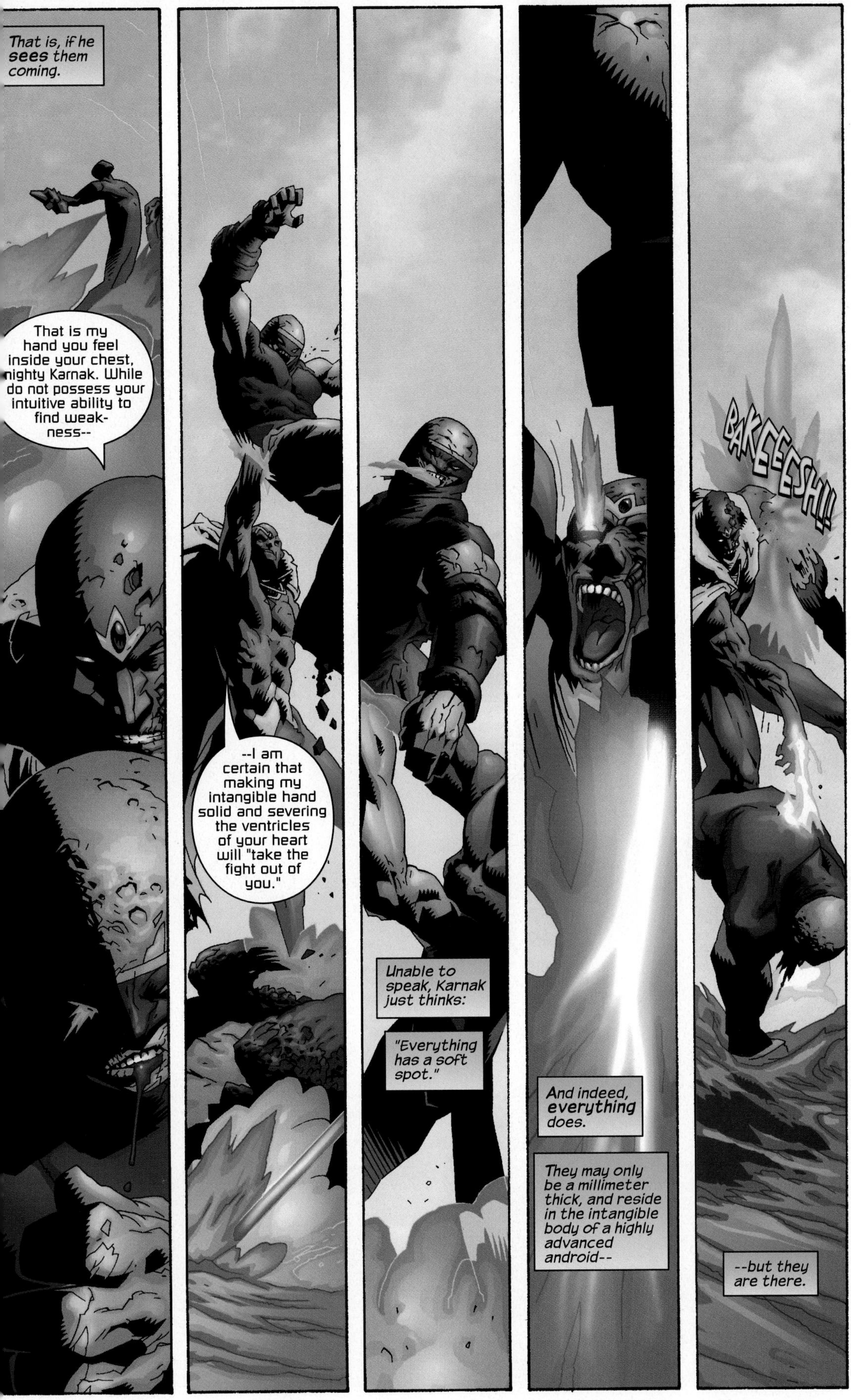

That is, if he sees them coming.
That is my hand you feel inside your chest, mighty Karnak. While I do not possess your intuitive ability to find weak-ness--
--I am certain that making my intangible hand solid and severing the ventricles of your heart will "take the fight out of you."
Unable to speak, Karnak just thinks:
"Everything has a soft spot."
And indeed, everything does.
They may only be a millimeter thick, and reside in the intangible body of a highly advanced android--
BAKEEESH!!
--but they are there.

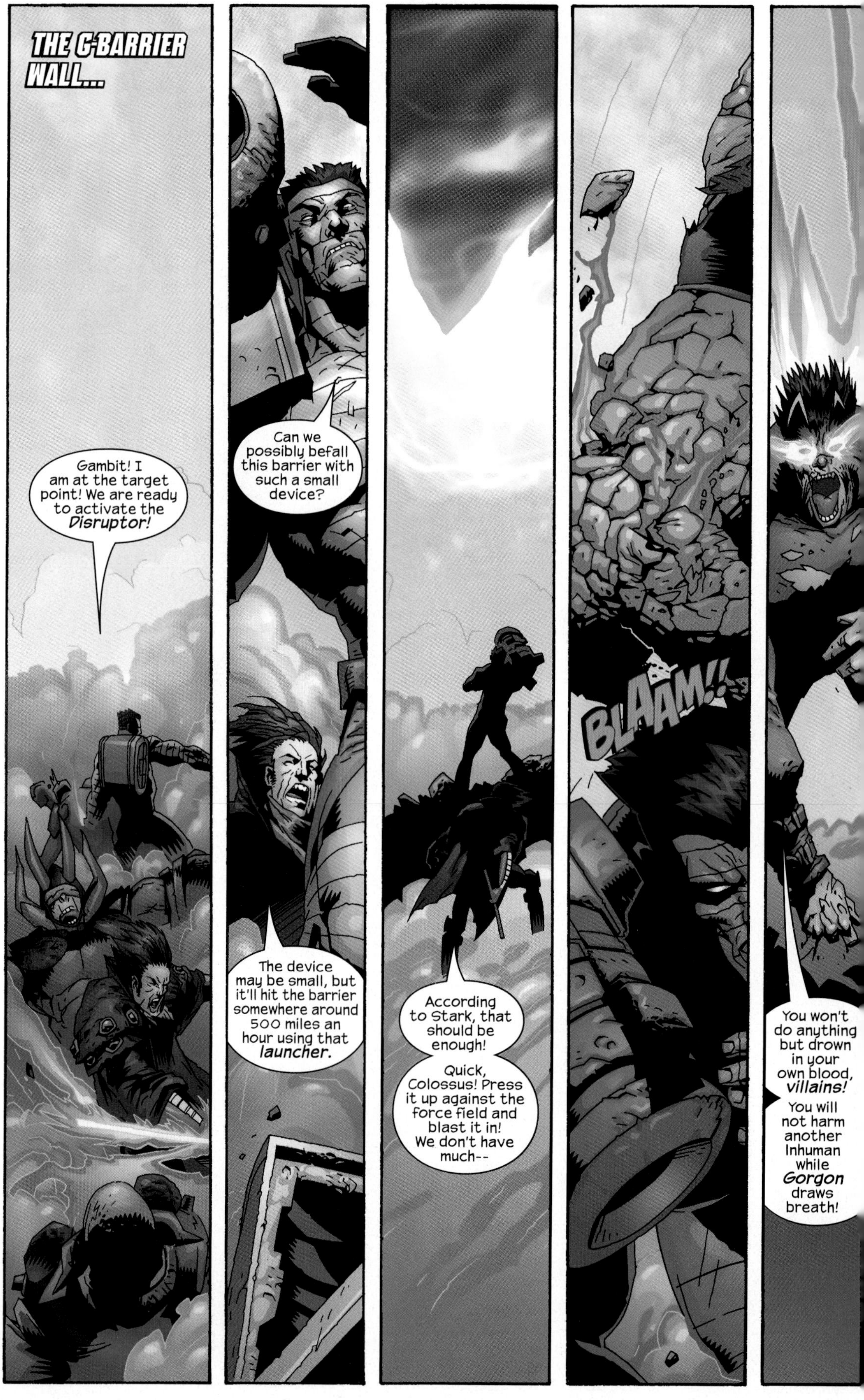
THE G-BARRIER WALL...
Gambit! I am at the target point! We are ready to activate the Disruptor!
Can we possibly befall this barrier with such a small device?
The device may be small, but it'll hit the barrier somewhere around 500 miles an hour using that launcher.
According to Stark, that should be enough!
Quick, Colossus! Press it up against the force field and blast it in! We don't have much--
BLAAM!!
You won't do anything but drown in your own blood, villains!
You will not harm another Inhuman while Gorgon draws breath!

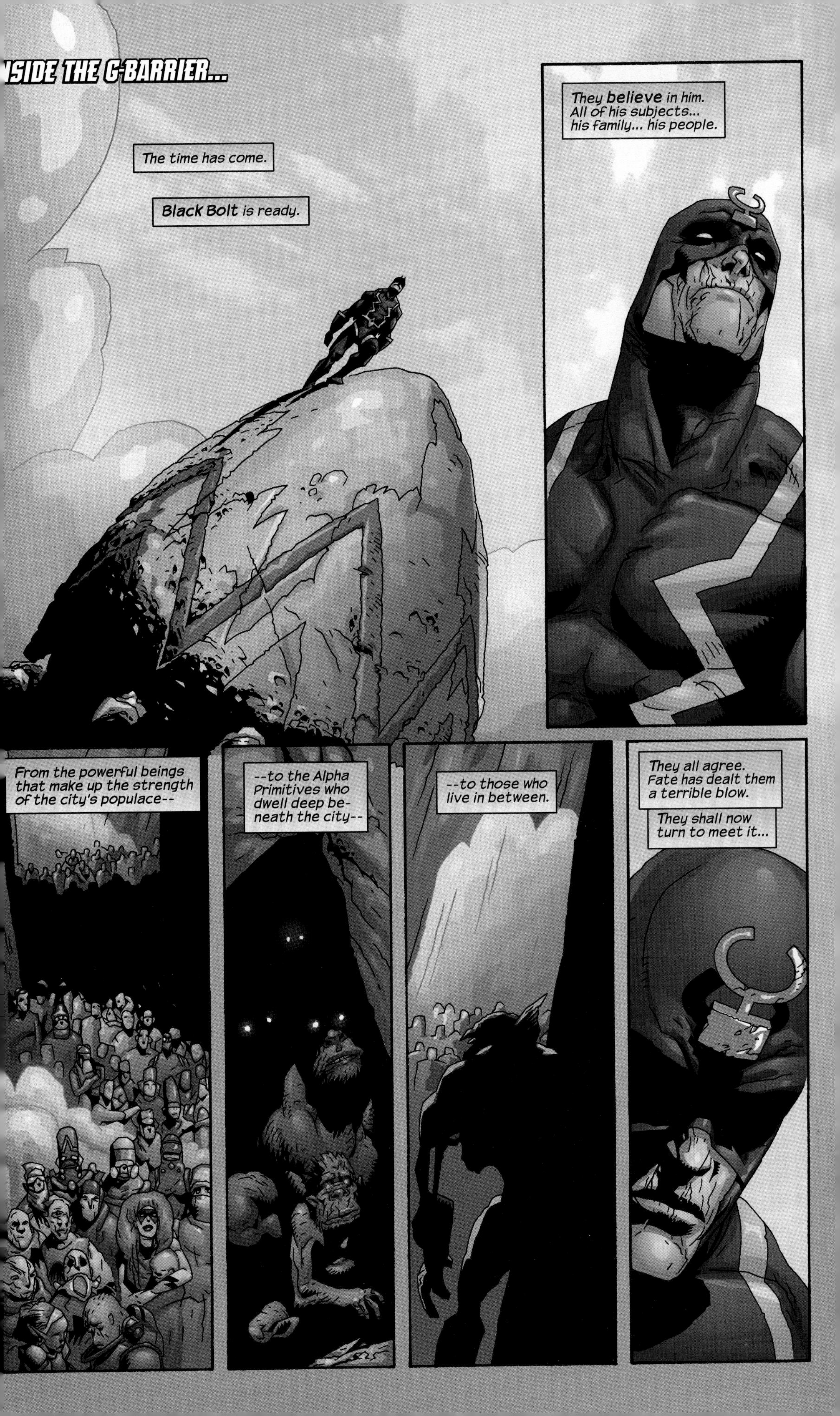

NSIDE THE G-BARRIER...
The time has come.
Black Bolt is ready.
They believe in him. All of his subjects... his family... his people.
From the powerful beings that make up the strength of the city's populace--
--to the Alpha Primitives who dwell deep beneath the city--
--to those who live in between.
They all agree. Fate has dealt them a terrible blow.
They shall now turn to meet it...

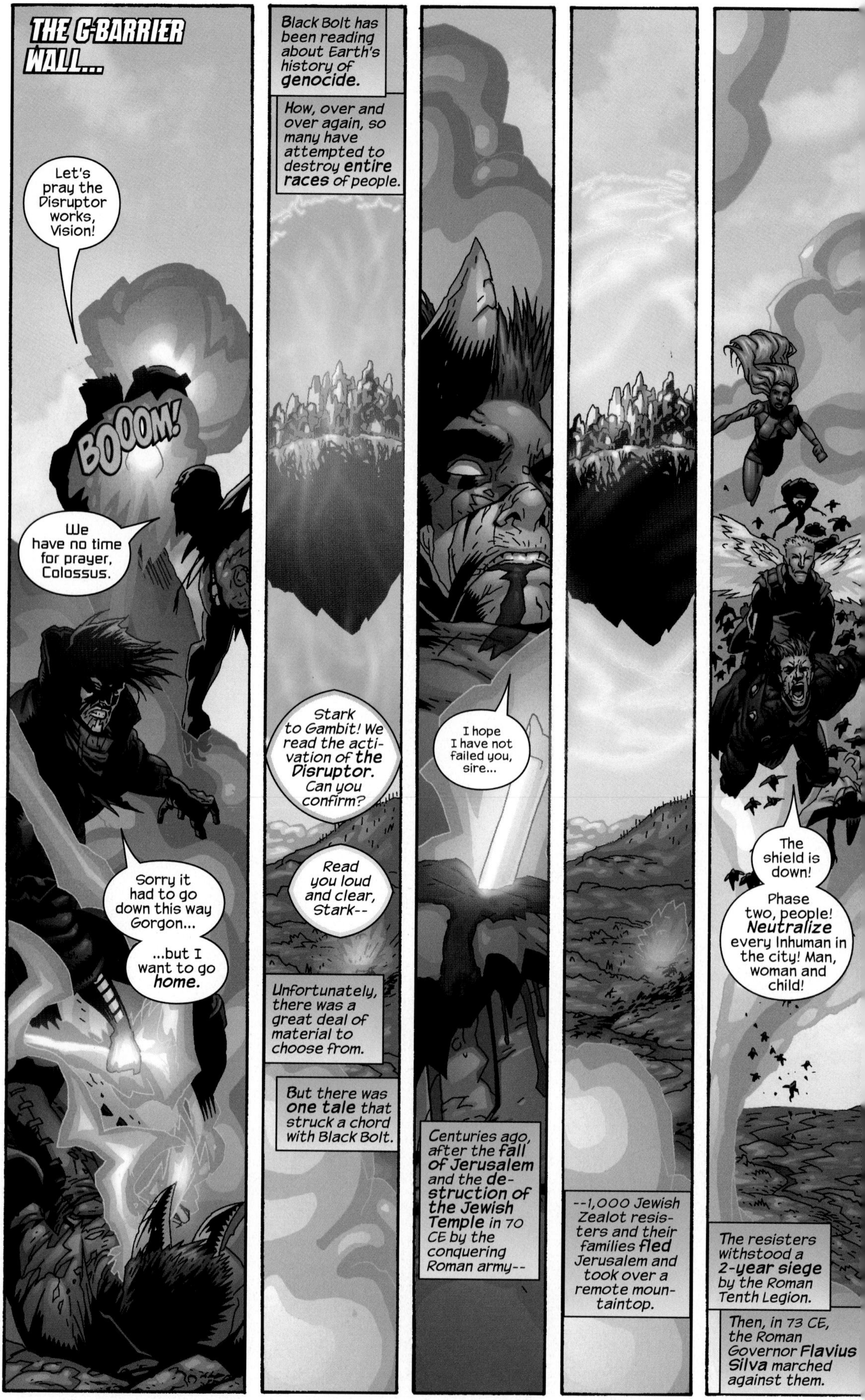
THE G-BARRIER WALL...
Let's pray the Disruptor works, Vision!
BOOOM!
We have no time for prayer, Colossus.
Sorry it had to go down this way Gorgon...
...but I want to go home.
Black Bolt has been reading about Earth's history of genocide.
How, over and over again, so many have attempted to destroy entire races of people.
Stark to Gambit! We read the activation of the Disruptor. Can you confirm?
Read you loud and clear, Stark--
Unfortunately, there was a great deal of material to choose from.
But there was one tale that struck a chord with Black Bolt.
I hope I have not failed you, sire...
Centuries ago, after the fall of Jerusalem and the destruction of the Jewish Temple in 70 CE by the conquering Roman army--
--1,000 Jewish Zealot resisters and their families fled Jerusalem and took over a remote mountaintop.
The shield is down!
Phase two, people! Neutralize every Inhuman in the city! Man, woman and child!
The resisters withstood a 2-year siege by the Roman Tenth Legion.
Then, in 73 CE, the Roman Governor Flavius Silva marched against them.

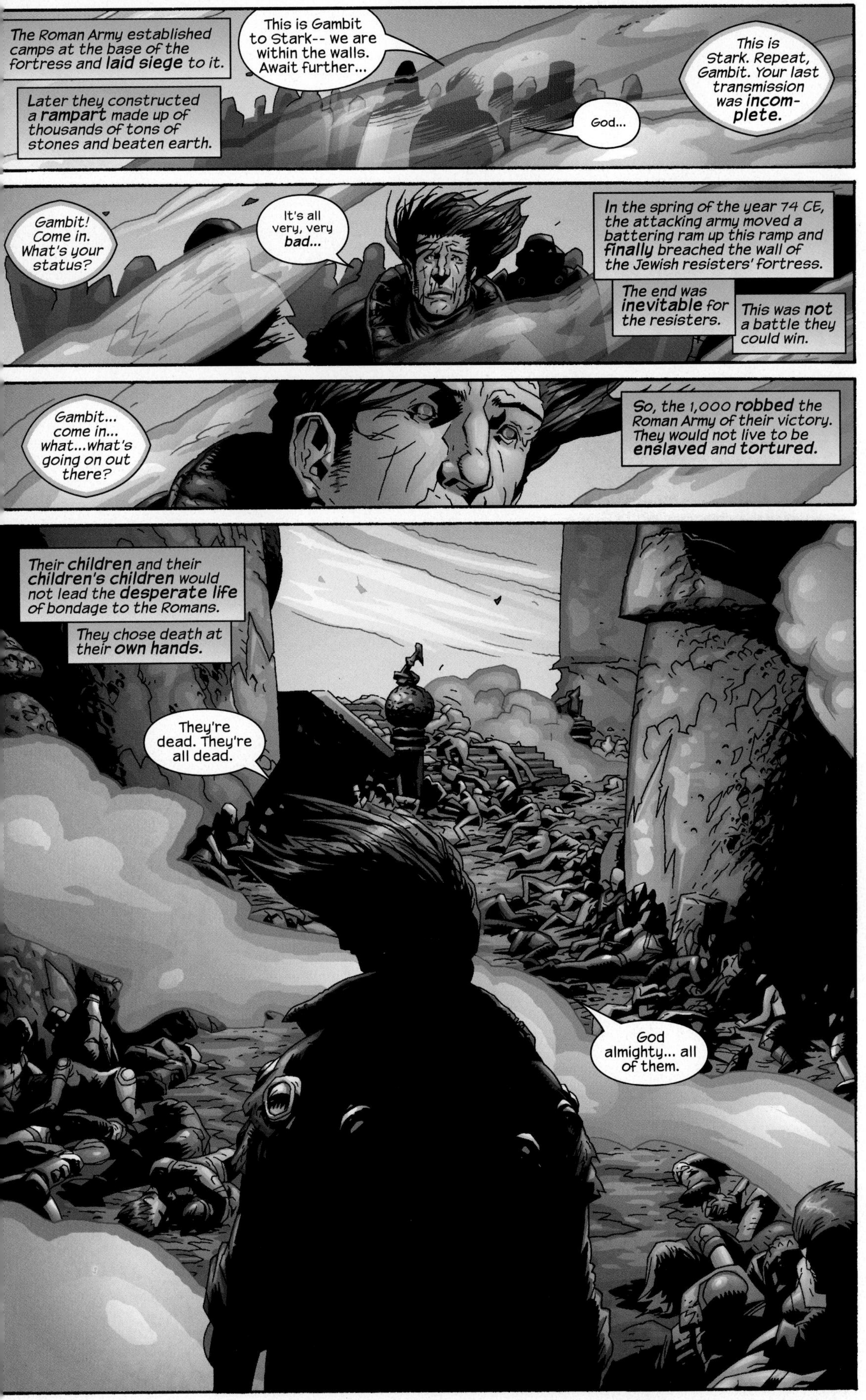
The Roman Army established camps at the base of the fortress and laid siege to it.
Later they constructed a rampart made up of thousands of tons of stones and beaten earth.
This is Gambit to Stark-- we are within the walls. Await further...
God...
This is Stark. Repeat, Gambit. Your last transmission was incomplete.
Gambit! Come in. What's your status?
It's all very, very bad...
In the spring of the year 74 CE, the attacking army moved a battering ram up this ramp and finally breached the wall of the Jewish resisters' fortress.
The end was inevitable for the resisters.
This was not a battle they could win.
Gambit... come in... what...what's going on out there?
So, the 1,000 robbed the Roman Army of their victory. They would not live to be enslaved and tortured.
Their children and their children's children would not lead the desperate life of bondage to the Romans.
They chose death at their own hands.
They're dead. They're all dead.
God almighty... all of them.

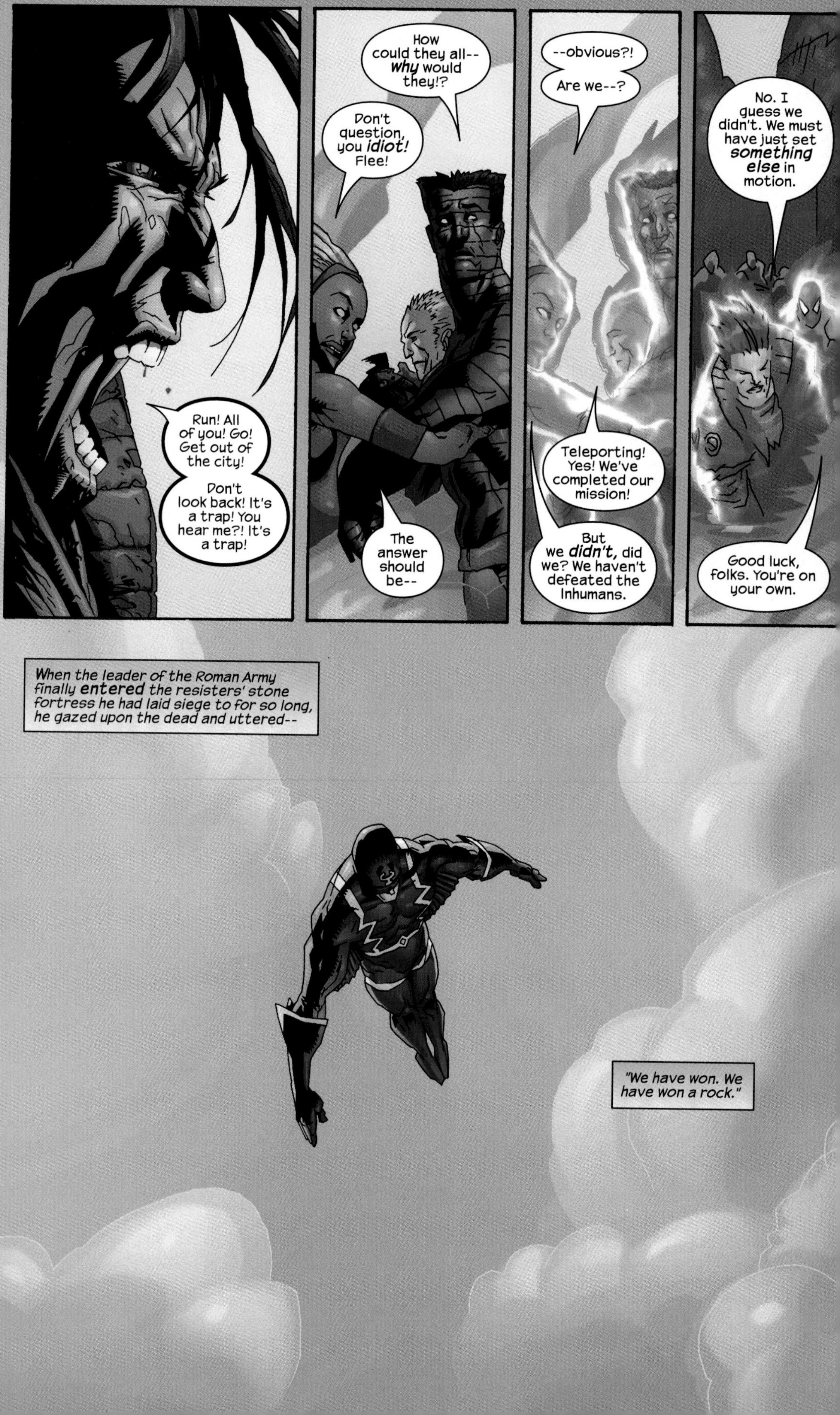

Run! All of you! Go! Get out of the city!
Don't look back! It's a trap! You hear me?! It's a trap!
How could they all-- why would they!?
Don't question, you idiot! Flee!
The answer should be--
--obvious?!
Are we--?
Teleporting! Yes! We've completed our mission!
But we didn't, did we? We haven't defeated the Inhumans.
No. I guess we didn't. We must have just set something else in motion.
Good luck, folks. You're on your own.
When the leader of the Roman Army finally entered the resisters' stone fortress he had laid siege to for so long, he gazed upon the dead and uttered--
"We have won. We have won a rock."

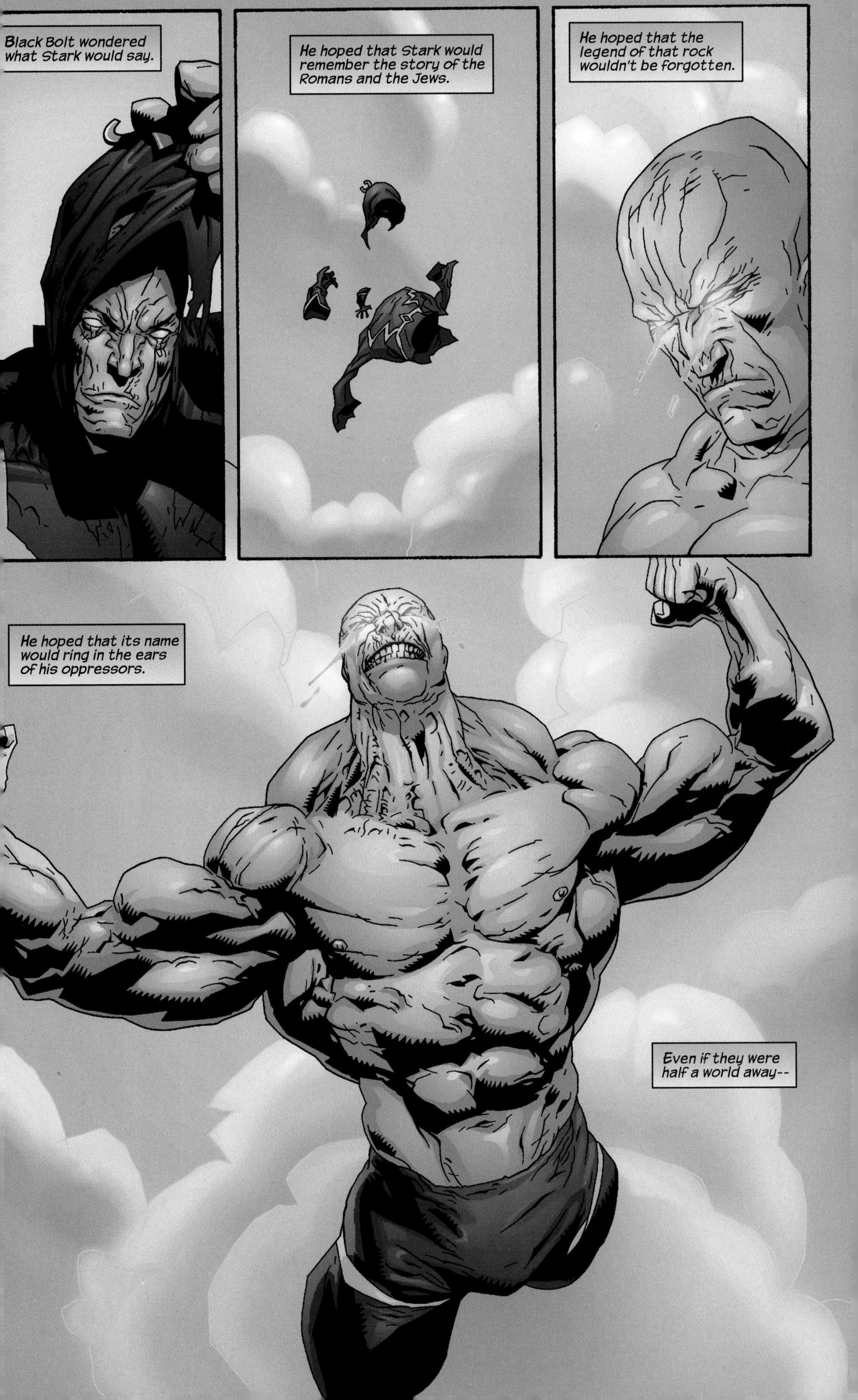
Black Bolt wondered what Stark would say.
He hoped that Stark would remember the story of the Romans and the Jews.
He hoped that the legend of that rock wouldn't be forgotten.
He hoped that its name would ring in the ears of his oppressors.
Even if they were half a world away--

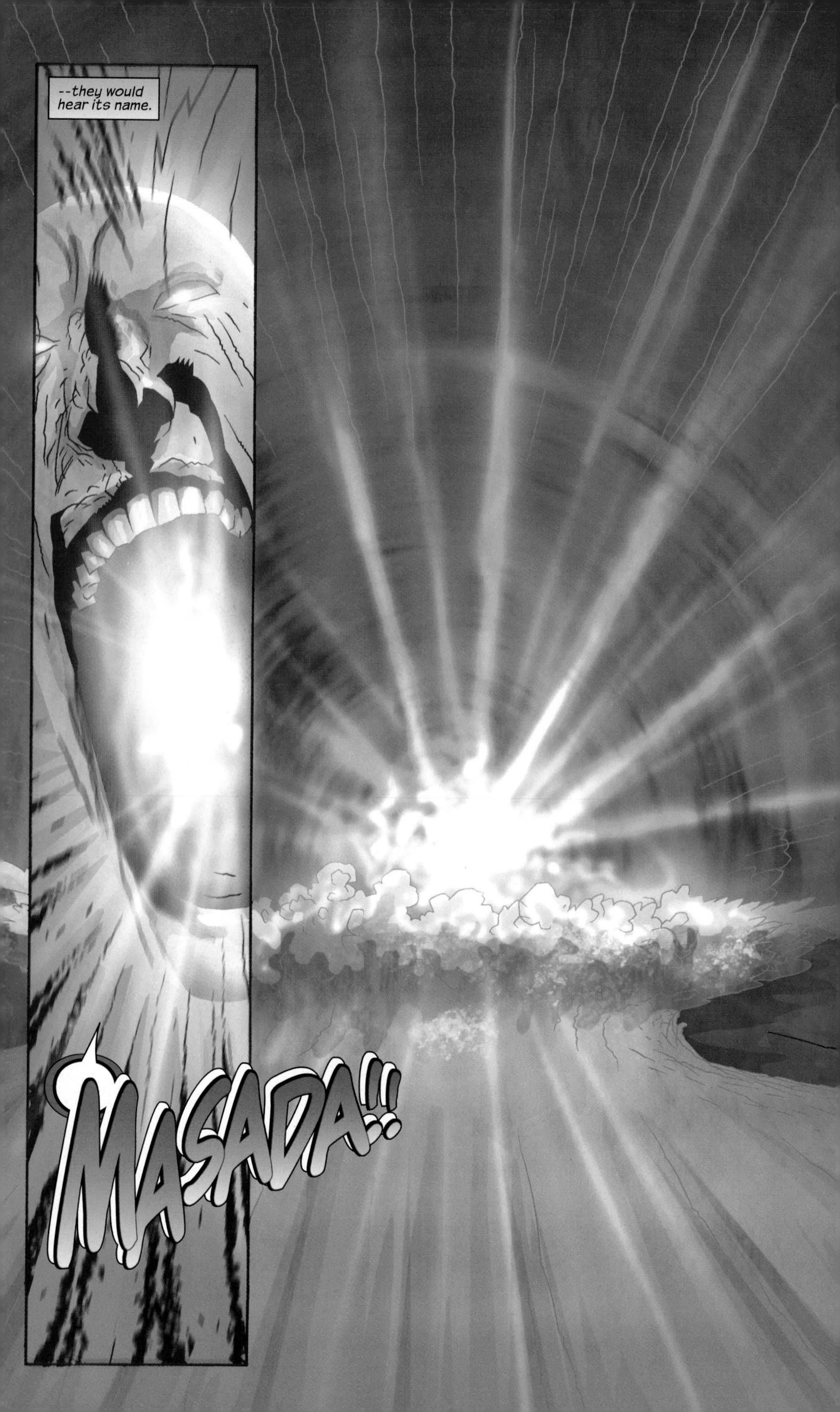
--they would hear its name.
MASADA!!

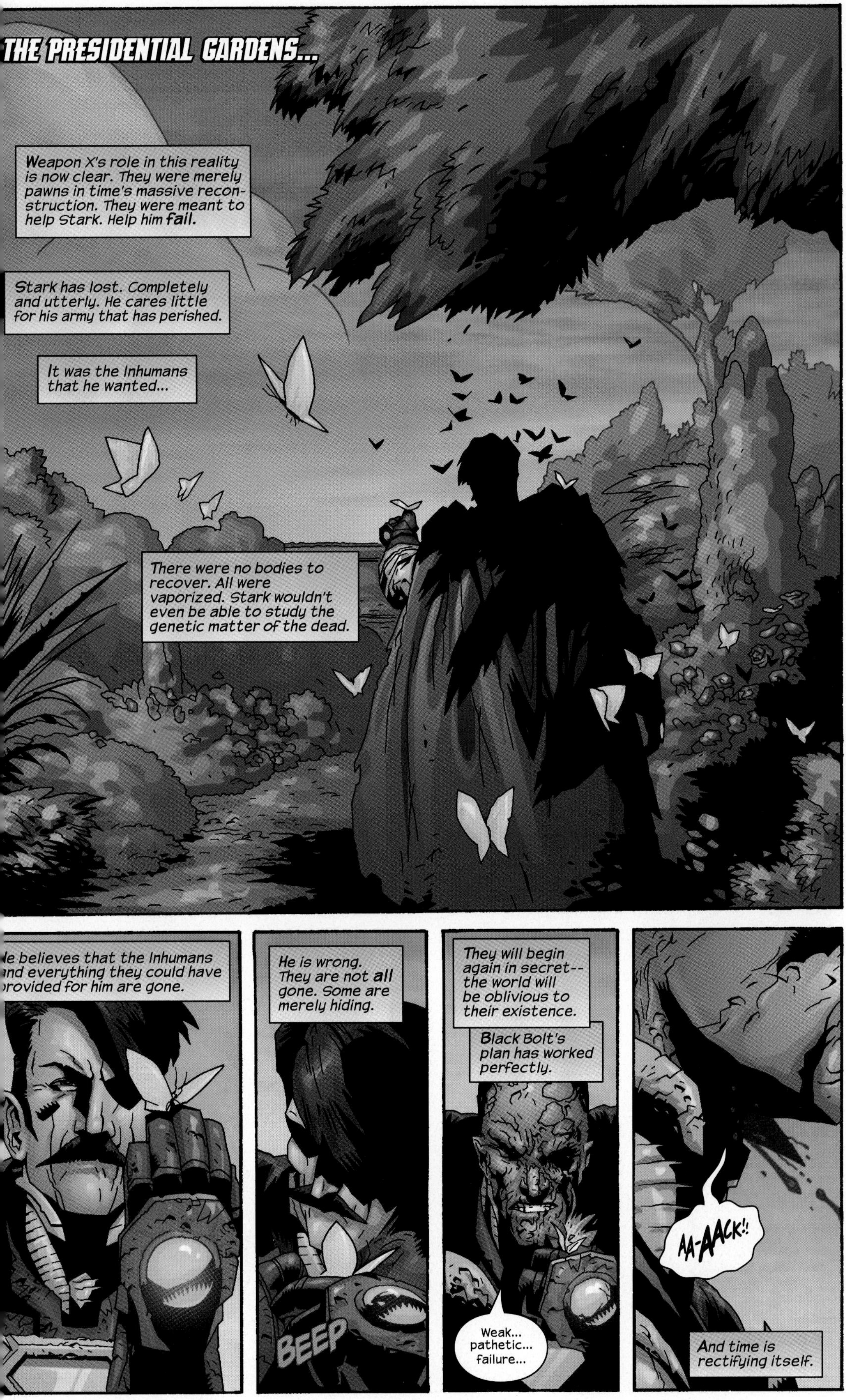
THE PRESIDENTIAL GARDENS...
Weapon X's role in this reality is now clear. They were merely pawns in time's massive reconstruction. They were meant to help Stark. Help him fail.
Stark has lost. Completely and utterly. He cares little for his army that has perished.
It was the Inhumans that he wanted...
There were no bodies to recover. All were vaporized. Stark wouldn't even be able to study the genetic matter of the dead.
le believes that the Inhumans nd everything they could have rovided for him are gone.
He is wrong. They are not all gone. Some are merely hiding.
BEEP
They will begin again in secret-- the world will be oblivious to their existence.
Black Bolt's plan has worked perfectly.
Weak... pathetic... failure...
AA-AACK!!
And time is rectifying itself.

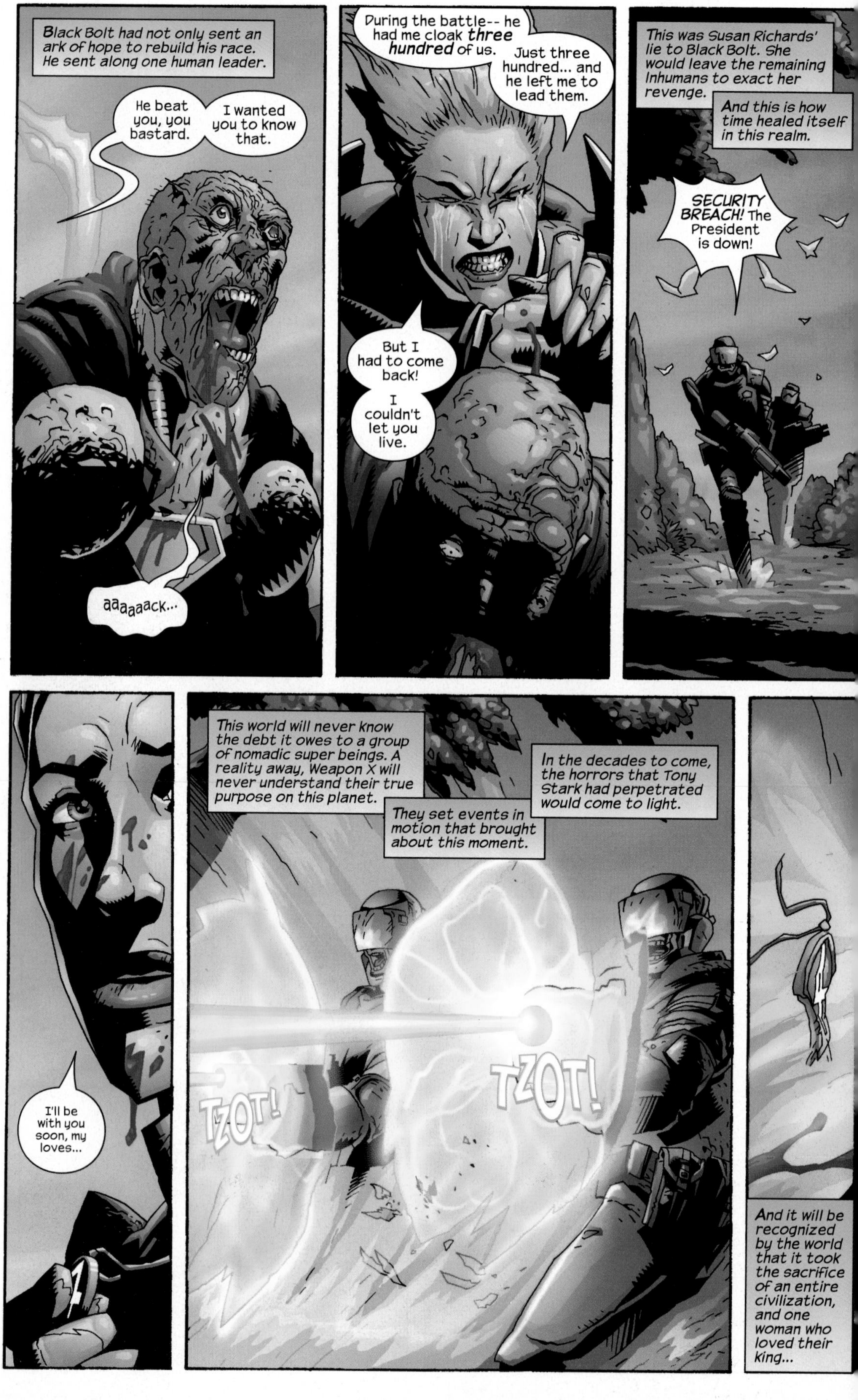
Black Bolt had not only sent an ark of hope to rebuild his race. He sent along one human leader.
He beat you, you bastard.
I wanted you to know that.
aaaaaack...
During the battle-- he had me cloak three hundred of us.
Just three hundred... and he left me to lead them.
But I had to come back!
I couldn't let you live.
This was Susan Richards' lie to Black Bolt. She would leave the remaining Inhumans to exact her revenge.
And this is how time healed itself in this realm.
SECURITY BREACH! The President is down!
I'll be with you soon, my loves...
This world will never know the debt it owes to a group of nomadic super beings. A reality away, Weapon X will never understand their true purpose on this planet.
They set events in motion that brought about this moment.
In the decades to come, the horrors that Tony Stark had perpetrated would come to light.
TZOT!
TZOT!
And it will be recognized by the world that it took the sacrifice of an entire civilization, and one woman who loved their king...

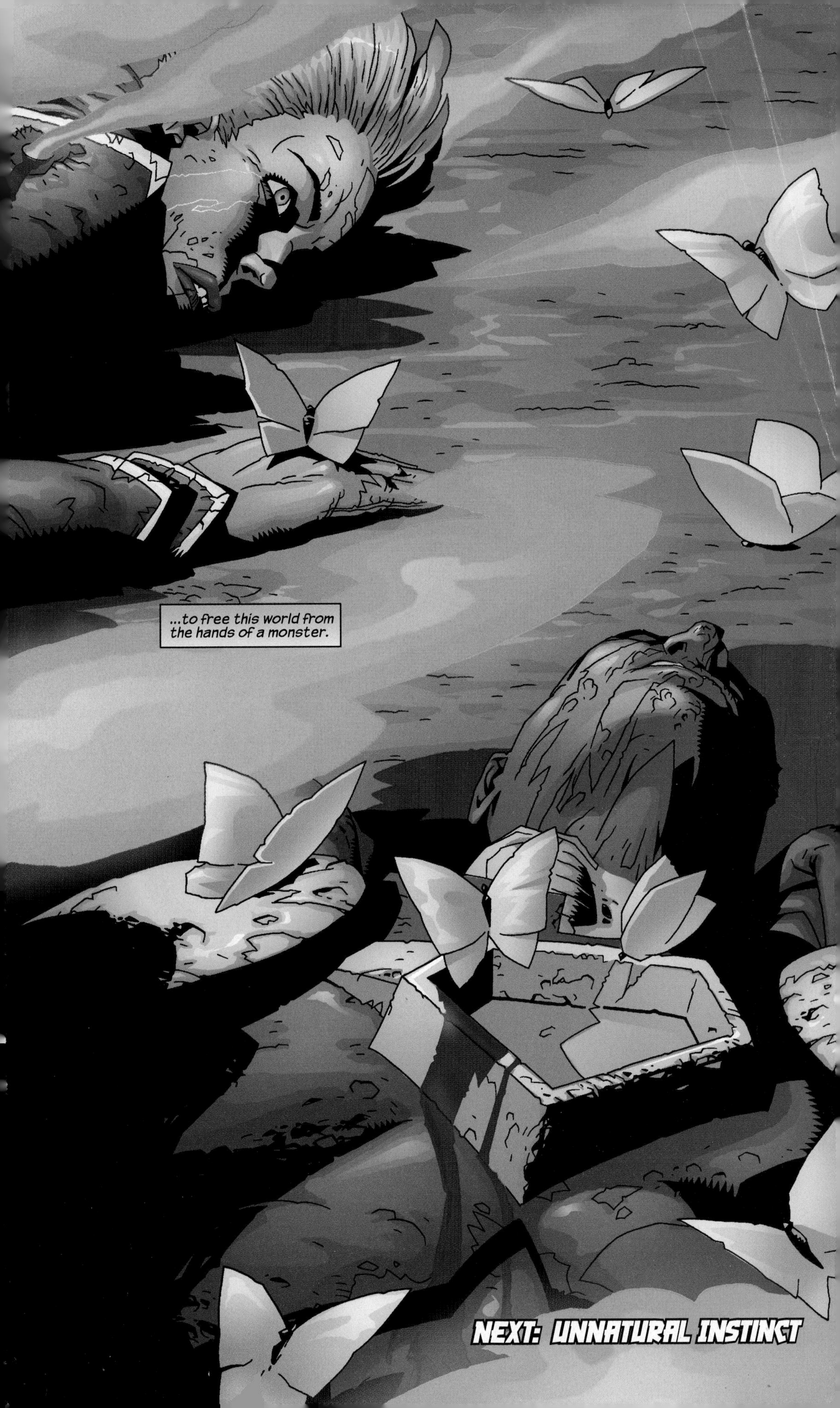
...to free this world from the hands of a monster.
NEXT: UNNATURAL INSTINCT

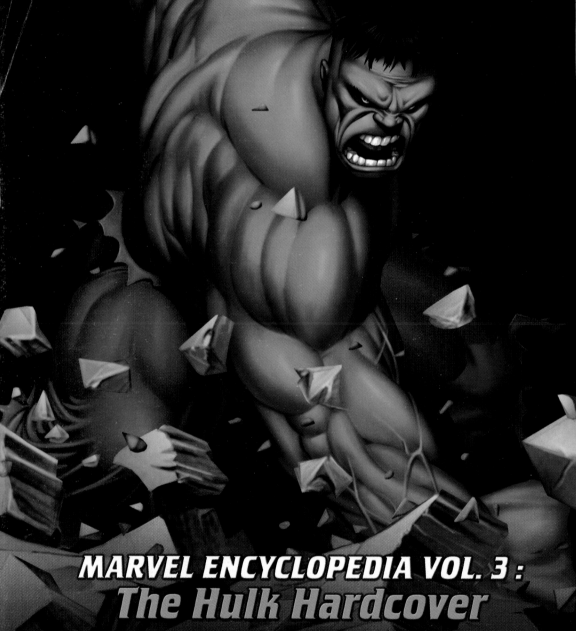

MARVEL
ENCYCLOPEDIA

MARVEL ENCYCLOPEDIA VOL. 3 :
The Hulk Hardcover

Everything you ever wanted to know about THE INCREDIBLE HULK
in one comprehensive, low-priced volume!

MARVEL